Bugs,
Bogs,
Bats, *and*
Books

D1534029

Bugs, Bogs, Bats, *and* Books

Sharing nature with children through reading

KATHLEEN T. ISAACS

an imprint of the American Library Association

HURON STREET PRESS

CHICAGO · 2014

Kathleen T. Isaacs spent many years as a teacher, with intermittent stints as a school and public librarian. She has taught in schools and universities in Baltimore, Washington, Hong Kong, and Xi'an, China, and has traveled extensively in many parts of the world. She has served on several award selection committees for the Association for Library Service to Children, including the Sibert Award, Notable Children's Books, and the Newbery Award. She is also the author of *Picturing the World: Informational Picture Books for Children.*

Printed in the United States of America
18 17 16 15 14   5 4 3 2 1

Extensive effort has gone into ensuring the reliability of the information in this book; however, the publisher makes no warranty, express or implied, with respect to the material contained herein.

ISBN: 978-1-937589-58-5 (paper).

Library of Congress Cataloging-in-Publication Data

Isaacs, Kathleen T.
   Bugs, bogs, bats, and books : sharing nature with children through reading / Kathleen T. Isaacs.
     pages cm
   Includes bibliographical references and index.
   ISBN 978-1-937589-58-5 (paperback)
   1. Nature—Juvenile literature—Bibliography. 2. Natural history—Juvenile literature—Bibliography. 3. Nature stories—Bibliography. 4. Children—Books and reading—United States. I. Title.
Z6827.I83 2014
[QH48]
028.5'5—dc23

2014001417

Book design by Kim Thornton in the Charis and Interstate typefaces.
Cover images © Shutterstock, Inc.

⊛ This paper meets the requirements of ANSI/NISO Z39.48-1992 (Permanence of Paper).

To Skip,
who has shared a love for nature and for books with me for fifty years.

Contents

Acknowledgments

Thanks to the children whose pictures appear here and to their parents: Adam, Emily, Jenny, Katy, Madison, Rachel, Robert, Sophie, Wesley, and William. Thanks to Catherine Isaacs for the story time picture on page 215. And many thanks to the Anne Arundel Public Library and the efficient people at MILO, the Maryland Public Library Interlibrary Loan Organization.

Inspecting a cicada

Chapter 1

Why Nature Books?

THE TWO CHILDREN PICTURED AT THE BEGINNING OF THIS CHAPTER ARE looking at a cicada, an insect that appears in parts of the United States in thirteen- or seventeen-year cycles in great swarms that produce a noisy buzz. The appearance of a new cicada brood generates wonder in children and adults alike, enough to cause a spike in media attention and Google searches. These youngsters were lucky enough to visit a place where these intriguing insects had emerged in stunning numbers. They came at the right time and with adults who encouraged them to look closely and admire, and who even provided tools.

We can't always be at the right place at the right time to show our children nature's spectacles, but we can encourage their interest in other ways. Spending time outside in backyards and nearby parks, in zoos and museums, and inside with books and videos that convey others' experiences, children become familiar and comfortable with the natural world and make personal connections.

There has been a lot of talk about the nature deficit of modern children. Their increasingly suburbanized and organized childhoods leave little time or space for exploration of the natural world. What we don't experience, we are less likely to appreciate. The phrase *nature-deficit disorder* was coined by the California writer Richard Louv, who made it part of the subtitle of his best-selling *Last Child in the Woods* in 2005. He observed that modern young people have become disconnected from the natural world for multiple reasons: parent fears, societal and legal barriers, and the competing lure of the Internet and video games.[1] Recently, the noted British naturalist and writer Steven Moss has concurred, suggesting that in his country, too, the growth of virtual play and the loss of freedom to venture outdoors and have hands-on experience with the natural world have led to a nature deficit.[2] This is not a national phenomenon, but an international phenomenon that needs to be addressed in a variety of ways.

The National Wildlife Federation has a website devoted to research about this issue and ways to counteract it, which parents and caregivers might find helpful. The site, called Be Out There (www.nwf.org/Be-Out-There.aspx), provides activities and includes an interactive Nature Find map that locates nature sites and events wherever you are in the United States (www.nwf.org/NatureFind.aspx). There are also dozens of books available in your public libraries suggesting things to see and do outdoors. I've annotated a few in the last chapter of this book.

For school children, hands-on environmental education and increased environmental literacy is the goal of the No Child Left Inside Act introduced by bipartisan coalitions of senators and representatives in 2009, again in 2011, and in July 2013. As of August 2013, the most recent twin bills were still in the Senate Committee on Health, Education, Labor, and Pensions and the House Committee on Education and the Workforce. There has been more legislative success at the state level. (The phrase *no child left inside* was coined by the Connecticut Department of Environmental Protection.) But developing an appreciation for the natural world should begin long before children go to school.

Beyond simple comfort and connection and appreciation, the natural world can stimulate curiosity and wonder. In 1969, just a few days after the birth of my third child, my mother purchased a copy of *The Sense of Wonder* and sent it to us, inscribed to all her grandchildren. The text of this book is Rachel Carson's essay "Help Your Child to Wonder," which first appeared in *Woman's Home Companion* in July 1956. Our copy was published by Harper & Row in 1965 and included photographs by Charles Pratt showing children in the natural world, especially on the Maine coast Carson loved so well. It was a perfect combination, but so was the second version with nature photographs by Nick Kelsh that came out in 1998. The essay encouraged adults to take children out of doors, to have them experience the natural world in all weathers and seasons, to "keep alive his inborn sense of wonder."[3]

Rachel Carson was not the first to use the phrase *sense of wonder.* Coleridge, writing in the nineteenth century about Wordsworth's view of nature, described his ability "carry on the feelings of childhood into the power of manhood; to combine a child's sense of wonder and novelty with the appearances which every day, for, perhaps, forty years, had rendered familiar."[4] But the phrase and the idea it implies are now inextricably connected to memories of Carson's life and her advocacy for the natural world.

To keep this sense, Carson said, a child "needs the companionship of at least one adult who can share it, rediscovering with him the joy, excitement and mystery of the world we live in."[5] Carson was encouraging adults to take children out of doors, even children who live in cities and lack a doting aunt with a coastal Maine cottage. I certainly agree. But adults can also encourage children's connection, wonder, and enthusiasm for the natural world as well as their own by sharing books with them.

Richard Louv's groundbreaking book is also all about going outside. But buried deep in its pages is support for reading as well. Arguing that adults, too, need to rediscover their sense of wonder at the natural world, he goes on to offer an endorsement of books at any age:

> Reading about nature with a child is another way, as an adult, to revive a sense of natural wonder. Reading is, of course, a form of indirect experience, but unlike television, reading does not swallow the senses or dictate thought. Reading stimulates the ecology of the imagination.[6]

On the website for the Children and Nature Network, an organization founded by Louv and dedicated to support both people and organizations working to reconnect the two, there's an extensive section called "Where Nature Meets Story" (www.childrenandnature.org/naturestory). Here are many suggested activities for different times and places—at night, in winter, on the beach, and so forth—connected with some older but well-loved titles that will also "stimulate the ecology of the imagination."

Even the youngest children can begin to make connections with the natural world. *Busy Gorillas* (John Schindel, Tricycle Press, 2010) is a board book with few words but actions that toddlers can imitate. Galbraith's *Where Is Baby?* (Peachtree, 2013) can inspire a game of peek-a-boo, as well as recognition of a variety of animals, while Edward Gibbs's *I Spy with My Little Eye* (Templar Books, 2011) offers a guessing game. A bedtime story like Mary Logue's *Sleep Like a Tiger* (Houghton Mifflin Harcourt, 2012) reminds listeners that animals go to sleep, too—and may leave them wondering about just what else is going on in the world of the illustrations. Later on, children will want to hear and read stories about other children who explore the out-of-doors with caring adults, as well as books about particular animals and natural places that they know.

Looking at books about the natural world can whet children's appetites and help them understand what they see, hear, touch, smell, and feel. Picture books and informational books for young readers are an ideal introduction to a subject, appealing to a broad range of ages and to readers, nonreaders, and listeners alike. They can ignite an interest or add depth to an experience. Books for children today include stunning art, photographs, and artists' renderings of the natural world that are full of Carson's "joy, excitement and mystery." Today's photo, art, and printing techniques make astonishing images available, and publishers take full advantage of them. There is, of course, no substitute for going outside, but reading aloud or simply looking at such books with young children is a terrific companion activity. Before or after a walk in the rain, a trip to the beach or zoo, or a nighttime search for fireflies, a book can make connections and add questions. When a television image has caught a child's imagination, a book can carry it further. The natural world is filled with wonders, not all of them available in the neighborhood or even visible to the child's eye, but many of them are pictured in books readily available in a public library.

Identifying animals is fun for children and adults alike, but it is not really the point. Carson says:

> If a child asked me a question that suggested even a faint awareness of the mystery behind the arrival of a migrant sandpiper on the beach of an August morning, I would be far more pleased than by the mere fact that he knew it was a sandpiper and not a plover.[7]

Books can help children learn stories behind the animals they see, and a story, attached to a particular animal, makes the animal more appealing, more memorable, more wondrous. "In children, cultivate the wonder as a foundation for facts," Carson amplified in later, unpublished writings.[8] She was probably opposing our adult need for facts first to a child's primary need for experience, but I think further information connected to recent personal experience enriches the experience at any age.

The titles I describe on the following pages are books a parent or care-giver might read or provide to encourage a child's curiosity, appreciation, and sense of wonder at the natural world. They appeal to a wide range of ages. There are books to share with a baby and books a ten-year-old would enjoy, and many titles for children in between. All have been published recently. You can find them at libraries around the country, at independent or chain bookstores in your neighborhood, and for sale (new or used) online. They range from board books to nonfiction for older readers illustrated with images that help tell the story. Some have been written for parents to read to toddlers, others for young people reading on their own. All would be, I think, a joy to share. Unlike other lists of suggested reading on the web or in books for adults about connecting your child with nature, these are all rel-atively new. I included a few of my favorites from as long ago as 2006, but most have been published in the last four years. They are titles you might not yet have heard of by authors and illustrators you may not yet have come to know and trust.

In selecting these titles, I looked for books that conveyed their own excite-ment, appreciation, and sense of wonder. I chose both stories and informa-tional books. I looked for stories in which the science was accurate, even if presented in the context of a fantasy (animals that talk or imaginary jour-neys, for example). I used the selection sources professionals use—starred reviews in reputable journals and lists of outstanding books from profes-sional reviewers. Some of the books were included in a selection of infor-mational picture books I did for teachers and librarians, *Picturing the World* (ALA Editions, 2013), but the majority are newly annotated for this book. Finally, I looked for books that would be readily available. Most of the books annotated here I borrowed from the Maryland public library system. Your state may not have as efficient and convenient an interlibrary loan system as Maryland has, but your local library probably has many of the books listed here. If you don't know where your nearest library is, the website www .askyourlibrary.org will tell you. Just enter your zip code. When you get there, ask a librarian for help.

The people shown in the photographs in this book are mostly family members: husband, children, grandchildren. These are pictures I've taken over the years while exploring the natural world with them. The sidebars in the chapters of annotations include relevant suggestions for activities you might enjoy trying with your children and children you care for. Titles annotated in chapter 16 as well as sites on the Internet will offer other ideas.

This is not meant to be a book to read straight through. The next chapter contains some suggestions for choosing just the right book for your own child. After that, the chapters have been organized into rough categories of suggested books, beginning where any good teaching begins—at home and in your own backyard. Use the table of contents and index to find books and subjects of particular interest. I hope it will prove useful in your efforts to revive your own and ignite your child's sense of wonder.

NOTES

1. Richard Louv, *Last Child in the Woods: Saving Our Children from Nature-Deficit Disorder* (Chapel Hill, NC: Algonquin Books, 2005).

2. Stephen Moss, "Natural Childhood," National Trust, 2012, www.national trust.org.uk/document-1355766991839.

3. Rachel Carson, *The Sense of Wonder*, illus. by Charles Pratt (New York: Harper & Row, 1965), 45.

4. Samuel Taylor Coleridge, *Biographia Literaria: IV*, in *The Portable Coleridge*, ed. I. A. Richards (New York: Viking, 1950), 475.

5. Carson, *Sense of Wonder*, 45.

6. Louv, *Last Child*, 164–65.

7. Carson, *Sense of Wonder*, 83.

8. Rachel Carson Papers, Yale Collection of American Literature, Beinecke Rare Book and Manuscript Library, Yale University; quoted in Rick Van Noy, *A Natural Sense of Wonder: Connecting Kids with Nature through the Seasons* (Athens: University of Georgia Press, 2008), 134.

A reader-to-be

Chapter 2

Choosing Good Nature Books

ALTHOUGH NOT YET READING, THE CHILD IN THE PHOTOGRAPH AT THE beginning of this chapter is enjoying a book. Parents or caregivers choose children's books in a variety of ways and for a variety of reasons. They may be seeking books to read aloud and share. They may hope to introduce or follow up a particular experience. They may be buying books as gifts, borrowing them from a library or a friend, or helping a child make his or her own choices. They may be looking for entertainment or instruction or something that will help the child fall asleep. Whatever the situation, there are four elements to consider in picking a children's book. Most important is the subject and its potential appeal for the child. The second element is the text, how the story is told. Third, and equally important, is the visual experience of the book: its illustrations, design, and production. Last, you should consider educational issues: factual accuracy, the author's and illustrator's use of sources, and provision of additional tools (such as puzzles and suggestions for further research) for a child's enjoyment or education.

7

Subject and Child Appeal

When choosing a good book for a child, the adult should, if possible, be guided by the child's own interests. Often this is easy. Two-year-olds who visit the aquarium where I volunteer as an exhibit guide are always looking for turtles. Older children are fascinated by dolphins. One child may love to dig in the garden; another wants to walk in the woods, lifting up logs to look for salamanders. A child who has just visited the seashore or the zoo may want to know more about what she has seen. Sometimes children don't know right away what they're interested in; they need to explore. The lists that follow include a wide variety of subjects, both familiar and unusual, that would usually be classified as part of the natural world. They are a place to start.

A good teacher, parent, or caregiver will also be thinking about the child's next step. Children's minds need stretching. Educators talk about the zone of proximal development—that area between the skills a child already has and what he or she still needs to learn, between what children can do on their own and what requires help. The best learning choices for children lie in that space. They build on what the child knows, and they offer the next step. But sometimes readers and listeners just want something comfortable, something that reinforces what they already know and enjoy. That's an appropriate choice, too.

Whatever the topic, it should be a subject of interest and value to children. Look for books that make a connection to the child reader. There should be some way the child can find himself, his interests, experiences, and understanding of the world in the book. Many of the titles I have annotated are about animal babies, building on a child's natural interest in childhood. Books for older readers often begin by making a human connection. Steve Jenkins sometimes uses human bodies or hands as measurements, as he did in *Down, Down, Down: A Journey to the Bottom of the Sea* (Houghton Mifflin Harcourt, 2009).

By necessity, a children's book is a limited experience, providing only a small slice of information about a subject. Which slice it provides matters a lot. The author's and illustrator's choices should have some purpose. Usually, the creator is using something small and particular to suggest or represent something larger. A book about an ecosystem will pick a few appealing species to represent the whole system. A description of an animal may well focus on the animal's family life, its childhood, and later child-rearing. A biography may concentrate on a few moments in the subject's life, moments that may be high points in the life story or that may connect with the reader in ways that invite further exploration. Patrick McDonnell's *Me . . . Jane* (Little, Brown, 2011) is the story of the child Jane Goodall and her stuffed chimpanzee.

Books for young readers also open doors. If what they learn engages them, children will want to read and learn more. For some subjects where there are lots of good titles (bird-watching, bears, and butterflies, for example), I've included several books that may be helpful for readers who want to know more.

Suggested age ranges and reading levels should be considered flexibly. What the book is about and how the book connects to the reader are far more important in gauging potential appeal. Librarians know that pictures make a huge difference. Children who have no hope of reading the text will often choose a book to look at the pictures. Visual literacy, the ability to make meaning from pictures, starts long before a child can decode words on a page. Children can follow the pictures and put together the information they need to ask and answer questions and to grasp a story. For early readers, pictures continue to provide helpful cues to the text. Even for adults, it's said, a picture is worth a thousand words. In today's world of ubiquitous screens and images, children expect to learn about their world through pictures. And that's a grand place to start. Later, maybe, the child will want to puzzle out the words. Or maybe not. That's OK, too. My annotations suggest broad age levels, based more on the book's appeal than its difficulty.

How the Story Is Told

Good writers write with passion and enthusiasm that leave the reader with a sense of adventure and discovery. They organize a story logically and tell it with clarity and directness. They choose a narrative style that is appropriate to the subject and intended reader, using rich, appropriate language and equally rich and appropriate examples. The information is accurate and truthful (even if imagined) and the writer and illustrator avoid demeaning stereotypes.

Naturalists who also write and illustrate for young people have a passion to share their own love for their subjects that comes through to their readers. Naturalists and wildlife photographers such as Jim Arnosky, Nic Bishop, and

Suzi Eszterhas came to writing for young people after years of experience exploring the out-of-doors. That experience and their continued enthusiasm shine through their work. But successful writers for children can convey enthusiasm and expertise even if the subject has not been part of a lifetime of study. Inspired by things he has read, Jason Chin, who began life as an illustrator and bookseller, has written about environments as disparate as the redwood forests, coral reefs, and the Galápagos island chain. Like many illustrators, Susan Stockdale has a background in art and design. On her website (www.susanstockdale.com/about-me) she notes that she came to making books about animals after reading picture books with her own children.

The choice of narrative style is part of how a story is told. Is it fiction, information, or poetry? Is it information with fictional elements, a real experience told through the eyes of an imagined child, like *Just Ducks!* by Nicola Davies (Candlewick Press, 2012)? Do animal characters represent humans, as in Nancy Elizabeth Wallace's *Pond Walk* (Marshall Cavendish, 2011)? Do the animals wear clothes? Or is the text straightforward exposition? *The Animal Book,* by Steve Jenkins (Houghton Mifflin, 2013), is a collection of facts; *Sharks,* by Beverly Macmillan (Simon & Schuster, 2008), is a topically organized introduction to this popular fish group, part of an extensive series. Ellen Bryan Obed's *Twelve Kinds of Ice* (Houghton Mifflin, 2012) is a memoir, looking back on childhood experiences. Other authors use poetry—sometimes a collection of poems about a particular subject, like Amy Ludwig VanDerwater's *Forest Has a Song* (Clarion, 2013), sometimes a single long poem like Helen Frost's *Step Gently Out* (Candlewick Press, 2012), or sometimes a story told in rhyming couplets like Kurt Cyrus's *Voyage of Turtle Rex* (Harcourt, 2011). Some writers are more comfortable with one form than another; some subjects seem to lend themselves better to one style than to others.

When children or adults say they prefer fiction, they are often thinking more about style than about content. Some readers like to skip around in their reading and amass facts; others love a good story and can retain background facts as they read; still others want to see information clearly organized so they can understand what's important. Some prefer photographs, something that shows the real thing; others like the additional emotional and informational content that a good illustration can convey. Research has shown that while some children prefer stories, others will choose information books and stories equally and that, in spite of popular belief to the contrary, this is true of both boys and girls.[1] My own experience both in reading aloud and in watching children choose their own books is that children typically don't care as much about how the story is told as about its subject. If the style seems to fit the subject and the writer, and the book is about something that intrigues them, the style or form is not usually a deciding point in a child's choice.

The children's books I have selected are made up of a series of pictures and poems or narrative text. Together or separately, they will tell a story, describe an object or an event, or explain some process or phenomenon. An important question is how the details have been arranged. Stories usually have a predictable narrative arc, with one action leading to another, rising to a climax, and leading to a resolution. Information books often approach a topic chronologically as Sandra Markle did in *Snow School* (Charlesbridge, 2013), which follows a pair of snow leopard cubs over the course of a year. Writers telling bedtime stories will often use the passage of time from morning to night as an organizing principle. Others use the seasons. Whether fiction or nonfiction, a story told chronologically or topically will often start with a narrative hook. Dereck and Beverly Joubert begin *Face to Face with Leopards* (National Geographic, 2009) with an encounter with an eight-day-old cub and its mother in the wild. The narrative hook, a common technique in fiction writing, draws readers into the nonfiction text. Other nonfiction books are topically organized with a different subject on each double-page spread. The table of contents in John Seidensticker's *Predators* (Simon & Schuster, 2008) shows that, like others in the Insiders series, the book has a clear topical organization, first presenting aspects of the subject in general and then describing particular species. Sometimes a one-topic-per-spread format can dictate the content so rigidly that some subjects seem slighted while others are overdeveloped. The designers of the Insiders series get around that problem by varying the amount of text on a page. Look carefully at nonfiction to be sure that the facts have dictated the organization and not the other way around.

The story should be told with interesting language that is appropriate to the child's language level. There is nothing wrong with technical words. Children are sponges, ready to soak up new vocabulary, but new words should be defined in context as they are used (and perhaps in a glossary in the back matter) or they may well be ignored. Clarity and directness make a text easier to understand. Look for language that isn't hackneyed, even in books for the youngest child. Lively verbs, fresh turns of phrase, precise language, and appropriate imagery all enhance both storytelling and exposition of facts. Here is Jean Craighead George describing the return of wolves to Yellowstone National Park:

> Flowers filled the valley. Bees and butterflies that fed on the flowers returned. Warblers sang. Hummingbirds brightened the valley. Like pieces in a kaleidoscope, the broken parts of the wilderness were tumbling into place.
>   The wolves were back.[2]

Here's what Kate Messner's narrator notices as she and her father ski cross-country through snowy woods.

> Over the snow, a deer has crossed our path. Deep
> hoof prints punch through the crust, up the hill,
> under a tree. An oval of melted snow tells the story
> of a good night's sleep.
>
> Under the snow, deer mice doze. They huddle up,
> cuddle up against the cold in a nest of feathers and fur.[3]

Stories should be told with rich, appropriate examples. Authors select an event or series of events and particular examples to make a general point, create a narrative arc or develop a larger theme. As you read books you want to share with your children, ask: Is the story cohesive? Do the examples work together to tell a story a child will understand? Think about what has been included and what was left out. Do the specific examples or story chosen for the child reader leave an appropriate general impression? This is especially important in biographies. Oceanographer Sylvia Earle has had a long, rich life. Adult biographies might spend more time on her work as a scientist or her political action, but, appropriately for the child audience, biographer Claire Nivola concentrated on the wonders of the water world that inspired her career in her beautifully illustrated *Life in the Ocean: The Story of Ocean-ographer Sylvia Earle* (Frances Foster/ FSG, 2012).

Good books for children should be truthful. In an informational book, the subject should not be so oversimplified as to leave a misleading impression, and the book should include enough of the significant facts to represent the subject accurately. Made-up elements may have a place, but handling them can be tricky. For example, avoiding anthropomorphism in describing animals seems simple, but it is difficult not to imagine that animals share our feelings and our motivations. Some excellent titles about the natural world use language suggesting that animals are thinking in ways that humans think or include images showing animals with human expressions. This may help very young children connect, but parents and caregivers can also encourage them to wonder if animals might have quite different motivations.

In an imagined story, there should be some underlying truth. Where fantasy elements combine with realism and the distinction may not be clear to the child, an adult can help a child make those distinctions. Writers often use animal characters in books that are otherwise factual. In Jerry Pinkney's recent interpretations of traditional stories his settings are filled with appropriate plants and animal, but in *The Tortoise & the Hare* (Little, Brown, 2013), unlike *The Lion & the Mouse* (Little, Brown, 2009), the animals wear clothes. Pinkney has explained that he clothed the hare and tortoise and their friends to make them stand out in the desert setting of the book. In real life, the animals would blend in with their environment and be hard to see.[4] Adults reading these titles with children can make that point.

How the Story Is Pictured

Illustrations should match the subject and tone, support the story, or add additional information. In the best nature books, the illustrations often convey far more about the setting than the text alone can. Illustrations can also bring children much closer to the subject than they are likely to get in real life. Artists such as Wendell Minor and Jim Arnosky and photographers such as Nic Bishop are skilled at showing animals in the context of their environment, adding a great deal to the text. Illustrators such as Patricia J. Wynne carefully research their subjects, going to great lengths to make sure that details in the illustrations are as accurate as those in the text.

Just as authors select details that are most appropriate to tell the story to a child reader—and perhaps to give a sense of its larger importance—illustrators need to choose carefully what they are going to show. The pictures may emphasize important points or add details that the words don't convey. They may even tell a whole separate story, but one that is still accurate and relevant.

Illustrations should be well crafted. This may seem an obvious point, but it still needs to be made. Children's book illustrations may be photographs, or they may be painted, drawn, carved, or etched and printed, scratched, pasted, and digitally generated or enhanced. Readers and parents who are curious can often find out about the materials the artist used by looking at the copyright page. Nowadays, many publishers include that information, sometimes in considerable detail. Illustrative styles vary from realistic to quite abstract. Wildlife photographers like Mark Newman and Suzi Eszterhas and wildlife artists like John Sill and Sylvia Long produce meticulously detailed images that could be used in a field guide. On the other hand, Meilo So's ocean backgrounds for Kate Coombs's *Water Sings Blue* (Chronicle Books, 2012) are abstract and allusive with gray watercolor clouds and colorful blotches that represent coral. Young children don't seem to have difficulty with abstractions, as long as the style is consistent. Babies are really only looking for eyes and a smile. Older children enjoy cartoons. What children don't like are realistic pictures that aren't realistic—awkwardly portrayed people or animals, or scenes that are hard to make out.

The choice of medium, the colors used, and the design should support the author's text and be appropriate for the intended audience. In Divya Srinivasan's *Little Owl's Night* (Viking, 2011), the page background is a nighttime black, with the simple text in white, bright enough to be easy to read. Illustrating the opening pages of Karen Fox's *Older Than the Stars* (Charlesbridge, 2010), Nancy Davis used special text effects that evoke the chaos of the beginnings of the universe. The idea of the big bang, which is complicated for very young readers, is made clearer by that image. Denise Fleming's textured pulp paintings, illustrating *Under Ground* (Beach Lane Books, 2012), give an authentic feeling of digging around in the dirt. In considering a book's design, look at the cover, too. Sometimes there is even a different cover under the paper jacket. Endpapers as well often offer story background or further information.

Illustrations that vary in size and placement on the page keep the reader's interest. Photographs should be well reproduced and large enough to see easily. The subject should be clearly identified. If an illustration spreads across adjoining pages, it should be carefully positioned so details are not lost in the gutter between the left- and right-hand pages. Text and illustration should be well integrated. Child readers should not have to leaf through the book to find an explanation for a picture. Books for young people are often their first introduction to new knowledge, so when the text mentions something unfamiliar, there should be a picture to help the reader understand what it is. Many children's brains record pictures even more effectively than words.

The keys to success for traditional picture books lie in the moments you turn the page. The pictures and graphic elements, including the font, will guide readers through the book. A good example can be found in Erin Stead's Boston Globe-Horn Book honor-winning illustrations for Julie Fogliano's *And Then It's Spring* (Neal Porter / Roaring Brook Press, 2012). The boy is almost always facing to the right, looking off the page to the next one. (While sowing seeds, he is facing the other way but clearly walking backwards, again into the page turn.) Only where the reader needs to slow down, to pay attention or think about the passage of time, does the boy look back.

Some modern informational picture books present material on two levels, with the information on a page summarized or introduced by words or simple sentences in a larger font. Nic Bishop does this regularly. Others, like many of Steve Jenkins's books, have a short picture-book text and several pages at the end that give a more thorough treatment to the subject.

Finally, a book for young readers should be sturdy enough to last through repeated readings. Foldouts, pop-ups, tabs, and the like should not tear after just a few sessions. Children reread books they like, often over and over. Invitations to interact with the physical book are very appealing, but they can also become a disappointment if parts of the book don't last.

Accuracy, Sources, and Additional Tools

As mentioned, books about the natural world should be accurate. Writers and illustrators choose the details they think appropriate to tell the story they want to tell. They may have to simplify ideas or omit events that seem irrelevant to their focus or inappropriate for the audience, but the narrative as a whole should not be misleading. The overall impression should be proportionate and balanced.

Parents and caregivers, and even librarians, bookstore purchasers, and reviewers normally can't know definitively how much effort the authors, illustrators, and editors have put into researching and verifying what appears in the book. But, looking at the creator biographies (often at the end or on the back flap) can sometimes give a sense of what backgrounds and experiences they brought to the subject. Many books will include a list of acknowledgments—thank-yous to experts in the field for contributing information and perhaps for checking the final product. Look for these acknowledgments. They are usually on the back of the title page or at the end of the book, wherever the cataloging information is, but sometimes they are in an author's note.

Even in a book for the youngest readers, an author can indicate where he or she got information. For middle graders, sometimes an illustrator's afterword explains his or her research as well. This can range from a list of sources to a detailed explanation of photographic methods, such as those provided in National Geographic's Face to Face with Animals series. As I evaluate books, I appreciate authors who have added information about their research methods and sources to their own or their publisher's website, but this information should be a supplement, not a substitute, for some acknowledgment in the book. For elementary school students, along with sources, the back matter in an informational book should provide suggestions for further reading. Having opened a door to a subject, the author should invite the young reader through it. Suggested web resources are grand, and there are many wonderful places to access information, videos, and even live-streaming images of the natural world, but even today many children, especially young children, don't have ready access to the Internet. The Census Bureau reports that 20 percent of U.S. households didn't use Internet inside or outside the home in 2010 (www.census.gov/compendia/statab/2012/tables/12s1155.pdf). Even in the 80 percent that do, easy access for children may not be convenient or appropriate.

In informational books for elementary school readers, maps and time lines are important. Every exposure to these graphical representations of space and time helps a child develop his or her own mental map or and sense of history. In families and preschools where map reading is encouraged, even preschoolers can find their own place in the world, a starting place for broader connections.

Finally, it is really helpful to have page numbers and an index. The index does not need to be traditional; it can be made of pictures. In *How to Clean a Hippopotamus* (Houghton Mifflin Harcourt, 2010) Steve Jenkins and Robin Page provided miniature reproductions of each double-page spread along with additional information about animals. These books are teaching young readers how to find information in books, with the index as their tool. In books for elementary school readers—who may be reading for school reports or to learn about a particular passion—an index should be required.

A Final Concern

There's one more consideration to keep in mind as you choose titles for the readers and listeners you know. Since the publication of Carson's essay, there has been increasing concern about the environment. That concern has filtered down from adults to children, who learn about environmental issues in the media, in their schools, and in children's books. The message, for many years, has been a succession of warnings: animals are disappearing; the thinning of the ozone layer (and its actual holes) affects human health; the water we drink and air we breathe have been tainted. It is one thing for a high school principal to say to graduates and their assembled relatives "We've found in recent years that progress is not inevitable and some problems might never be solved" and "We're all facing a century full of challenge and uncertainty."[5] It is quite another to lay that burden on young children for whom environmental problems are beyond their understanding or control.

Constantly repeating the litany of environmental losses has led to a phenomenon called ecophobia, which I encountered in my own teaching. Sixth graders would tell me they simply didn't want to hear anything more about the Chesapeake Bay, good or bad. It was all just too depressing. If you distance yourself from things that hurt, you can sometimes keep the pain at bay. There is substantial research available showing that children in many countries have become "fearful, cynical, and pessimistic about environmental issues."[6] It is not unreasonable to assume that just as positive environmental experiences in childhood have been shown to correlate with environmental concern, careers, and activism in adulthood, negative experiences and negative information will lead to less concern on the part of adults. Stories that reflect a writer's and illustrator's enthusiasm and sense of wonder are more likely to help young readers and listeners share those attitudes. Most of the titles in this list are not stories about what's going or gone, but about what's in the world today. It is impossible to exclude all mention of threatened species and lost habitat, but my preference was for books that limited that information to the back matter unless it was a book for older readers. I also included a few that offer environmental good news.

Where to Get Suggestions

Public libraries and independent bookstores with large children's collections are excellent places to start. Public libraries often have children's specialists, people who have read hundreds and even thousands of books written for young people and can not only identify trusted authors and illustrators but also suggest a title that a particular child might want. Those librarians also have access to read-alike sources and can help your child find a book to follow one he or she particularly enjoyed.

In choosing books to consider for this selection of informational picture books, I looked at a variety of notable book lists as well as starred reviews and end-of-the-year honors from children's book review magazines. Publishers' and authors' websites often give more complete lists of a particular title's awards. But this is not terribly helpful when you are standing in front of a shelf full of potential choices. The book itself lets one evaluate the design, the illustrations, and the level of the text. But how can one judge the accuracy of its content? Nowadays, digital library catalogs often include book reviews, some from readers and some from professionals. Many book review sources online are behind pay walls, but Kirkus Reviews (kirkus reviews.com) are free after the first month they appear. The National Science Teachers' Association puts its best-books lists online, with free access (www.nsta.org/publications/ostb). So does the Association of Library Service for Children, a division of the American Library Association (www.ala .org/alsc/awardsgrants/notalists). Public libraries may offer access to databases of children's book review compilation sources such as NoveList K–8 or the Children's Literature Comprehensive Database.

The books on this list reflect a wide range of formats and styles of presentation. There are puzzles and pop-ups and lift-the-flaps books that encourage a child reader's interaction. There are stories in which people interact with animals, portrayed accurately, and stories in which somewhat personified animals function in an identifiable natural setting. There are picture albums and photo essays and books that just provide the facts, sometimes in digestible bites and sometimes in straightforward exposition. Not every format works for every subject or every child, but in the variety there should be something for most tastes.

The chapters that follow are loosely organized by subject but also by format (poetry and biography) and age appeal (a separate chapter with titles for babies and toddlers and another with titles for their caregivers). The index will help you find bedtime stories, books for beginning readers, and titles about animal babies and particular subjects in any chapter. Sidebars with each chapter suggest just a few of the many possible activities that might go along with each subject—things to do before or after reading. Some are family projects; others connect your family to citizen scientists across the country. "What, after all, do parents owe their young that is more important than a warm and trusting connection to the Earth?" the historian Theodore Roszak once wrote.[7] Sharing nature with children through reading is another way to help that connection grow.

NOTES

1. Marilyn Chapman, Margot Filipenko, Marianne McTavish, and Jon Shapiro, "First Graders' Preferences for Narrative and/or Information Books and Perceptions of Other Boys' and Girls' Book Preferences," *Canadian Journal of Education / Revue canadienne de l'éducation* (2007): 531–53.

2. Jean Craighead George, *The Wolves Are Back.*, illus. by Wendell Minor (New York: Dutton Children's Books, 2008), n.p.

3. Kate Messner, *Over and Under the Snow,* illus. by Christopher Silas Neal (San Francisco: Chronicle Books, 2011), n.p.

4. Jerry Pinkney, *The Tortoise & the Hare* (New York: Little, Brown, 2013), author's note.

5. Nancy Starmer, head of George School, commencement address, Newtown, PA, May 26, 2013; see www.phillyburbs.com/news/local/courier_times _news/student-s-back-flip-one-of-george-school-graduation-highlights/ article_6c5d3bca-844c-5491-a5ca-16fe2fec1fe9.html and www.georgeschool .org/NewsAndEvents/2013/Commencement%20Celebrates%20Class%20 of%202013.aspx.

6. Susan Jean Strife, "Children's Environmental Concerns: Expressing Ecophobia," *Journal of Environmental Education* 43, no. 1 (2012); published online November 14, 2011, www.tandfonline.com/doi/full/10.1080/00958964.20 11.602131.

7. Theodore Roszak, *The Voice of the Earth: An Exploration of Ecopsychology,* 2nd ed. (Grand Rapids, MI: Phanes Press, 2001), 293.

Found deer skeleton

Chapter 3

Nature Encounters

THE SIX-YEAR-OLD PICTURED HERE LED ME DIRECTLY TO THE DEER SKELE-
ton in the woods where she'd seen it the day before. She knew just where it
lay, though there was no obvious path through the undergrowth. She is not
likely to forget this find, even as a grown-up. Childhood encounters with
the natural world are often treasured memories for adults. Indeed, they can
be among their earliest remembrances. I still remember the froglets that
appeared as if by magic in the stairwell to the laundry room of the apartment
project where we lived when I was barely three.

Preschoolers will tell you eagerly about the ducks they've fed, the owl they
heard, the deer that came into their yard. They enjoy keeping a nature table
with bits and pieces from their explorations. Although adults are encouraged
to take nothing but pictures, children can be taught to collect judiciously,
and in appropriate places. The feathers and shells and interesting rocks in
their display serve as reminders of an enjoyable experience. Older children
can be encouraged to keep nature journals as in *Ellie's Log* (Oregon State
University Press, 2013), where they can document their experiences in both

words and pictures. In the back matter of numerous titles annotated here are suggestions for keeping nature journals as well as for making appropriate art.

The stories in this chapter focus on children's personal experiences with the natural world. In some stories, kids are on their own or exploring and playing with other kids. In others, family members and other adults are making the experience possible and, in the process, forging treasured connections. These may be organized trips—hunting or fishing or helping to conserve a species—or they may be simple walks in the woods or on a beach. Barbara Kerley's album of photographs, *The World Is Waiting for You,* reminds us all how such childhood experiences can connect to future adult lives.

CHILDREN MOSTLY ON THEIR OWN

A Perfect Day
Picture book

By Carin Berger. Illustrated by Carin Berger.
 Greenwillow Books, 2012. Ages 3–7.
Subjects: Snow, Play, Winter, Seasons

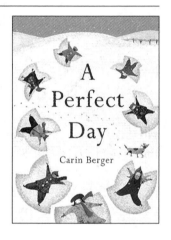

"It snowed / and snowed / and snowed / and snowed." The opening text of this appealing celebration falls down the first pages like snowflakes. Then, from dawn to dusk, children ski, skate, sled, throw snowballs, make forts and snowmen, sell icicles, and make snow angels before going home for hot chocolate. The delights of fresh new snow are made extra special by Berger's intriguing cut-paper collages, scenes of eighteen children and a dog at play, done on old ledgers painted in shades of white. The round-headed children look similar but can be distinguished by their outfits. Words (mostly entries in script) peek through the scenes, adding to the mystery and the distance. This simple story, a catalog of activities with just one line of text per spread, opens and closes with scenes of the small-town setting. This perfect day is a snow day of childhood dreams.

Just Ducks! *Informational picture book*

By Nicola Davies. Illustrated by Salvatore Rubbino. Candlewick Press, 2012.
   Ages 4–9.
Subjects: Mallards, Ducks

This charming child's-eye view of the ducks that share her world is, in fact, an informational book, complete with an index which reveals that the text covers appearance, habits, families, and behavior. But it reads like a story told by a girl who has spent plenty of time watching ducks that wake her in the morning with their quacks. The text is on two levels: the narrative, which spans a day in the girl's life with some memories of other seasons, and extra informational notes in a different font. "Drakes don't sit on eggs, so they don't need to be camouflaged." The voice is completely believable and the information accurate. Surprisingly realistic, watercolor-like, earth-toned illustrations show the narrator going on with her daily activities but continually connected to the natural world around her thanks to her mallard neighbors.

Gobble, Gobble *Informational picture book*

By Cathryn Falwell. Illustrated by Cathryn Falwell. Dawn Publications, 2011.
   Ages 4–7.
Subjects: Stories in rhyme, Turkeys

Lucky Jenny finds a surprise in her own backyard. After a flock of turkeys visits in the spring, she continues to watch them throughout the year. A simple rhyming text describes the turkeys' appearance and behavior as they nest and raise their young in the nearby woods. Illustrations with the appearance of painted block prints include other inhabitants of the turkeys' surroundings—a deer, chickadees, cardinals, squirrels. Plants and trees from the author-illustrator's home state of Maine are recognizable, and the season is indicated with a vignette: apple blossoms, dandelion flower, red leaf, snowflake. The book concludes with "Jenny's Journal," more facts about turkeys for the older reader. As she has done in previous books, the author-illustrator includes suggestions for artwork and other activities. A Guess These Tracks puzzle provides an appealing conclusion.

Infinity and Me
Picture book

By Kate Hosford. Illustrated by Gabi Swiatkow-
ska. Carolrhoda Books, 2012. Ages 5–10.
Subjects: Infinity, Grandmothers, Schools

Big mathematical ideas are part of the wonder
of the natural world. This intriguing title takes
a stab at introducing one such concept to the
picture book audience. Looking at the stars one
night, Uma begins to think about infinity, ask-
ing friends, people at school, and her grandmother, and finally coming to
an understanding that works for her. This child's-eye way of contemplating
infinity includes enormous numbers, the uninterrupted track of the infinity
symbol, music that goes round and round, eating ice cream endlessly, and
staying eight forever. Uma's grandmother thinks of family, stretching backwards and forwards in time. The child settles on boundless love. Expressive
paintings filled with detail, sketches, and portraits demonstrate the suggested interpretations and show Uma (with her new red shoes) along with
recurring details that will invite repeated attention.

In the Meadow
Picture book

By Yukiko Kato. Illustrated by Komako Sakai. Enchanted Lion Books, 2011.
Ages 3–6.
Subjects: Meadows, Nature

A preschooler explores the natural world as part of a family outing. In this
first of a promised series of Japanese imports, a small child wanders away
from the river into a meadow where the plants are higher than her eyes.
She looks, listens, and gets just a little worried until her mother finds her.
Onomatopoetic sounds add realism to this charming, simple story. Pastel
illustrations have a texture that suggests that this is a well-worn memory.
They show the child admiring an orange-and-black butterfly, surprised by
a grasshopper, and listening to birds and bees. Feeling alone and lost is far
more scary than are the animals she encounters. Quiet and expressive, this
is a perfect natural world experience—and it ends well.

Ellie's Log: Exploring the Forest Where the Great Tree Fell

Fiction

By Judith L. Li. Illustrated by M. L. Herring. Oregon State University Press, 2013. Ages 8–11.

Subjects: Oregon, Forests, Nature journals

Budding young naturalists might be particularly interested in this combination of science and storytelling that describes and models keeping a nature journal. After a winter storm causes an old Douglas fir to fall in the forest behind her home in Oregon, Ellie and her fifth-grade classmate Ricky visit and revisit this Pacific Northwest woods over the next few months, drawing and learning about changes there. Each chapter describes one of their seven trips, opening with an artist's illustration of the area and closing with two pages from Ellie's field notebook. Page margins are also decorated with wildlife sketches. Unusually for such an exploration, there is much consideration of tiny things—the world inside the moss, for example, and the insects and fungi that contribute to tree rot. Instructions for keeping your own nature logbook are included.

Snowflakes Fall

Picture book

By Patricia MacLachlan. Illustrated by Steven Kellogg. Random House, 2013. Ages 3–7.

Subjects: Snow, Seasons

Children romp in falling snow, worry in a nighttime storm, slide, make snow angels in the shining day, and recognize the snow's contribution to the water cycle and summer flowers. Reminding readers that, like snowflakes, no two children are the same, this poignant picture book was written and illustrated as a memorial for the children of Newtown, Connecticut, but it could also be read to young children as a simple appreciation for the joy of winter snow. The front endpapers show children playing hide-and-seek in the changing seasons; in the back, snow angels ascend heavenward. Kellogg's paintings, on double-page spreads, show a wide variety of kids and dogs in action in the changing small-town landscape. Understated and moving.

The Perfect Gift   *Picture book*

By J. Samia Mair. Illustrated by Craig Howarth. Islamic Foundation, 2010.
   Ages 5–8.
Subjects: Gifts, Nature—religious aspects, Islamic stories

Seeking a perfect gift for her mother for Eid ul-Adha, Sarah walks into the snowy woods and finds a beautiful spring flower. Tempted to pick it, she decides to leave it there with a sign reminding everyone that such beauty is a gift from Allah. This Muslim child's story is a reminder that respect for the natural world extends across cultures and religions. Though the flower has not yet returned the following year (when Eid falls earlier in the winter), Sarah's family finds an icicle with a rainbow of light and adopts a new family custom, a walk in the woods to find a perfect gift every year. Eid is a holiday on the Islamic calendar; it falls earlier each year on the calendar most of us use. But looking for some special beauty in the natural world can happen in any season, and Sarah's story can connect us all.

Green
Picture book

By Laura Vaccaro Seeger. Illustrated by
   Laura Vaccaro Seeger. Roaring Brook
   Press, 2012. Ages 2–6.
Subjects: Green, Stories in rhyme, Colors,
   Concepts

The wonder in this book is both in the natural world and in the artist's creation. With a text that is only two words per spread and die-cut pages, Seeger reflects on the many meanings we have for the word *green.* Each picture leads into the next and uses elements of the one before. Seemingly textured paintings invite readers to touch and to immerse themselves in a world that is mostly natural. A forest leads to a sea, and then to green foods. A tiger peers through a jungle; a khaki salamander almost matches its background. On these two pages, words in the painted background become part of the text. There are some manmade objects: a stop sign is "never green" and an old painted wall is faded. Finally, after the "no green" of winter, a boy plants a tree: "forever green." Irresistible.

No One But You

Picture book

By Douglas Wood. Illustrated by P. J. Lynch.
Candlewick Press, 2011. Ages 3–8.
Subjects: Nature, Senses and sensation

Addressed directly to the young listener, this glorious oversize album of portraits is an invitation to personal discovery of the wonders of nature. "No one but you can remember your own memories." A diverse group of children, painted so realistically you would recognize them on the street, have individual encounters with natural phenomena. Opening with a small boy looking closely at a ladybug, this goes on, engaging all the senses in a variety of memorable experiences including (among others) walking in a rain puddle, holding a turtle, smelling a dandelion, tasting a drop of water from a rose blossom, listening to frogs, and wishing on a star. The narrative arc takes the reader from morning till night, with the final spread showing a child walking with others on a moonlit night and saying "I love you, too." This should inspire listeners to collect some magical moments of their own.

Go Outside!

TAKE A WALK with a child. Walk around the block or into a park. Notice the sky and the weather, the wind in the trees and on your faces. How does the air feel?

Find a place to sit down. Close your eyes and listen. What do you hear? Sometimes it takes a minute or two for all the small sounds to register.

What do you smell? Are there natural smells, even in a city?

Look at a small patch of ground. Challenge the child with you to find all the different living things that are making use of that patch of ground.

Can they imagine what it would be like to be as small as the ants and bugs you see? And what would a bird, flying overhead, see down here?

Sitting still for a long time is hard. Is there a hill to run up or roll down?

In a wood, there may be stones or logs to move with critters living underneath.

Don't forget to bring something home—a drawing, a photograph, a leaf rubbing, or a pinecone—something for the child's nature notebook or nature table. And bring a memory for yourself!

CHILDREN AND ADULTS

The Deer Watch
Picture book

By Pat Lowery Collins. Illustrated by David
    Slonim. Candlewick Press, 2013. Ages 3–7.
Subjects: Deer, Fathers and sons, Nature

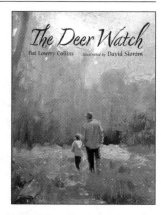

A boy and his father set out early one morning
to see a deer. They explore the shore, the marsh,
a new development, and an area of conservation
land where shadows allow a mother and her
twin fawns to hide. This quiet story of a shared
experience in the natural world is very reminiscent of Yolen's *Owl Moon*
(Philomel, 1987), right down to the child's determination to be quiet and
still—hard for this boy. At one point, when he thinks nothing is moving, his
father reminds him of what might be hidden: baby birds, little foxes, mother
squirrels. The boy tells his story with considerable detail, remembering the
sound of seagulls, the egret and pheasant they spotted, and the warmth of
a sudden rain shower. But he sets it in an unidentified past. Textured oil
paintings place the whole episode in the mists of memory—a treasured one.

The World Is Waiting for You   *Picture book*

By Barbara Kerley. Illustrated with National Geographic Society (U.S.) pho-
    tographs. National Geographic, 2013. Ages 4–10.
Subjects: Discoveries in geography, Photographs

Images of adults engaging with the natural world combine with those of
children simply enjoying the out-of-doors to illustrate this ode to exploration. "The whole wide world is waiting for you," Kerley says, and the
pictures she's chosen, mostly from National Geographic archives, reveal its
possibilities. "Follow the path around the next bend. / Who knows where
it might lead?" Children play in water and mud, climb rocks and trees, and
peer into snow holes and hollow logs. Strikingly composed and beautifully
reproduced, these images have been carefully arranged so that the children's
actions lead to those of adults. A paleontologist unearths dinosaur bones,

and Sylvia Earle dives deep. An astronaut floats outside the International Space Station, and a bunch of spelunkers clamber about in a giant crystal cave. The back matter identifies the adults, explains their activities, and provides a geographic location for all the images, which, together, celebrate the opportunities in our world.

Big Night for Salamanders   *Picture book*

By Sarah Lamstein. Illustrated by Carol Benioff. Boyds Mills Press, 2010.
    Ages 6–9.
Subjects: Salamanders, Vernal pools, Ecology

A family works together to give nature a hand. On the night of the first warm spring rain, Evan can hardly wait until after dark, when he and his parents will go out to slow traffic and help spotted salamanders cross from their winter burrows to the vernal (temporary) pool where they will lay their eggs. The dual text of his experience and salamander facts introduces the Big Night of amphibian migration in the Northeast. Paintings show the salamanders in their habitat, a mixed-race boy whose enthusiasm shows in his body language, and even, once, a dog slyly stealing a cookie from the boy's plate. Parents (only parts of their bodies appear) are involved in this crossing activity and remind Evan of road safety from time to time. An afterword describes the spotted salamander's life cycle and gives more information about Big Nights and vernal pools.

The White-Footed Mouse
Picture book

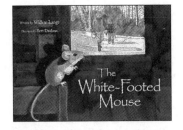

By Willem Lange. Illustrated by Bert Dodson.
    Bunker Hill Publishing, 2012. Ages 5–9.
Subjects: Mice, Fathers and sons, Outdoor
    life, Hunting

On a winter hunting trip, a boy applies his father's rule: don't kill anything you don't want to eat. This gentle father-and-son story celebrates the natural world. The narrator's father—"the greatest dad that any kid has ever had"—teaches him to find birds' nests, to paddle a canoe, and to shoot a .22 rifle. When he's eight, he's deemed old enough to go hunting with his father at their mountain camp in the woods. There he finds, and feeds, a white-footed mouse, an animal his father doesn't want in the cabin. But the rule holds. The realistic pencil-and-watercolor illustrations support the story's nostalgic air. This is a piece of memory, but also a reminder of the respect for nature that goes along with a love for hunting in many families. This is the third collaboration between these two Vermonters reflecting north-country life.

One Frozen Lake   *Picture book*

By Deborah Jo Larson. Illustrated by Steve Johnson and Lou Fancher. Minnesota Historical Society Press, 2012. Ages 4–7.
Subjects: Ice fishing, Fishing, Grandfathers, Counting

Appropriately dressed for the weather, a small boy and his grandfather spend a day ice fishing. The spare description of their day enumerates the depth of the ice; the strength of the fishing line; the number of canvas fishing shacks, jig sticks, and trays in the tackle box; the number of fishing holes, friends, cups of cocoa consumed, and hours that pass. Ice fishing hasn't changed much over the years: the shack has a coal stove; grandfather uses a hand drill; the two play cards while they wait. But this is a modern story with a catch-and-release ending. Johnson and Fancher's digital collage art balances the expanses of ice with plenty of colorful plaids, including a red Stewart patchwork on the endpapers and some fantasized plaid fish. Though this activity is limited to northern states, all readers can appreciate the intergenerational connection.

Puffling Patrol
Informational picture book

By Ted Lewin and Betsy Lewin. Illustrated by Ted Lewin and Betsy Lewin. Lee & Low Books, 2012. Ages 5–9.
Subjects: Atlantic puffins, Wildlife rescue, Iceland

On Iceland's Westman Islands, children patrol the streets in August to rescue puffin chicks who have landed there, confused by the town lights, and whose wings are not strong enough to take off again. The Lewins, who have made it their life's work to introduce children to other parts of the world, here follow eight-year-old twins Dáni and Erna as they participate in a natural environmental cycle—the fledging of seabirds—along with others in their small town. They feed one tiny puffin. In the dark and rain they search for and find another. The rescue and release of even one small bird is satisfying. Ted Lewin's watercolors effectively convey the majestic scenery as well as more intimate indoor moments. Betsy Lewin's pen-and-ink sketches add detail. The back matter includes additional information, resources, glossary, and a pronunciation guide for older readers.

Butterfly Tree   *Picture book*

By Sandra Markle. Illustrated by Leslie Wu. Peachtree, 2011. Ages 4–8.
Subjects: Monarch butterfly, Butterflies, Migration, Lake Erie

Markle, who has written about nature all around the world, offers a never-to-be-forgotten moment based on an experience she remembers from her own childhood. Her gentle free verse description slowly reveals the nature of a cloud Jilly and her mother saw from a Lake Erie beach. First it looks like black rain. Could it be a volcano? When the cloud comes closer and turns a shimmering orange, they follow it into the woods where it becomes a tree full of monarch butterflies, "an explosion of golden-orange bits that fills the sunlight." Impressionistic pastel illustrations add to the mystery. While a two-page explanation at the end describes the facts of monarch migration, this dreamy, evocative memory approaches this scientific wonder with appropriate awe. This is a grand companion to more literal accounts of butterfly behavior.

Over and Under the Snow   *Informational picture book*

By Kate Messner. Illustrated by Christopher Silas Neal. Chronicle Books, 2011. Ages 4–8.
Subjects: Animals, Snow, Winter, Hibernation, Nature stories, Seasons

In a day's skiing with her father cross-country through the snowy woods, a child learns about the animals living over and under the snow. There are tracks in the snow. Squirrels and voles, frogs, even beaver and a queen bee hide underneath; a great horned owl sits in a tree overhead. This beautifully written text is a pleasure to read aloud. "We stand like statues carved in ice till a bushy-tailed fox steps from a thicket. Tips his ear to the ground. / listens . . . / listens . . . / listens still . . ." The simple outlines of the animals and the muted colors of the mixed media illustrations on matte paper add to the quiet effect. There's plenty of snowy white space. The back matter adds more detail about the animals in this "secret kingdom under the snow." For lap listeners and small groups, this charming celebration of the winter world could easily prompt similar outings.

Turtle Summer: A Journal for My Daughter

Nonfiction

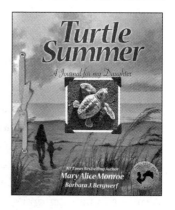

By Mary Alice Monroe. Illustrated by Barbara
    J. Bergwerf. Sylvan Dell Publishing, 2007.
    Ages 5–10.
Subjects: Scrapbooks, Loggerhead turtle, Sea
    turtles

The imagined premise of this informative and engaging book is that a turtle watcher and rehabilitator has made this journal for her daughter to recall a summer they spent at their beach cottage watching for nesting and hatching sea turtles. After the mother turtle leaves, her nest is marked to keep it safe, and the eggs are carefully moved if necessary. Pastel sketches and photographs show step-by-step documentation of a modern turtle-watching experience as well as calendar pages to mark the months, and labeled flowers and shells. Along the way, readers learn to recognize other seashore treasures: sea stars, sand dollars, and some of the common birds. A double-page spread shows activities at the Sea Turtle Hospital. Gently and simply told, the text flows along comfortably as the summer passes and they wait for the hatching. Finally the young turtles emerge and slowly make their way to the sea.

Good Night, Laila Tov

Picture book

By Laurel Snyder. Illustrated by Jui Ishida. Random House, 2012. Ages 3–6.
Subjects: Stories in rhyme, Camping, Family life, Nature—religious aspects,
Bedtime, Jews—United States

On a family camping trip, the waves on the beach, the meadow sky, a surprise rainstorm, and the long road home all lull the children to sleep, wishing them good night in both English and Hebrew. On this trip, the family plants trees near a campsite, in line with the Judaic tradition of *tikkun olam*, repairing the world. This is mentioned on the jacket flap but not in the library-bound edition. It's unfortunate that this idea and the translation of *laila tov* (given in agate type in the copyright information) were not included in an author's note, because understanding that would help readers. Still, both rhyming story and colorful, stylized illustrations show a family enjoying the natural world. The illustrations include symbols that some readers will recognize as Jewish, but both story and pictures have broader appeal.

Carpenter bee on phlox

Chapter 4

Backyard and Garden

CHILDREN'S EXPERIENCES WITH THE NATURAL WORLD OFTEN BEGIN AT home. An infant might have a colorful bird mobile or a flower in a pot. There might be a fish tank or a pet, or several. Board books (annotated in another chapter) may be a first connection, too. Very young children can and do look out windows. Even in big, busy cities, there are birds. There's the sun in the morning, the moon at night, and all kinds of weather to see and talk about. Maybe there is a yard or garden or (for a lucky few) a family farm or country camp. Young children are taken for walks in the neighborhood and, if there is one nearby, to a local park. Just as a social studies curriculum for young children will usually start with the child, the family, and the community, parents can connect their very young child to the natural world with activities in and around their home. The activities can be as simple as observing a bee on a flower, as seen in the photograph in this chapter.

These books, too, take place around the home. Some take place entirely in the imagination, some chronicle an activity, and some describe patient observation of the natural world by children and grown-ups alike.

INSIDE AND OUTSIDE

Inside Outside   *Picture book*

By Lizi Boyd. Illustrated by Lizi Boyd. Chronicle Books, 2013. Ages 3–7.
Subjects: Dogs, Play, Stories without words, Toy and movable books

If you're inside, do you wonder what's going on outside? Can you bring your outdoor play inside? Peek through the windows, or turn the pages to find out in this charming wordless picture book. One boy, one dog, one cat, and two mice take advantage of each season. A turtle, found in a spring rain, joins them. Inside and outside, there's much going on, and the activities echo each other. Even prereaders will find many story lines to follow. The birds, fed seeds in the winter, build nests, raise babies, and even join the boy's games. Someone builds a tree house. Everyone dresses up for Halloween. Planting, building a snowman, painting, flying a kite, making model boats, reading, raking leaves, performing, and going for a night time walk—there's no end of things to do inside and out in this celebration of children's connection to the natural world.

Sleep Like a Tiger   *Picture book; Bedtime story*

By Mary Logue. Illustrated by Pamela Zagarenski. Houghton Mifflin Harcourt, 2012. Ages 3–7.
Subjects: Sleep, Animals—sleep behavior

Making a clear connection to the natural world, parents of a little girl who says she's not sleepy help her get ready for bed by doing the appropriate preparations and thinking about how animals sleep. These soothing thoughts send her off to dreamland, comfortably curled up with her stuffed cat next to a tiger with its stuffed girl. The pictures of this Caldecott Honor book are intriguing, with details that will set readers wondering. Where is the train on the endpapers going? What's with the wheels everywhere? And the coffeepot? The narrative includes some dry humor and appealing imagery: The dog is on the couch "where he's not supposed to be." Snails "curl up like a cinnamon roll inside their shell." This should lead children to curl up in their "cocoon of sheets" and "nest of blankets" ready for dreams of their own.

Waiting Out the Storm
Picture book

By JoAnn Early Macken. Illustrated by Susan
Gaber. Candlewick Press, 2010. Ages 3–7.
Subjects: Stories in rhyme, Rain and rainfall,
Mother and child, Weather

In a story told entirely in dialog and rhyme that
reads comfortably aloud, a mother assures the
daughter she calls Buttercup that both the ani-
mals out-of-doors and the child inside will be safe during a thunderstorm. The
mother's imaginative explanations will appeal especially to a young listener
with a vivid imagination. While they gather daffodils outside, and the wind
picks up, mother reassuringly tells her daughter, "The wind calls the raindrops to come out and play." Later, indoors, thunder's loud noise is explained:
"Thunder stomps. Thunder stumbles and bumbles around." Gaber's softly lit
paintings show the dark clouds and flashing lightning but also a pair of mallards paddling in the rain, chipmunks snuggling in a burrow, and a mama
chickadee sheltering her nestlings. A storm is "a wonder to see," Mama says.
Calming and soothing, this is just right for reading on a rainy day.

Once Upon a Northern Night   *Picture book*

By Jean Pendziwol. Illustrated by Isabelle Arsenault. Groundwood Books /
House of Anansi Press, 2013. Ages 3–6.
Subjects: Winter, Night, Snow

From mother to child, perhaps, a lyrical description of a nighttime snowfall
in a Canadian winter. Fine lines and muted colors characterize the dreamy
illustrations of this free-verse poem. They show the earth "wrapped in a
downy blanket, / just like you," the snowflakes like stars, tracks in the
woods, a deer and her fawn, a great gray owl, snowshoe hares, a fox and
more. There's a picnic table "mounded with snowy white / like vanilla ice
cream" and even northern lights. Spots of color appear on each page, though
much is in shades of black, brown, and white; so the blue of frost decorating
the window comes as a welcome surprise. And then there's the wonder of a
snowy morning, seen through the window. This is winter in many parts of
North America and a lovely, soft rendition of its magic.

The Snow Day
Picture book

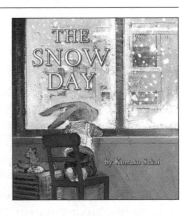

By Komako Sakai. Illustrated by Komako
Sakai. Arthur A. Levine Books, 2009.
Ages 3–5.
Subjects: Snow, Mother and child, Rabbits

With kindergarten closed, a bunny enjoys an
unexpected snow day although it keeps his
(or maybe her) father's plane from coming
home. This bunny child wears pants, but the
first-person narrative gives no clue to its gender. The story is quiet, appropriate to the sound of falling snow and the tedium of a long day, and it's
unusual in that the rabbit family lives in an apartment. At first, mother and
child only go out on the balcony. "Mommy, we are all alone in the world,"
the bunny says. After a long day of watchful waiting, the snow stops and
they venture outside in the dark to make snowballs, snow dumplings, and
even snow monsters. Many of the painted illustrations are framed; others
spread wordlessly across two pages, showing the snow in all its glory. These
rabbits have particularly expressive ears; the child's ears, for example, often
strain forward in excitement. This five-year-old's wonder at the magic of a
snowy day is catching.

NATURE IN THE YARD

Wolfsnail: A Backyard Predator *Informational picture book*

By Sarah C. Campbell. Illustrated by Sarah C. Campbell and Richard P.
Campbell. Boyds Mills Press, 2008. Ages 4–7.
Subject: Snails

This beautiful photo essay describes the drama one can find in one's own
backyard. Unlike most garden snails that chew on plants, the rosy wolfsnail
of the southern United States eats other snails and slugs. Astonishing photos
taken by the author show a wolfsnail's slow journey up a hosta plant, its discovery of another snail's slime trail, its consumption of a smaller land snail,
the empty shell left behind, and the carnivorous snail's return to rest. The

steady pace of its journey is occasionally interrupted by a different picture: an expanse of hosta leaf, a threatening bird, a worm. The large-font text is written in relatively simple sentences but uses appropriate vocabulary (*mucus*, *radula*) defined in context or in the glossary at the end. Further facts can also be found in the back matter. A splendid nature book for beginning readers.

Look Up! Bird-Watching in Your Own Backyard *Nonfiction*

By Annette LeBlanc Cate. Illustrated by Annette LeBlanc Cate. Candlewick
    Press, 2013. Ages 8–15.
Subject: Bird-watching

Bird-watching is simple, says the enthusiastic author. You can start in your own backyard or neighborhood with no more equipment than a sketchbook. (Not because drawing birds is easy, but because it forces close attention.) This chatty, appealing invitation is packed with accurate information and cartoon-like sketches of an extraordinary variety of birds from across the country. (The page on bird color alone has sixty different species.) The author covers basics like color, shape, and actions before going on to distinguishing markings and using a field guide. She even introduces some scientific names. These are very talkative birds. Speech bubbles carry much of the information, and there's plenty of humor. A potential birder will find much to learn and enjoy in this informative, accessible introduction, and the bibliography includes good suggestions for birders of any age.

What Bluebirds Do *Informational picture book*

By Pamela F. Kirby. Illustrated by Pamela F. Kirby. Boyds Mills Press,
    2009. Ages 4–10.
Subject: Bluebirds

From a blind in her North Carolina yard, photographer Kirby observed and photographed a pair of eastern bluebirds. She introduces them to young readers, carefully distinguishing male from female and both from other blue birds they might encounter. This photo essay describes their courtship behavior, their nest box, their eggs, and their feeding of their five nestlings. A scrawny newborn chick with a collar of down is shown in a human hand, and we see all five, nestled together in their small quarters, after their first brown spotted feathers had grown. Both parents feed the babies, first in the nest box and then outside as they gradually move away and learn to find food on their own. The simple sentence structure will help the fledgling reader, and the sharply reproduced photographs also tell the story. Extensive back matter includes more detailed information.

If You Want to See a Whale   *Picture book*

By Julie Fogliano. Illustrated by Erin E. Stead. Roaring Brook Press, 2013. Ages 2–6.

Subjects: Whale-watching, Patience

Imagining yourself into the natural world is another way to get there. In this quiet tribute to the imagination a small boy describes—to his dog, perhaps, or to the reader—what you must do to see a whale. You need a window, an ocean, and a "not-so-comfy chair." You need to disregard the distracting paths your imagination might follow: "if you want to see a whale / you'll have to just ignore the roses." Be patient and focus, though the distractions are goals in themselves. The gentle repetition makes for a grand read-aloud

Do Some Planting

AN AVOCADO PIT, suspended by toothpicks with its broad end in a glass of water and its pointy end up, will sprout in three to six weeks. It's best to change the water every few days. An avocado tree will grow satisfactorily indoors for some years if it has enough light, though it won't fruit.

If there is room outside, give a child a small plot of land. Digging is fun! Planning, preparing the ground, and lots of watchful waiting will be necessary. Weeding, too, is essential in many parts of the country.

In pots in the window or a little plot of land, even toddlers can plant seeds. Radishes, lettuce, and marigolds sprout reasonably quickly. The first two can be eaten less than sixty days later. Marigolds, cut regularly, will flower all summer. Beans are easy seeds to handle and have sturdy sprouts.

Check out KidsGardening, from the National Gardening Association, for more ideas (www.kidsgardening.org).

Or adopt a plant and record important data like date of leaf out and flowering for the National Science Foundation's Project BudBurst (www.budburst.org).

Join another ongoing citizen science project by planting a tulip garden; see Journey North's Tulip Test Gardens (www.learner.org/jnorth/tm/tulips/AboutFall.html).

experience. Stead's illustrations use the textures of block printing to provide depth for the ocean and the sky and precise pencil lines to show the boy, the dog, a bird, an inchworm, shapes in the clouds, and possible pirates in the sea. Charming.

GARDENS AND FARMS

Quiet in the Garden
Picture book

By Aliki. Illustrated by Aliki. Greenwillow
   Books, 2009. Ages 3–6.
Subjects: Gardens, Animals—food, Nature study

Sitting quietly in his garden, a small boy observes the plants and animals, listens to the sounds, and imagines conversing with the critters around him. Each explains his actions with versions of the explanation that he was hungry. Young listeners who enjoy predictability will appreciate the somewhat repetitive text, and they won't mind the seasonal improbability. Strawberries, cucumbers, daffodils, and tomatoes all at the same time? The story ends with a list of the fruits and vegetables the boy has picked for himself and his twelve garden friends. This bountiful garden also yields a lovely harvest of eating words, from *nibble* and *chomp* to *swallow* and *munch*. This blue-eyed, brown-skinned boy starts out with sandals and soon sheds them; he has a bandage on one elbow, a nice touch.

And Then It's Spring
Picture book

By Julie Fogliano. Illustrated by Erin E. Stead. Roaring Brook Press, 2012.
   Ages 3–7.
Subjects: Spring, Gardens, Seasons

A boy plants seeds. Tenderly, uncertainly, and somewhat impatiently, he waits for them to sprout. He wonders, worries, and waits some more, and finally "all around / you have / green." The action is in the boy's imaginings.

In early spring, after planting and a rain, the ground is "still brown, / but a hopeful, very possible sort of brown." Will bears stomp on the seedlings? Preschoolers who have waited endlessly for their own seeds to sprout will recognize the concern here in the boy, dog, rabbit, turtle, and bird, especially as they listen for the "greenish hum" underground. The voles and worms underground are listening, too. This lovely, understated poem has pictures to match, done with woodblock prints and pencil, showing a bespectacled boy whose blank face could be any child who has tried to hurry spring.

Molly's Organic Farm

Picture book

By Carol Malnor and Trina L. Hunner. Illustrated by Trina L. Hunner. Dawn Publications, 2012. Ages 4–7.

Subjects: Organic farming, Farms, Cats

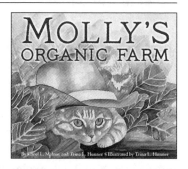

This cat's-eye view of an organic farm is based on the true story of a homeless cat that wandered into a California organic farm and spent the summer there and the following winter with a farm neighbor, the illustrator. The story of the cat, told in couplets, is intertwined with an introduction to organic farming, including the role of compost, beneficial bugs, companion planting, crop rotation, and animal helpers. Hunner's realistic watercolors show both the once-homeless orange cat and the plants and animals of the farm from Molly the cat's perspective. The text, too, emphasizes the sensations of living outdoors on a farm from Molly's point of view: the smell and texture of the compost, the sounds of the insects, the heat of the sun, the cool shade provided by sunflowers, the nighttime animals, and the changing temperatures of the seasons. Sweet.

It's Harvest Time!   *Informational picture book*

By Jean McElroy. Illustrated by Tilde. Little Simon, 2010. Ages 4–7.

Subjects: Seeds, Plants, Plant life cycles, Lift-the-flap books, Toy and movable books

This interactive lift-the-flap guessing game demonstrates how five different seeds will become plants and food we eat. Simple in concept and appearance, it is surprisingly effective in connecting seeds to plants and food. Each of the five sections begins with a description of a few seeds and a question—what will you become?—opposite a photograph of the seeds and a statement about how they will grow or what they need. Open up the first set of flaps to see what the sprout looks like, and open again to a larger picture of a child with the produce: yellow corn, red apples, orange carrots, purple grapes, and orange pumpkins. The color of the question page and the arrow indicating which flap to turn matches the ultimate color of the fruit or vegetable. The format looks young, but the content will intrigue primary-grade readers.

The Honeybee Man

Picture book

By Lela Nargi. Illustrated by Kyrsten Brooker.
Schwartz & Wade Books, 2011. Ages 5–8.
Subjects: Honeybees, Bees, Beekeepers, Brooklyn (New York)

Nature can be found in surprising places. On the roof of his home in Brooklyn, Fred raises honeybees, sending them off to forage in his neighbor's gardens and maybe even some blueberry bushes across town. This sweet story shows him saying good morning to his queens, admiring the sister bees as they fly off, and dreaming of flying along. Later in the year, he harvests his honey and shares it with neighbors. The author based her imagined story on two real-life Brooklyn beekeepers. Moderately realistic illustrations, a combination of oil paintings and collage, play with perspective and size to give a slightly surreal effect. But accurate information about bees—even their waggle-dance communication—is built into the story, and more is added in an afterword. Endpaper diagrams show bee and flower and beehive parts. Charming and unusual.

Twelve Kinds of Ice

Memoir

By Ellen Bryan Obed. Illustrated by Barbara McClintock. Houghton Mifflin Books for Children, 2012. Ages 6–9.
Subjects: Ice skating, Family life, Winter, Seasons

Memories of a Maine childhood glisten in this evocative series of vignettes. From the first skim of ice in a water bucket to the soft and splotchy skating rink surface at the end of the season, the author's nostalgic description of winters on the family farm will resonate for any reader who grew up in a part of the world with seasonal freezing temperatures. A series of scenes recalled in poetic language combine to form a narrative arc with some suspense, a surprise winter thaw, and a culminating ice show. Numerous line drawings add to the appeal, showing children sledding, a father waltzing with a broom, the narrator figure skating at night, and more. Old-fashioned but timeless, this is a sparkling celebration of family, friends, and a magical season.

Maple Syrup Season
Informational picture book

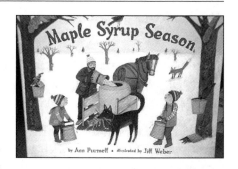

By Ann Purmell. Illustrated by Jill
    Weber. Holiday House, 2008.
    Ages 5–9.
Subjects: Maple syrup, Family life

In late winter, when the sap is running in the maple trees, it's maple syrup season. A fictional extended family gathers to tap the trees, collect the sap, boil it down, and make syrup and delicious sugar on snow taffy. Although the illustrations add some fanciful details, this is a clear and informative explanation of the traditional maple syrup-making process. The straightforward text is relatively simple. The art could represent almost any time period, but the setting is probably present-day New England. The characters are easily recognizable: Dad with his glasses and neatly trimmed beard, Hannah with her plaid shirt and braids, and Hayden with his green and yellow cap and mittens. A cat and dog follow the process, too. Two pages of end matter, including a glossary, add more specific details about the process and the product. Pair this with Purmell's earlier *Christmas Tree Farm* (Holiday House, 2006).

Compost Stew: An A to Z Recipe for the Earth *Picture book*

By Mary McKenna Siddals. Illustrated by Ashley Wolff. Tricycle Press,
 2010. Ages 4–7.
Subjects: Alphabet book, Stories in rhyme, Gardening

Aided by a goose and a spotted dog, four children add ingredients to their
pot of compost stew throughout the year in this cheerful, environmentally
conscious book that may encourage young gardeners to do the same. Working inside and outside, the children collect materials, moisten, stir, and cover
their concoction. The author has included some that readers might not have
thought of themselves—hair clippings, dryer lint, paper shreds, and quarry
dust—and a note in the front adds a little more information. The rhyming
instructions for composting use an alphabet of ingredients from apple cores
to zinnia heads. Reused materials for the collage-and-gouache illustrations
provide a perfect background and accompaniment. Fun to read aloud, this
alphabet song is broken up along the way with a refrain: "Just add to the pot
/ and let it all rot / into Compost Stew."

Secrets of the Garden: Food Chains *Informational picture book*
and the Food Web in Our Backyard

By Kathleen Weidner Zoehfeld. Illustrated by Priscilla Lamont. Alfred A.
 Knopf, 2012. Ages 4–9.
Subjects: Gardens, Gardening, Food chains (Ecology)

While Alice describes how her family plants, nourishes, and enjoys a large
backyard garden, chickens explain food chains and the food web the garden represents. This clever presentation of information about the relationships among plants and animals accompanies an activity that will already
be familiar to some readers. Text and appealing pen-and-watercolor illustrations work together to show Pete and Alice, their parents, cat, and two
chickens working in what Alice calls their "summer home." The plants they
choose are those that might be grown in a home garden in a temperate zone.
The children watch and wait, notice the rabbit nibbling lettuce, insects both
helpful and harmful, the robin, and the worms. Finally, all enjoy the harvest, putting some away for the winter when they will plan what they'll do
next year. Both factual and fanciful, this should make readers want to grow
something themselves.

Partial eclipse of the moon

Chapter 5

From the Earth to the Sky and Beyond

HOW DO CHILDREN BEGIN TO MAKE THE CONNECTION BETWEEN THEIR OWN lives and the earth we all live on, and the sun and the stars? First, of course, there's day and night, and the appearance and disappearance of the sun and moon. Bedtime stories often make a nighttime-moonlight connection, though parents can point out to their children that for much of a month the moon is also visible during the day and doesn't always light up the night. There is hardly ever an eclipse, even partial, as pictured here. That would be an event to remember. So are nights spent looking for falling stars. The Perseid shower, in August, is one of the best to observe because it is known for producing a large number of bright meteors and comes at a time of year when it is usually comfortable to be outside in the middle of the night. Beyond the moon and highly publicized meteor showers, though, the workings of the sun, moon, and stars often seem mysterious even to adults. The growth of mountains, the making and unmaking of rocks, the causes of weather, the importance of water and the water cycle to life on our planet—these complicated subjects are not very often addressed in books for younger readers. It is difficult to explain them simply, but it can be done, and the information is valuable. Understanding at a beginning level will make learning easier later.

THE SUN, THE MOON, AND THE STARS

Max and the Tag-Along Moon   *Picture book; Bedtime story*

By Floyd Cooper. Illustrated by Floyd Cooper. Philomel Books, 2012.
   Ages 3–6.
Subjects: Moon, Grandfathers

Just before Max left his Granpa's house, the two admired a big yellow moon together. The moon stayed visible during the car ride home, apparently following him, disappearing into clouds, and returning to shine into his bedroom window. "'That ol' moon will always shine for you'" Granpa had said. This quiet, warm story about a grandfather and grandson has a nature connection, too. The idea that the moon follows you is one that youngsters latch on to early, part of their first awareness of the workings of the outside world, long before they know why. Cooper's illustrations are full of curved lines and brown colors as the family car winds through the landscape between the two homes. There are plenty of natural images—a silhouetted bird, a sparkling river, cows sleeping quietly. A comforting bedtime story.

Older Than the Stars   *Informational picture book*

By Karen C. Fox. Illustrated by Nancy Davis. Charlesbridge, 2010. Ages 5–9.
Subjects: Cosmology, Big bang theory, Atoms

"These are the blocks that formed from the bits that were born in the bang when the world began." A catchy, cumulative "House That Jack Built" rhyme is the entry point for introducing some current theories about the origin of the universe. Pointing out that we are all made of star stuff, the author concludes, "You are as old as the universe itself," a staggering concept for a young reader or listener. Sidebars offer a fuller explanation of the stages presented in the hand-lettered poem, still using vocabulary appropriate to the intended audience. A glossary defines concepts like *atom, proton,* and *universe.* The combination of lettering and pictures supports the gradual coming together of the random bits and blocks into the universe we now recognize. Energetic and imaginative, these appealing illustrations and memorable text beg to be shared.

You Are Stardust

Informational picture book

By Elin Kelsey. Illustrated by Soyeon Kim.
   Owlkids Books, 2012. Ages 5–10.
Subjects: Human ecology, Connections to nature

"Every tiny atom in your body / came from a star that exploded / long before you were born." That mind-blowing statement is illustrated with a visualization of an explosion, with open-sided octahedrons carrying figures of children. This is a photograph of one of the seven dioramas Kim made to represent the many examples of human connections to the natural world Kelsey offers. Her message is not uncommon, but her particular details resonate. She speaks directly to the reader, noting that dinosaurs once drank the water we drink. Blow a kiss to the world; the pollen in your breath might take root. Humans and animals both know what it is to be a friend. The endpapers include sketches and notes that reveal more about the construction of the illustrations. Warm and positive, this celebration of our connection to nature deserves a wide audience.

Boy, Were We Wrong about the Solar System!

Informational picture book

By Kathleen V. Kudlinski. Illustrated by John Rocco. Dutton Children's Books,
   2008. Ages 5–9.
Subject: Solar system

This quick history of scientific theories about the solar system emphasizes changes in our understanding since the time of the Greeks and Romans— from the discovery that the earth was round and not the center of the system to the recognition that Pluto is not a major planet. The author also makes a point of describing changes in the tools scientists use. The naked eye yielded to the telescope; records were kept over time revealing the recurrence of comets; radio telescopes, space exploration, and the Hubble space telescope all have contributed new information. Rocco's computer-enhanced caricatures add humor, showing astronomers through the ages and even a group of future children at a space museum on the moon. This reminder that our knowledge about the natural world is still growing is a companion to Kudlinski's, *Boy, Were We Wrong about Dinosaurs!* (Dutton, 2005).

ROCKS AND MOUNTAINS

A Rock Is Lively
Informational picture book
By Dianna Hutts Aston. Illustrated by Sylvia
   Long. Chronicle Books, 2012. Ages 5–10.
Subjects: Rocks, Minerals

Rocks star in this descriptive introduction to geology, combining surprising adjectives and hard facts. This imaginative author-illustrator pair can make even stones fascinating. In the tradition of earlier titles about eggs, seeds, and butterflies, annotated in later chapters, Aston and Long introduce rock science with adjectival phrases, short, informative paragraphs, and glorious watercolor illustrations, here of rock and mineral varieties. A double-page spread of fifty-one different samples introduces and closes the book. Each specimen is labeled in the illustrations and on the repetition of the multi-rock spread. The varied visual presentations add interest and information, keeping readers engaged. An unusual picture book subject handled in an engaging fashion. With its hand-lettered look and ending surprise, this could create another generation of rock hounds.

If Rocks Could Sing: A Discovered Alphabet

Alphabet book

By Leslie McGuirk. Illustrated by Leslie McGuirk. Tricycle Press, 2011. Ages 4–10.

Subjects: Rocks

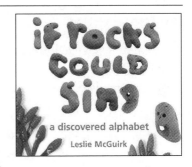

A whimsical alphabet book illustrating both letters and items representing those letters with pieces of sandstone, mostly from a Florida beach, suggests a new way to look at the natural world. For the purposes of this book, where the rocks aren't immediately like the initial object (such as the *e* for elephant) there are other images on the page to help viewers make the connection. The bird stone sits in a nest; the mitten-shaped rock goes with a knitted mitten; the stone rabbit has a carrot. A short afterword called "Rock Talk" discusses the collection process. McGuirk gathered her rocks over a period of ten years; for children, this might be the beginning of a lifetime's habit of looking for shells and stones with unusual shapes.

Volcano Rising

Informational picture book

By Elizabeth Rusch. Illustrated by Susan Swan. Charlesbridge, 2013. Ages 6–10.

Subjects: Volcanoes

"Ka-boom!" "Pow!" "Hisssss!" When people think of volcanos they think of explosions, but this author argues that volcanos create as well as destroy, making mountains, new islands, and fertile fields. With a two-level text that begs to be read aloud, she explains volcanic activity, giving examples along the way for curious and more able readers. Swan's colorful collages, a combination of various media and digital scans, make for striking illustrations that have occasional helpful labels. From a potential volcano in the making in Oregon to submarine volcanos explored by robots, with stops along the way at Paricutin in Mexico, Surtsey and Grimsvötn in Iceland, Mt. St. Helens in Washington, Kilauea in Hawaii, Yellowstone Park, and more, young readers can experience the range and power of volcanos in our world.

An Island Grows   *Informational picture book*

By Lola M. Schaefer. Illustrated by Cathie Felstead. Greenwillow Books,
    2006. Ages 3–7.
Subjects: Islands, Stories in rhyme, Geology

"Magma glows. / Volcano blows. / Lava flows / and flows / and flows. / An
island grows." Simple rhyming couplets and stylized illustrations combine
here to introduce the process of volcanic island formation from undersea
eruption to the island's eventual colonization by plants and people. Geology
is an unusual subject in the picture book world. While the text includes some
appropriate scientific terms that will be unfamiliar, it has been set invitingly
with only a phrase or two on a page, in large type. The illustrations vary in
size and placement on the pages; some grow like the island, and some stretch
across the spread. Done in cut-paper collage with the look of folk art, these
document the process and the change from seascape to thriving community
with farms, markets, and celebrations. "Busy island in the sea, where only
water used to be."

SUN ENERGY AND THE WATER CYCLE

Living Sunlight: How Plants   *Informational picture book*
Bring the Earth to Life

By Molly Bang and Penny Chisholm. Illustrated by Molly Bang. Blue Sky
    Press, 2009. Ages 4–10.
Subjects: Photosynthesis, Sunshine, Plants

In Bang and Chisholm's highly regarded *My Light* (Blue Sky Press, 2004), the
sun explained energy and electricity. In this companion, the sun goes on to
explain how its light energy becomes the energy for life on earth. Plants use
sun energy and carbon dioxide to build sugar (glucose); they breathe out
oxygen. Humans and animals get sun energy by eating plants. We breathe
in oxygen, and breathe out water and carbon dioxide, which plants breathe
in. This is the circle of life on earth. Bang illustrates this with vibrant, colorful paintings. Both illustrations and text are clear and precisely designed
with the young reader in mind. The process of photosynthesis is depicted
in squares that represent close-ups of each step. The authors emphasize this

cycle's importance: "Without plants, you would have no oxygen. Without plants, you would have no food. Without plants, you could not live."

Ocean Sunlight: How Tiny Plants Feed the Seas

Informational picture book

By Molly Bang and Penny Chisholm. Illustrated by Molly Bang. Blue Sky Press, 2012. Ages 5–11.
Subjects: Photobiology, Marine animals, Plants, Sunshine

There are a billion billion billion phytoplankton in the ocean, constantly reproducing themselves and constantly being eaten. This astonishing fact is part of the wonder of photosynthesis and the chain of life that the authors describe in this, their third book about energy in our world. Simple words and information-packed pictures combine to explain how the energy of sunlight creates food in the water through the photosynthesis of the bottom of the food chain, and how it powers the winds that mix the seas. Careful viewers will see that the illustrations support the chemical explanation, with water, carbon dioxide, sugar, and oxygen molecules depicted as combinations of atoms. Yellow dots of sun energy surround the sugars and the creatures that can take it in. In the back, the authors provide a more detailed explanation of the same concepts, for older readers and parents.

All the Water in the World

Informational picture book

By George Ella Lyon. Illustrated by Katherine Tillotson. Atheneum Books for Young Readers, 2011. Ages 4–7.
Subject: Water cycle

"Water doesn't come. / It goes. / Around." This poetic portrayal of the water cycle reminds us that all the water in the world is all the water there is in the world. Rain comes as a "Tap dance / avalanche / stampede of drips and drops and drumming." Elsewhere "dry grasses rustle / dirt's just dust." The design and digitally rendered illustrations of this charming read-aloud enliven a lyrical text arranged dramatically in varying shapes and fonts. The colors are grand—the blue and purple swirls of waters, the browns of dry lands. On one amazing spread green shapes form both trees and tigers, with mountains and a stream. The reader or listener is directly addressed as "honey." The message here, to keep the earth green, is so beautifully presented it makes you want to listen.

Why Do Elephants Need the Sun? *Informational picture book*

By Robert E. Wells. Illustrated by Robert E. Wells. Albert Whitman & Co., 2010. Ages 5–9.
Subjects: Sun, Water cycle, Photosynthesis

A series of engaging pen-and-acrylic illustrations of monkeys frolicking around a large elephant illustrates this relatively simple explanation of the importance of the sun in elephant's lives as well as our own. Touching on photosynthesis, the water cycle, gravity, the sun's composition and the way it generates energy, as well as the many ways humans use solar energy, the text of this appealing book breaks down some important scientific con-

Observe the Changing Sky and Seasons

LOOK AT THE moon at some time every day for twenty-eight days. Record how it changes. Using a blank four- or five-week calendar page, draw the visible shape of the moon. (Sometimes, of course, it won't be visible.) Write in the date and time of observation. Older children can also record moonrise and moonset, available in many weather apps, newspapers, and from the U.S. Naval Observatory's Astronomical Applications Department (see http://aa.usno.navy.mil/data/docs/RS_OneDay.php).

Where it snows, go outside to catch snowflakes. An old piece of black velveteen is perfect for this, but I have also used a dark-colored washcloth or my sleeve. A rougher texture allows air under the flake, which makes it last longer, but black construction paper will work, too. Look at the flakes with a hand lens. If you search for a few minutes and the flakes aren't distinguishable, wait for another snowfall.

Observe and track seasonal changes like trees leafing out and their leaves changing color. Report your observations as a citizen scientist. Participate in the international data collection of Journey North (www.learner.org/jnorth/sunlight/tm/about.html).

Look up at the night sky. From January through May, the Globe at Night project records how many stars can be seen in the constellations Orion, Leo, and Crux (the Southern Cross). Send observations to www.globeatnight.org.

cepts and connects them to a child's life and imagination. With one to three sentences on each double-page spread, the information is well-paced. The book must be turned vertically to appreciate some illustrations, another way to keep the child reader engaged. Though simple, some of the vocabulary is challenging. The child reader may need some adult support. Part of the Wells of Knowledge Science Series.

WEATHER

The Story of Snow:
The Science of Winter's Wonder
Informational picture book

By Mark Cassino and Jon Nelson.
  Illustrated by Nora Aoyagi.
  Chronicle Books, 2009. Ages 4–10.
Subject: Snowflakes

Highly magnified photographs of snow crystals form the heart of this excellent introduction to many children's favorite part of winter. The text is presented on three levels: a simple sentence with the main idea for reading aloud, a more detailed paragraph of explanation, and captions for the illustrations. It explains snow formation, illustrates the variety within the three basic forms, and gives instructions for catching and observing them yourself. Aoyagi's drawings help make the explanations clear. But readers will be most fascinated by the endless variations in Cassini's spectacular photographs. While the book encourages readers to follow up by exploring snow crystals themselves, the publisher's website offers a particularly well-thought-out teacher's guide. Notable not only for its subject but for the author's obvious enthusiasm, this offers a nice complement to Jacqueline Briggs Martin's 1998 biography of the man who pioneered snowflake photography, *Snowflake Bentley* (Houghton Mifflin).

Hurricane Hunters!   *Informational picture book*
Riders on the Storm

By Chris L. Demarest. Illustrated by Chris L. Demarest. Margaret K.
   McElderry Books / Simon & Schuster, 2006. Ages 5–9.
Subjects: Hurricanes, Meteorologists

Taking readers into the eye of a hurricane, this book documents scientific
investigation of potential natural disasters. As a hurricane approaches the
Atlantic coast, members of the Air Force's 53rd Weather Reconnaissance
Squadron take off in a specially equipped WC-130 Hercules turboprop air-
plane to fly into the eye and measure the storm. The simple text serves as
captions for illustrations appropriately large-sized for the large-sized storm.
They show the plane taking off, the force of the winds on a small tropical
island, the deployment of the crew among their many instruments, the drop-
sonde with its parachute descending into the storm, and civilian preparations below. One particularly effective spread contrasts the small size of the
plane, shown in the hurricane's eye, with the huge and chaotic ocean swells.
The book opens with a labeled line drawing of the plane and closes with an
extensive author's note.

Tornado! The Story Behind These Twisting,   *Nonfiction*
Turning, Spinning, and Spiraling Storms

By Judith Bloom Fradin and Dennis B. Fradin. Illustrated with photographs. National Geographic, 2011. Ages 8–12.
Subjects: Tornadoes, Weather, Disasters

Nature's most violent storms, tornadoes, are more common in the United
States than anywhere else in the world, but scientists have found new
methods to predict and study them. Beginning with a gripping description
of a disaster in Kansas and illustrated with dramatic photographs, this is
both informative and accessible enough for able middle-grade readers. The
authors have interviewed witnesses, survivors, and scientists and provide
intriguing short quotations both in the text and in text boxes. A page of
"tornado talk" defines terms in both words and pictures. Maps show where
tornados are common, in the United States and around the world. Appropriately, the authors also include do's and don'ts for responding to a tornado

warning. The text is challenging but the images are so powerful that they will prompt both awe and admiration for what nature can do.

Thunderstorm

Picture book

By Arthur Geisert. Illustrated by Arthur
   Geisert. Enchanted Lion Books, 2013.
   Ages 6–10.
Subject: Storms

This wordless book chronicles the progress across a midwestern farm landscape of a damaging July thunderstorm and a family driving home with a wagonload of baled hay. The story begins and ends on the covers. The action takes place in the course of one Saturday afternoon; each spread includes the time of day. The storm spawns tornadoes, which tear apart the homes of animals and people alike, and a flood. It is both scary and awe-inspiring in its power. But in this world, families help each other. Meticulously executed etchings, hand printed and water-colored, stretch across each spread. They emphasize the vast and changing sky and landscape but also include cutaways showing underground animal dens, birds in trees, and people's homes and barns. The spreads are contiguous; this could be a single scroll. Geisert has also described the rural Midwest in *Country Road ABC* (Houghton Mifflin, 2010).

Prairie Storms   *Informational picture book*

By Darcy Pattison. Illustrated by Kathleen Rietz. Sylvan Dell Publishing,
   2011. Ages 6–10.
Subjects: Prairie ecology, Storms, Prairie animals

Month by month, this combination of meteorology and prairie ecology provides a fresh, new way of looking at a familiar habitat. From the prairie chicken roosting in January's drifting snow to the bison herd facing into the wind of a December blizzard, the author's lively text and illustrator's images introduce the seasonal changes on American grasslands and the animals that endure them. Creatures described include sandhill cranes and burrowing owls, prairie dogs, fox, deer, skunk, cougar, and even a burrowing lizard.

Fog and flood, light showers and cloudbursts, dust storms, thunder storms, heat lightning, and a tornado—the variety of storms is surprising. Rietz's realistic paintings are framed appropriately with textures and sometimes images from the illustrations. The back matter includes further information about grasslands, seasons, and weather; a map; and several quizzes that add informational value.

SEASONS

What child doesn't love the advent of fall, with its piles of leaves? Or winter, with its snow, or for that matter any change of seasons? For those who live where seasons change, this is another dramatic demonstration of their own connection to a larger system. Even (or maybe especially) parents and care-givers who live in parts of the country where the seasons don't change dra-matically will also want to share such books with their children. (Other titles that use seasons as an organizing principle have been annotated throughout this book and can be found by using the index.)

In Like a Lion, Out Like a Lamb

Picture book

By Marion Dane Bauer. Illustrated by Emily
    Arnold McCully. Holiday House, 2011.
    Ages 4–8.
Subjects: Stories in rhyme, March (Month),
    Spring

March literally comes in as a lion and goes out as a lamb in this charming picture book depiction of the changing sea-son. The familiar saying is brought to life in rhyme with an actual lion charging around on the pages. "March comes with a roar. / He rattles your windows / and scratches at your door. He turns snow to mud, / then tromps across your floor." The lively lion refuses to leave until suddenly spring buds make him sneeze. The lamb appears, bringing a shower of flowers, and the lion falls asleep. The rhyme and rhythm are slightly erratic, fitting March's changeable weather. McCully's illustrations add atmosphere and humor as the lion rampages around and, later, the lamb leads a parade of baby animals. Bleak backgrounds give way to pastels, promising a gentler time, until the lamb's sneeze produces both the flowers and bugs of summer.

Seasons

Picture book

By Anne Crausaz. Illustrated by Anne Crausaz.
   Kane Miller, 2011. Ages 4–7.
Subjects: Seasons, Senses and sensation, Nature

A young girl reflects on signs of the changing seasons, from the green of spring to the last taste of snowflakes before spring returns. With simple, poetic words set on flat, stylized illustrations, this joyful French import invites children to wonder and to enjoy the natural world all year around. The imagery is captivating: "Fireflies, like flying stars. Summer has arrived!" So are the ways the child interacts with the world: tasting cherries in the spring and blackberries in the fall, and, in summer, the "sand in your mouth!" All the senses are engaged. Feel the tickle of a ladybug, listen to a summer storm, smell the tomato and basil in the garden, watch and follow the dandelion seeds. Notice the ants riding along. There is play, too. In fall, "the leaves make a wonderful crackling sound. Jump in!" Lap-sized and just right for sharing.

Under the Snow   *Informational picture book*

By Melissa Stewart. Illustrated by Constance Rummel Bergum. Peachtree,
   2009. Ages 4–8.
Subjects: Snow, Animals—wintering, Winter, Seasons

In winter, when snow covers the fields, forests, ponds, and wetlands, a hidden world of animals lies underneath. Using examples, including ladybugs in a stone wall, centipedes and a bumblebee queen in a rotting log, bluegills, a frog and a turtle buried in mud, and a wetland beaver family inside their lodge, Stewart describes how some animals spend their winters in hibernation or frozen solid, while others are resting, slowly swimming, or active as always. The lyrical text packs a lot of information, describing a broad range of environments, animals, and activities. Appropriately for the intended audience, the narrative begins and ends with humans enjoying the winter and getting ready for spring. Bergum's muted watercolor illustrations often show activity on two levels, above and below the snow and ice. Animals are shown close-up and in realistic detail. A charming read-aloud or read-alone book.

Naturalists in training

Chapter 6

Naturalists

SOME ARTISTS AND PHOTOGRAPHERS WERE NATURALISTS IN THE FIELD long before they came to write and illustrate children's books about the natural world. Many began their love affair with nature as children. They draw on long and continued experience to produce books that stand alone or appear in series. Many of them have produced series that children, caregivers, teachers, and librarians have turned to over and over, knowing from experience that a new book on an unfamiliar subject will be as appealing as one they already know. This chapter focuses on an artist, two photographers, an artist and writer team, and a group of wildlife researchers, explorers, and photographers employed by National Geographic.

JIM ARNOSKY

Not quite "born in a tree and raised by bees" like his character Crinkleroot, Arnosky has been exploring the natural world all his life. Since the publication of his first book in 1988, he has been writing, drawing, and sometimes singing about nature for children in school visits and other programs. As of March 2013, he had 125 different titles listed in the Library of Congress catalog—a body of work that has earned him several lifetime achievement awards, but keeps on growing. Describing his career for TeachingBooks.net he said, "I make books about wild animals in wild places for young people" (www.teachingbooks.net/content/interviews/Arnosky_qu.pdf). He and his wife, Deanna, make their home in Vermont, spend two months each year in the Florida Keys, and have traveled extensively, exploring, sketching, and photographing. Her photographs, along with sketches he's done in the field, are the basis for the amazing wildlife drawings and paintings that fill his books, accompanied by descriptions of the animal behavior.

Whether titles are parts of a series or stand alone, what distinguishes his work is its accuracy. "I don't ever want to put anything in my book that kids will have to unlearn later," he explained to an audience at *School Library Journal*'s Day of Dialog in 2013 (https://twitter.com/wl_heather/status/339750600017317888). This accuracy is a result of hours, days, and years of patient observation. "It takes forty gallons of sap to make one gallon of maple syrup," he noted (www.slj.com/2013/06/books-media/authors-illustrators/sharing-the-love-librarians-authors-talk-kid-lit-slj-day-of-dialog-2013).

His books feature full-page and double-page close-ups, scenes showing creatures in their habitats, sketches showing details, and even foldout pages to add interest and make life-sized portraits possible. Even when he is not producing titles that can be used as field guides, his plants and animals are always recognizable. The author's website, www.jimarnosky.com, includes a wide variety of supporting materials, coloring pages, drawing lessons, photographs from the couple's travels, a memoir, and the like. A recent series and some nature guides are listed below; other titles can be found in other sections.

Wild Tracks! A Guide to Nature's Footprints

Informational picture book

By Jim Arnosky. Illustrated by Jim Arnosky. Sterling, 2008. Ages 6–10.
Subject: Animals—tracks

The naturalist's one hundredth book is a guide to animal tracks, showing how these marks in the snow, sand, or mud not only identify the animal, but also reveal its behavior. Running deer spread their hoofs wide for stability; their back toes show in their tracks. A skunk's running pattern is diagonal, while fox keep all four feet in line. Each chapter displays and describes the tracks of a different animal family, and each is illustrated with a page of pencil sketches, selections from a nature journal with handwritten labels and measurements that frame a few paragraphs of explanatory text. Opposite, a painting shows a member of that family in its natural habitat. The table of contents will make it easy for budding trackers to find the animal they seek, at least in the book. Though oversized for a field guide, this could send young readers out to do some tracking and sketching themselves.

Slither and Crawl:
Eye to Eye with Reptiles
Informational picture book

By Jim Arnosky. Illustrated by Jim Arnosky.
    Sterling, 2009. Ages 6–10.
Subject: Reptiles

From the toothy alligator that illustrates his introduction to the concluding story of the Burmese python he didn't find in Key Largo, Arnosky distills years of watching snakes, lizards, turtles, and crocodilians in this introduction to the "richness of reptiles." It features a straightforward, rather general description of each of these families, detailed close-up paintings, pencil sketches, and four foldout pages, each with an array of life-sized depictions of these animals' heads. Most species pictured can be found in North America, but the naturalist includes some famous ones from around the world: a South American anaconda, a cobra from Asia and Africa, and the Galápagos tortoise. One spread features gigantic lizards, including the Komodo dragon from Indonesia. He has solid advice for budding reptile watchers: follow his example and watch dangerous reptiles with binoculars or a camera with a telephoto lens.

Creep and Flutter: The Secret World of Insects and Spiders

Informational picture book

By Jim Arnosky. Illustrated by Jim Arnosky.
    Sterling, 2011. Ages 6–10.
Subject: Insects, Spiders

Displaying his own boundless curiosity about the natural world, Arnosky here examines insects, describing more than 200 species of creeping, crawling, fluttering, and flying creatures. Detailed pencil drawings and colorful paintings, often larger than life-size, accompany an extensive text organized by insect families. From dragonflies, beetles, and butterflies to wasps and spiders, he covers the major familiar groups. Every page is full of images, and six fold out spectacularly. Who could resist a rainbow trout leaping for a mayfly or a golden silk spider on a web full of dewdrops? This is another book that works both for the browsing child drawn to the images and for the student looking for facts.

Thunder Birds: Nature's Flying Predators

Informational picture book

By Jim Arnosky. Illustrated by Jim Arnosky. Sterling, 2011. Ages 6–10.
Subject: Birds of prey

The fierce osprey looking out from the cover, trout held in his talons, is an appropriate beginning for this introduction to birds of prey. Inside, a golden eagle looms against the orange-red background of a western butte. Five different owl faces are shown life-size, with labels explaining their size and where they can be found. A black vulture perches on an alligator carcass on which he and his companions will soon feast. "Nature's flying predators are magnificent creatures," Arnosky writes, proving it with these striking intricate, and accurate illustrations of eagles, hawks, owls, vultures, herons, pelicans, and three diving birds. Detailed drawings and beautiful paintings, some on foldout pages, show birds up close and in context. Short explanations include numerous personal experiences. This is an elegant and awe-inspiring tribute.

Crinkleroot's Guide to Giving Back to Nature

Informational picture book

By Jim Arnosky. Illustrated by Jim Arnosky. G. P. Putnam's Sons, 2012. Ages 5–10.

Subject: Nature conservation

Crinkleroot, inspired by nineteenth century naturalist John Burroughs, may be familiar to today's parents from the PBS series "Backyard Safari," used in many schools, or from books published during their own childhood. Arnosky's lovable guide may be even more needed today. This book is full of suggestions for things that children themselves can do to protect and give back to nature: feeding wild animals and providing a welcoming habitat, picking up after themselves, keeping stream waters clean, planting trees, putting animals back where they were found, composting, and conserving energy. There are clear instructions for specific activities and solid explanations. The illustrations show many of the plants and animals young explorers might see outdoors (especially, but not solely, those who live in the eastern part of the country). With his beard and feathered hat, Crinkleroot looks like a man to follow into the natural world.

Shimmer & Splash: The Sparkling World of Sea Life

Informational picture book

By Jim Arnosky. Illustrated by Jim Arnosky. Sterling, 2013. Ages 6–10.

Subjects: Fish, Sharks, Marine animals

Arnosky turns his attention to the water world, describing animals he and his wife have observed in years of fishing and exploring from jetties, shores, and boats. As he has done in similar titles, he combines sketchbook drawings and dramatic paintings with short essays. Double foldout pages display inshore and deep-sea hunters, coral reef denizens, and sharks. From feisty fiddler crabs and stingrays hiding in the sand to sailfish leaping from the waves, his choices reflect his personal experiences but will also intrigue young readers who will surely be infected by this longtime nature observer's continuing love for the out-of-doors. The drawings and silhouettes in the margins of the text reveal identifying details like the difference between the rounded tip of a dolphin's dorsal fin and the sharper fin of a shark. An author's note and suggestions for further reading round out this appealing introduction.

NIC BISHOP

Clear text, crisp, colorful design, and astonishing photographs characterize Nic Bishop's species books. Combining stunning images of animals he has raised at home with photographs of animals he has observed in the wild, Nic Bishop's photo essays capitalize on his worldwide experience as naturalist and nature photographer. His introductions appeal to a broad spectrum of readers and listeners, providing basic information about habitat, behavior, physical characteristics, and specializations. Three levels of succinct text describe each picture. There's an identifying caption and a paragraph of explanation in which one describing sentence is bold-faced for younger readers or listeners. This makes for an easy read-aloud. "I really like a book that moves fast, that is set out in a very clear, logical fashion, and doesn't leave the child at any sort of dead end. When you tell children something in a book, you want the child to know why they've been told this," Bishop told an interviewer for Teaching Books.[1]

Solid color backgrounds complement the colors of the photographs when they don't stretch across both pages. Foldout pages highlight particularly striking images. The photographs include carefully planned close-ups that are well-lit and sharply focused, as well as equally thoughtfully chosen shots taken in the field. He uses both natural and artificial light, movement detectors, and high-speed flash. Most photos include some detail of the animal's natural environment. An explanation of his working methods can be found in the end matter in these books and in more detail on his website, www.nic bishop.com. These books also include an index and a glossary, making them particularly useful for young researchers. Bibliographies of his research for titles published since 2008 are also available on his website. Two of these books have been redone for an early reader series. Shaped and sized to appeal to beginning readers, they add an attractive nonfiction option. These easy readers use simple vocabulary and only a few short sentences on a spread, but they preserve the colorful design. Some of the photographs are repeated but others are new for these versions. Again, there are photographer's notes, an index, and a glossary.

Frogs   *Informational picture book*

By Nic Bishop. Illustrated with photographs by Nic Bishop. Scholastic Nonfiction, 2008. Ages 5–12.
Subject: Frogs

In a narrative that works both for reading and reading aloud, Bishop introduces frogs from all over the world—deserts and rain forests, Africa and
Australia—though many were raised in his home in this country. As always,
his photographs are the main attraction. Frogs appear in the context of
their environment, demonstrating their ability to blend in. Close-ups reveal
details: the four front toes, the circle of skin that covers the ears. Bishop is
a master at capturing the moment. A horned frog swallows his dinner; only
the tail of the mouse sticks out of his mouth. An African bullfrog, tongue
out, leaps to catch a caterpillar. (This image is repeated and enlarged so you
can see the tongue joined at the front of the mouth.) A gatefold shows four
images of the frog jumping. Bishop's enthusiasm for his subject is infectious.

Marsupials

Informational picture book

By Nic Bishop. Illustrated with photographs
  by Nic Bishop. Scholastic Nonfiction, 2009.
  Ages 4–10.
Subject: Marsupials

"Most people know about lions, zebras, monkeys, and bears, but what about bettongs and
bilbies?" Bishop begins his intriguing introduction to marsupials with this question, drawing
readers in immediately and keeping them there
with his amazing facts and close-up photographs of animals you've never
heard of, let alone encountered in the wild or even in a zoo. Who can resist
learning about a baby who feeds on its mother's poop? Appealing furry faces
look out at the reader alongside interesting descriptions of the animals'
activities, specialized body parts, and likely environment. The gatefold here
shows a flying possum called a sugar glider. There are kangaroos, koalas,
wombats, and wallabies but also plenty of rarities. There are marsupials

with upside down pockets and no pockets at all, marsupials that hop and climb and burrow, and even an animal readers may have encountered in an American backyard: the Virginia opossum. Beaut!

Butterflies and Moths   *Informational picture book*

By Nic Bishop. Illustrated with photographs by Nic Bishop. Scholastic Nonfiction, 2009. Ages 4–10.
Subjects: Butterflies, Moths

After Bishop explains some of the differences between these two species, his simple text is organized through a life cycle description from egg to caterpillar, to pupa, to mating and egg-laying adult. There are surprising images of what we might think of as familiar creatures: a much-magnified, newly hatched caterpillar eating its own eggshell; a luna moth's feathery antennae; a rain forest caterpillar puffed up to look like a poisonous snake. A beautiful set of foldout pages provides a four-page spread showing the different wing positions of a peacock butterfly in flight. The variety shown is stunning—the creatures come from around the world, but they are not all identified. This is not a scientific introduction. It is the wow factor, the fascinating facts and magnificent photographs, that makes this worthwhile. In *Butterflies* (Scholastic, 2011), part of the publisher's series for developing readers, Bishop uses many of the same striking images but concentrates on the life cycle of butterflies alone.

Lizards

Informational picture book

By Nic Bishop. Illustrated with photographs by Nic Bishop. Scholastic, 2010. Ages 4–10.
Subject: Lizards

Lizards from all over the world are the subject of this series entry. Opening with an image of a gliding gecko parachuting from branch to branch, the biologist/photographer captures one revealing moment after another. The center spread shows a brown leaf-tailed gecko almost indistinguishable from the leaf where it has curled up. This opens on both sides to four shots of a basilisk walking upright on water. Some images feature small details: the ear opening that distinguishes lizards from snakes; a chameleon's body-long tongue in action; the spiky skin and tiny claws of the desert-dwelling Australian thorny devil. The text describes lizard habitats, egg-laying and lack of child-rearing, their specialized body and behaviors, their feeding and mating. Bishop concludes with a description of the difficulties of getting several particular photographs. Another winner.

Snakes

Informational picture book

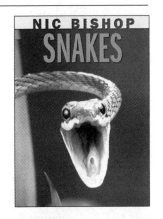

By Nic Bishop. Illustrated with photographs
   by Nic Bishop. Scholastic Nonfiction, 2012.
   Ages 5–10.
Subject: Snakes

The text in this introduction to snakes from around the world covers their body size and shape, skin and scales, locomotion, senses, cold-bloodedness, eating, hunting and defense mechanisms, and eggs. But what children will remember are the pictures—close-ups of snakes of all kinds, many magnified for effect: a feathered bush viper with leafy scales; an African egg snake swallowing an egg whole; a carpet python eating something like a mole; a double-page foldout of a rattlesnake, tongue out to sense the world; and the author with a young milk snake curled around his camera lens. Skin colors and patterns stand out. These creatures may be "strange, secret, and surprising," but they are also beautiful. Words defined in the short glossary are italicized in context, and they are important: *ambush, molt, predator, prey, venom.* You do not need to be a budding herpetologist to be fascinated.

Spiders   *Early reader*

By Nic Bishop. Illustrated with photographs by Nic Bishop. Scholastic, 2012.
   Ages 5–8.
Subject: Spiders

Bishop has recast his award-winning *Spiders* (Scholastic, 2007) into an appealing introduction to the arachnid world for developing readers (level

2 in the Scholastic Reader series). Using many new pictures and completely redoing his text, he manages, just the same, to describe physical features and behaviors, illustrating them appropriately. Spiders jump and dance and spin silk and eat insects they've trapped. He shows spider egg cases and new baby spiders. New and appropriate vocabulary is italicized and defined in context and in a glossary. Identifications for each photograph in the back matter include page numbers, working as a kind of index. Readers intrigued by this will surely want to go on to the more comprehensive title, with its larger pages and surprising foldout images.

SUZI ESZTERHAS

At six years old, Suzi Eszterhas already knew she wanted to be a wildlife photographer. "I spent a lot of time as a kid photographing my pets as well as the birds, squirrels, deer and raccoons that lived in my backyard," she told the San Francisco *Chronicle*. She started her wildlife photography career by abandoning her day job with the SPCA to spend nearly three years on her own in the Maasai Mara in Kenya photographing cheetahs. Since then she has traveled around the world to photograph endangered animals, sometimes on her own and sometimes leading others on photography expeditions. Her specialty has been baby animals. Even before going into the field, she does extensive research to know when and where these animals can be seen. Then she spends long periods of time with the animals—days, weeks, and even months—to get just the right shot. Her Eye on the Wild series is the culmination of more than ten years of such work.

The six titles in this series introduce six different mammals. Their focus on each animal's childhood is unique, and the photographs, taken in the wild, are stunning. With relatively simple language and a child-centered approach, she describes each baby and its family. The parents are called Mom and Dad. She uses familiar words like "tummy" and "snuggle" and sometimes ascribes human emotions: an orangutan is "a bit lonely without her mom"; a sea otter finds friends. This approach isn't excessively anthropomorphic and it builds the connection between the child reader and the animal baby. The front endpapers usually show portraits of the animal baby, the back shows the animal fully grown. Topics covered include litter size and family relationships, length of nursing, early explorations, learning to feed themselves in their environments, and development of independence. These sharply focused photographs show the pups, cubs, and babies in their environment, relating with others of their species and, often enough to maintain the connection, looking directly at the reader. A page of fast facts about each animal, including why they are considered endangered, and a website for further information is included at the end. "I really had a vision about getting kids jazzed about seeing these endangered animals," she told a San Francisco public radio interviewer.[2] Reading or being read any of these irresistible titles would certainly do that.

Orangutan

Informational picture book

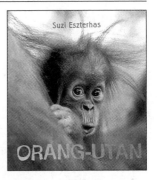

By Suzi Eszterhas. Illustrated with photographs by Suzi Eszterhas. Frances Lincoln Children's Books, 2013. Ages 4–8.

Subjects: Orangutans, Baby animals

Here, the photographer documents the life of a baby orangutan living in the rain forest of a Sumatran national park. The cuteness factor is high, as the red-haired baby peers out from within her mother's arms. Soon she's determinedly hanging onto her acrobatic mother's back as she swings through the trees. A series of five images shows the year-old baby's first climbing attempts; her mother stays by her side just in case. There's also a grand photograph of what a viewer could interpret as a baby's glee at jumping on her mother in her nest bed. There's the baby's first experience with solid food (prechewed by Mom), time for meeting other babies, and plenty of play. At four, a young orangutan goes out on her own, spending time with "friends," but continuing to meet up with her mother, from time to time, for the rest of her life.

Sea Otters
Informational picture book

By Suzi Eszterhas. Illustrated with photographs by Suzi Eszterhas. Frances Lincoln Children's Books, 2013. Ages 4–8.

Subjects: Baby animals, Sea otters

A baby sea otter, distinguished by its messy fluff, lies on her mother's belly in the Pacific Ocean. She doesn't even know how to swim, but she's so fluffy she floats in the cool water. These photographs show the mother otter carrying her pup in her mouth, as cats do, and letting her ride on her back when strangers approach. Not until the pup is four months old will she swim and dive on her own. As in all these books, the author documents the baby's increasing independence, here, exploring the coast on her own at six months old, joining up with others of her kind, grooming herself, and, amusingly, floating on her back in the sun, protecting her eyes with her paws. The fastest to mature of all the animals in this series, this pup will be fully grown in a year.

Brown Bear   *Informational picture book*

By Suzi Eszterhas. Illustrated with photographs by Suzi Eszterhas. Frances
    Lincoln Children's Books, 2012. Ages 4–8.
Subjects: Baby animals, Brown bear, Bears

For this title, the nature photographer followed a pair of brown bear cubs on foot, putting herself in considerable danger. Born in the middle of an Alaskan winter, they don't even leave their den until spring, five months later. For the next two years they stay with their mother. Nursing, they hum "rather like happy cats purring." Photos show them exploring, playing, and eating fresh grass. Their mother will catch fish for them, and later teach them to dig for clams and catch salmon themselves. Looking sometimes like overgrown teddy bears and other times like the bears they will become, the cubs in these photos engage in a wide variety of activities and finally set out together, away from their mother, to have a last joint winter nap before taking off on their own in their fourth year.

Cheetah   *Informational picture book*

By Suzi Eszterhas. Illustrated with photographs by Suzi Eszterhas. Frances
    Lincoln Children's Books, 2012. Ages 4–8.
Subjects: Cheetahs, Baby animals

Cheetah babies sound like baby birds chirping; their den is called a nest. Six to eight babies are born at a time and stay safely in the nest until they are two months old. Then they go out with their mom to explore the grasslands. The striking photographs in this title are a result of nearly three years the author-photographer spent on her own in the Maasai Mara, following the cheetah family and getting the mother accustomed to her presence. Her patience has paid off with surprising images: cubs nursing; a mother licking her wet baby dry; older cubs playing with each other, with Mom, and even with a visiting tortoise; and Mom streaking after a gazelle—dinner for all. They will stay with her for two years until they are fully grown and able to feed and protect themselves.

Gorilla   *Informational picture book*

By Suzi Eszterhas. Illustrated with photographs by Suzi Eszterhas. Frances
    Lincoln Children's Books, 2012. Ages 4–8.
Subjects: Gorillas, Baby animals

In the mountains of Africa a baby gorilla is born, then nurtured by her mother and entertained by siblings and cousins until she reaches adulthood. Remarkable close-up photographs, taken over seven years of visits, follow these early years of a baby gorilla. A simple text describes its growth, introduces its silverback father and other relatives, and documents its games and explorations. Many moments will have special appeal. Who could resist the three-month-old baby gorilla sucking her thumb, and, on the facing page, suckling from her mother who looks out at the reader with patient eyes? Later, when the baby is too old to be carried in her mother's arms, she rides piggyback through the jungle and, even later, wrestles with the other young ones. At six, she's ready to have babies of her own.

Lion

Informational picture book

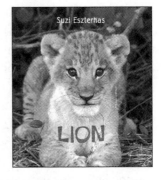

By Suzi Eszterhas. Illustrated with photographs
    by Suzi Eszterhas. Frances Lincoln Children's
    Books, 2012. Ages 4–8.
Subjects: Baby animals, Lions

Eszterhas spent three months with a pride of lions on the Maasai Mara, the African savannah where she also photographed the cheetahs. The book opens with a picture of a mother lion snuggling with a newborn cub whose eyes are still closed. After two months, the mother takes her cubs outside to meet the rest of the pride. One striking shot here is a seven-week-old cub meeting her father for the first time. But the story of the young cub goes beyond its mother's love. She explores her environment; she plays; she learns to hunt. We see young lions eying a small group of topi, a kind of antelope. "But sometimes the young cub is clumsy and the prey animals spot her and run away," the author reassuringly explains. After two years, fully grown, she will be capturing such prey successfully.

CATHRYN AND JOHN SILL

Cathryn and John Sill have combined her long expertise as an elementary school teacher with his wildlife artistry to create two successful series for their publisher. John Sill has worked as a freelance artist and illustrator since 1971, particularly known for his pictures of birds. Their joint About . . . series introduces all kinds of animal families, species, and groups—from birds and mammals to marsupials and even mollusks. The newer series, About Habitats, focuses on biomes, using examples from around the world to define their characteristics and demonstrate their diversity. They include both plants and animals and always begin with a map. The format for both these series is similar. On the left-hand page, a simple sentence or two states a fact, such as "The roots of desert plants have special ways of gathering and storing water." The painting on the facing page will be labeled. Usually the illustration shows an animal in its environment, using realistic details and colors. In *About Habitats: Deserts* (Peachtree 2007, 2012, annotated in this chapter), for example, opposite the statement quoted, you can see the raindrops falling on the puddle in which a spadefoot toad is partially submerged. In the About Habitats series, both plants and animals will be labeled and the location given. In the About Animals series, other animals in the picture will also be named. Occasionally there are several images on the picture page, providing some variety. In the afterword, the plates are repeated as smaller images accompanied by a paragraph of information. A glossary defines important words, and there are suggestions of books and websites for further study.

The first volume in the About . . . series appeared in 1991, and many were written in the first decade of the twenty-first century. Older titles in both series are now gradually being revised and reissued. *About Habitats: Mountains* and *About Mammals* will be issued in 2014 along with a bilingual edition of *About*

Birds. I have annotated eight newer titles from the two series, but readers who like their approach will be able to find many more in public libraries.

About Habitats: Wetlands

Informational picture book

By Cathryn P. Sill. Illustrated by John Sill.
Peachtree, 2012, 2008. Ages 5–9.
Subject: Wetlands

Plants and animals that live in areas that are, at least sometimes, covered with shallow water—wetlands—are the stars of this series entry. Wetlands, we learn from the simple text, may be salty or fresh water and may be permanent or seasonal. Some have trees; some look dry but have soggy ground. From mangrove swamps to bogs to freshwater wetlands, various plants and animals thrive in these specialized habitats. John Sill's finely crafted paintings show details of the plant and animal life, sometimes relatively close-up but more often from enough distance to get a sense of the different kinds of areas normally referred to as wetlands. Readers may be surprised to see a cityscape in the background of one plate; wetlands are all around us.

About Habitats: Oceans   *Informational picture book*

By Cathryn P. Sill. Illustrated by John Sill. Peachtree, 2012. Ages 5–9.
Subjects: Oceans, Marine ecology

This series entry presents seventeen simple facts about oceans and their inhabitants in a way that would work well for both early and struggling readers. The author has done an exceptional job of condensing her vast subject into important descriptive facts and a few memorable details. She even compares the ways ocean dwellers move and protect themselves. Each concept, expressed in a simple sentence, stands alone on the left-hand page except for the label of the detailed watercolor illustration on the right. Except for the iconic image of ocean-covered earth as a big blue marble, each plate includes animals flying over or swimming in ocean waters. The labels include both the ocean and the animals depicted. The author ends by pointing out the importance of oceans for people throughout the world.

About Habitats: Grasslands   *Informational picture book*

By Cathryn P. Sill. Illustrated by John Sill. Peachtree, 2011. Ages 5–9. *Grasslands*

Subject: Grassland ecology

Once again, this experienced educator distills her subject into a few important concepts and presents it in an accessible and memorable way. Here, she introduces grasslands around the world and some of the animals that live there with one or two simple sentences on the left-hand page of each spread. The realistic paintings on the right-hand page show grassland varieties and one to three species in their vast habitat. The species include familiar ones—buffalo, giraffes, deer—and less commonly known animals like regal fritillaries, saiga deer, and budgerigars. She touches lightly on the importance of grasslands to human beings and their need for protection. Like others in this series, which also includes deserts and mountains, this works for a broad range of readers and listeners.

Be a Naturalist

Go outside and observe!

- Adopt a tiny patch of ground and look at it in all weathers and seasons.
- Hang a sheet on a line at night. Shine a flashlight on it and wait to see what comes to the light.
- Get young people in the habit of recording their observations.
- Instill the habit of drawing as well as writing to encourage careful observation. Taking photographs is also a good way to keep track of what you see.
- Adults working with preschoolers can start out by helping them journal; even preschoolers can begin to draw pictures of what they see. A composition notebook or other notebook with blank pages works well for a nature journal. Always include the date and time. The weather is often a good idea, too.
- Consider contributing your family's observations to citizen science programs on the Web such as iNaturalist (www.inaturalist.org). This website collects observations from all over the world and other members will help people identify their findings.
- Project Noah, www.projectnoah.org, sponsored by National Geographic, is a similar website collection program full of interesting particular missions. A related smartphone app allows you to send your sightings or look for identifications.

About Birds:
A Guide for Children

Informational picture book

By Cathryn P. Sill. Illustrated by John
Sill. Peachtree, 2013. Ages 3 and up.
Subject: Birds

This beginner's guide offers simple state-
ments and beautiful, clearly labeled,
water-colored plates, usually showing the bird in context. It is a revised edition of a long-popular work. This opens with the most important fact about
the species—"Birds have feathers." This is set opposite a glorious image of
a male cardinal on a snowy evergreen branch in winter. There are close-ups
and landscapes, and, besides individual images, there are pairs and groups—
enough variation in the illustrations to keep the eye's interest and to allow
for comparisons. Finally, there's a human connection, a shadowy person
peeks out her window at a variety of birds feeding in her yard and at her
feeders. An afterword adds more about the birds shown in each plate. A
grand introduction.

About Penguins: *Informational picture book*
A Guide for Children

By Cathryn P. Sill. Illustrated by John Sill. Peachtree, 2013. Ages 5–9.
Subject: Penguins

Though penguins cannot fly, these seabirds swim well under water, using
their wings as flippers. In this newly revised version of this title, the Sills
describe and show penguin family physical characteristics and behavior as
well as some differences among penguin species. While most live in the icy
areas shown in the majority of illustrations, some live in warmer climates,
even tropical Galápagos. (That painting also shows a marine iguana and a
Sally Lightfoot crab, animals common to that part of the world.) Illustrated,
too, are nest variations, from rocky nests on the ground surface to burrows
to small caves and even no nests at all. (Here is a familiar image: king penguins with their eggs tucked under a warm skin flap on their feet.) This complements other books about specific bird families in the series.

About Hummingbirds: A Guide for Children

Informational picture book

By Cathryn P. Sill. Illustrated by John Sill. Peachtree, 2011. Ages 5–9.
Subjects: Hummingbirds, Animals, Birds

Twenty-five species of hummingbirds are illustrated in this informative introduction to an intriguing bird family found only in the Americas. Unlike other birds, these nectar and insect eaters can hover for long periods and fly in every direction, even upside down. These and other facts are presented, one to a page, in a format accessible even to quite young children. For the young listener or reading beginner, the pictures help tell the story. The text covers physical characteristics and behavior. Information in the afterword introduces important science concepts such as adaptations, camouflage, food chains, life cycles, and habitats as well as specific physical characteristics and behaviors.

About Raptors

Informational picture book

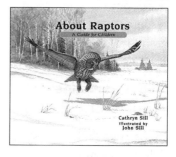

By Cathryn P. Sill. Illustrated by John Sill.
    Peachtree, 2010. Ages 5–9.
Subject: Birds of prey

Eagles, owls, hawks, vultures, falcons, a kite, and a secretary bird are examples of the mighty hunters called raptors, carnivorous birds of prey. As always, the Sills combine simple sentences, gorgeous watercolors, and explanatory back matter into an accessible introduction to this especially varied group. Their species come from all over the world. The text points out similarities and differences: their strong feet and sharp claws, their differing hunting methods, and their various nests or lack of nest. Each plate shows one or more raptors, usually in its habitat. An elf owl brings a grasshopper to its mate in a hole in a cactus in the American southwest; griffons and vultures feast on a dead zebra on the African savannah.

NATIONAL GEOGRAPHIC'S FACE TO FACE WITH ANIMALS SERIES

National Geographic publishers turned to their explorer-photographers for their Face to Face with Animals series of books first published between 2007 and 2010; most are still in print. Wildlife photographers, often in husband-and-wife teams, describe their experiences with a particular species. Many have studied their subject for years; others have photographed many different animals over long careers. These oversize books feature striking photographs of animals in the wild as well as plenty of personal anecdotes. Each opens with a dramatic face-to- face encounter. A second chapter, "Meet the . . . ," introduces the animal, sometimes one the researchers followed. A third provides information about the animal family in general, and a final one looks toward the future. Extensive end matter includes "How You Can Help," about helping the animals; "It's Your Turn," about researching the animals; "Facts at a Glance," which includes a map, glossary, and index; and a section titled "Research and Photographic Notes." While these books usually cover basic topics like physical characteristics, habits and habitats, reproduction, and family structures, they are more valuable for their enthusiasm than for their information. They offer a glimpse into the life of an animal researcher and describe some of the methods used. The emphasis is strongly on the wonder of animal observation and the potential loss of these iconic species in the world. Although the books are promoted for seven-to-ten-year-olds, many of them would be more suitable for middle-school readers who are ready for the sobering environmental news.

Face to Face with Sharks
Nonfiction

By David Doubilet and Jennifer Hayes. Illustrated with photographs by
David Doubilet and Jennifer Hayes. National Geographic, 2009. Ages
7–10.
Subject: Sharks

The gaping, toothy mouth of a great white shark on the cover of this Face to Face series entry will surely draw readers in, just as it would the shark's prey. Though the image confirms all stereotypes, the authors, who have photographed sharks around the world, reassure readers early on: "We have never been bitten by a shark." Like others in this series, this describes the photographers' research experiences; this one includes a day with seventeen different great whites. The text offers a general introduction to the species, talking especially about reproduction (slow), senses, feeding habits, and threats. Their pictures are fascinating. They show everything from a lemon shark pup still attached to the mother by a placental cord to a spotted whale shark accompanied by a tiny human diver not much longer than its tail. More sensational than informational, this book has plenty of reader appeal nonetheless.

Face to Face with Leopards   *Nonfiction*

By Beverly Joubert and Dereck Joubert. Illustrated with photographs by Beverly Joubert and Dereck Joubert. National Geographic, 2009. Ages 7–10. *Subject:* Leopards

In the course of their field studies of leopards in Botswana, the Jouberts follow a leopard they call Legadema (a local word for lightning) whom they first met as an eight-day-old cub with its mother. In four brief chapters, the Jouberts cover leopard habits and habitats, their role as top predators, and the threats to their survival. This husband-and-wife team of filmmaker and conservationist have been observing big cats in Africa for over twenty-five years. Their other titles in this series include *Face to Face with Cheetahs, Face to Face with Elephants,* and *Face to Face with Lions,* all published by National Geographic in 2008. The Jouberts' photographs are appealing. Some show the researchers in the wild; others focus on the leopards. There are endearing shots of mother and cub: in one, the mother licks the cub's face, in another, she carries her cub, sharp teeth around the baby's neck.

Face to Face with Orangutans   *Nonfiction*

By Tim Laman and Cheryl Denise Knott. Illustrated with photographs by Tim Laman and Cheryl Denise Knott. National Geographic, 2009. Ages 9–12. *Subject:* Orangutans

In Borneo, where orangutans live in the rain forest, a pair of researchers follow them through the forest to document and record their lives. Wildlife photographer Laman and his anthropologist wife introduce the ape Indonesians call "person of the forest." The biologist describes watching a large male eat termites from their mound and hold leafy branches to make an umbrella. For a moment, human and ape looked directly into each other's eyes. The orangutans the researchers follow live in the forest canopy, a terrain difficult to explore. Readers will be intrigued by details of their work. Photos of orangs in their forest home, including appealing images of babies, add to the attraction, but the sight of captured orphans in a rehabilitation center may be upsetting. The message of threat and loss in this and in *Face to Face with Gorillas* (Michael Nichols, National Geographic, 2009) may limit use of these two titles.

Face to Face with Wild Horses
Nonfiction

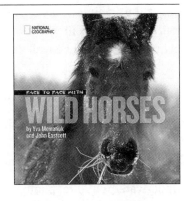

By Yva Momatiuk and John Eastcott.
Illustrated with photographs by Yva
Momatiuk and John Eastcott. National
Geographic, 2009. Ages 7–11.
Subjects: Wild horses, Photography

A husband-and-wife team of National Geographic photographers describe the wild horses they have observed and photographed in Wyoming's Red Desert. Opening with a suspenseful encounter with a stallion, Momatiuk talks about her lifelong love for horses and goes on to describe the horses she and her husband have gotten to know in the wild. She describes horse arrival and survival in North America, their physical characteristics, and their family lives, especially focusing on a newborn the couple named Flag and followed as he grew up. Photographs show horses feeding and fighting, touching and grooming, lying peacefully in the grass and racing across the desert. A final chapter explains modern wild horse management. These photographers have worked in other parts of the world as well. Their *Face to Face with Penguins* (National Geographic, 2009) is another in this series.

Face to Face with Butterflies   *Nonfiction*

By Darlyne Murawski. Illustrated by Darlyne Murawski. National Geographic, 2010. Ages 7–12.
Subjects: Butterflies, Insects, Migration

Research biologist Murawski followed up her *Face to Face with Caterpillars* (National Geographic, 2010) with this intriguing introduction. Using many of her own photographs, she begins by describing her early research in Costa Rica. She goes on to explain the differences between butterflies, skippers, and moths and to discuss their behaviors, migration, and mimicry. The text is appropriate for middle-grade readers who will be intrigued by the unusual images. There's a butterfly sticking its proboscis all the way down the long tube of a flower; another who's just kicked a rival off the flower it was feeding on; and an array of similar specimens in a museum collection showing surprising variety in the small details. Her very clear explanation of monarch migration includes maps. One shows the various stages of the northward journey. She encourages readers to go out to look for butterflies on their own, and they will be well prepared.

Face to Face with Manatees   *Nonfiction*

By Brian Skerry. Illustrated with photographs by Brian Skerry. National
     Geographic, 2010. Ages 8–12.
Subjects: Manatees, Marine mammals, Mammals

Underwater wildlife photographer Skerry describes personal encounters with manatees in Florida and offers an introduction to this intriguing, slow-moving mammal. In a touch that will especially appeal to young readers, he includes among his photographs two of his daughter swimming with a manatee calf under her arm. These images clearly show the adaptations that make possible this mammal's survival in an underwater environment. In his afterword he notes that tourists are allowed to swim with manatees in some places, but he also suggests observing them in zoos or marine parks and watching videos. Most closely related to elephants, these thick-skinned swimmers were once mistaken for mermaids. These photographs, some of manatees in groups, and others close-up, even showing the animal's large and bristly flexible snout, will keep readers from ever making that mistake!

NOTES

1. TeachingBooks.net In-depth Written Interview | Nic Bishop, June 30, 2009,
   www.teachingbooks.net/interview.cgi?id = 60.

2. Ben Trefny, "Photographer Documents Baby Animals Growing Up,"
   KALW Public Radio, San Francisco, May 14, 2012, http://kalw.org/post/
   photographer-documents-baby-animals-growing.

Wading in the Dog River, Vermont

Chapter 7

Habitats

FOR CHILDREN WHO LIVE NEAR THE DOG RIVER IN VERMONT, SHOWN IN THE photograph here, this doesn't seem like a habitat. It's familiar territory— home. It's home, too, to dace and other small fish that live in the water, the painted turtles that bask on floating logs, the white-throated sparrows that sing from the trees, and the raccoons and deer that roam the cultivated or overgrown farmlands and the remnants of deciduous forest. This *is* a habitat, even if it is familiar to residents of northeastern states. It is different from a riverbank in Florida or Arizona or Brazil or Australia. For a visitor from elsewhere, even common features may seem unusual. The shores have interesting rocks, the water is cold and clear, and so, relatively, is the air. Habitats are like neighborhoods, and it's not difficult for young children to grasp this concept and to think about what makes one like and unlike another. The titles in this chapter will take young readers from the Arctic to the tropics, from coral reefs to the bottom of the ocean, and from prairies to forests as well as to two places where volcanoes have been followed by slow, but remarkable, change.

Nature's Patchwork Quilt: Understanding Habitats

Informational picture book

By Mary Miché. Illustrated by Consie Powell. Dawn Publications, 2012. Ages 7–10.

Subjects: Habitat (Ecology), Natural history, Nature study

This interestingly illustrated book weaves an explanation of important nature study concepts like adaptations, food chains, and survival mechanisms into a description and illustration of a variety of habitats around the world. Consie Powell used a variety of geometric patterns to divide up her pages to show the many components of nature's quilt. From forests and deserts, to prairies and seashores, oceans and lakes, rain forests and tundra, plus cities and farms, each habitat illustrated includes distinctive plants as well as animals. There is much to look for on each spread including, always, at least one human being. A final spread shows twenty-two noted environmentalists. The book ends with extensive suggestions for educators. The text reads more like a series of definitions than a narrative, and would be especially suitable for curricular use.

Wild Animal Atlas: Earth's Astonishing Animals and Where They Live

Informational picture book

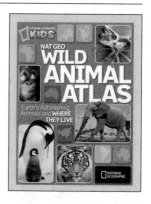

By National Geographic Society (U.S.). Illustrated with photographs from National Geographic, 2010. Ages 6–10.

Subjects: Zoogeography, Habitat (Ecology), Animals—maps

Continent by continent, this fascinating oversize volume presents ecosystems and iconic animals in a predictable and appealing format. Each section begins with a full-page photograph of a single animal—a bison for North America, a yellow-footed tortoise for South America, and so on. This is followed by a page of short descriptions of the ecosystems found on that continent together with an iconic animal for each ecosystem. Opposite that is a physical map of the continent with the animals shown where they might be found. Finally, there is a spread describing one particular ecosystem, such as the Great Barrier Reef for Australia, and introducing more creatures who live there. Each animal is shown with a small picture and a fact or two. Throughout the book red dots are used to indicate animals at risk, but this not a grim prediction. It's a glorious celebration.

THE FAR NORTH

North: The Amazing Story of Arctic Migration

Informational picture book

By Nick Dowson. Illustrated by Patrick Benson. Candlewick Press, 2011. Ages 7–10.
Subjects: Animals, Migration, Arctic regions

Lyrical prose and lush illustrations simply but effectively show the natural world of the Arctic, from its dark, lonely winters to its short, lush summers filled with creatures that have journeyed there from all over the world to reproduce. The poetic text provides examples of migrations from all over the world: from nearby, like the caribou, and from as far as New Zealand and Antarctica, like the godwits and terns. Benson's paintings, done in icy blues, grays, and greens, will add to the reader's sense of wonder. Sometimes filling a spread, and often showing the animals slightly veiled by snow, mist, or water, they are realistic enough for animal identification but also dramatic, emphasizing the vast expanses of the Arctic landscape and the way it teems with life in the summer. The text reads smoothly and the oversized illustrations show well, making this a particularly effective read-aloud.

Ocean's Child
Picture book; Bedtime story

By Christine Ford and Trish Holland. Illustrated by David Diaz. Golden Book, 2009. Ages 3–6.
Subjects: Beaufort Sea Coast (Alaska), Marine mammals, Canoes and canoeing, Mother and child

As a warmly dressed and obviously pregnant mother paddles through the evening, she sings a goodnight to the young child accompanying her as well as to a variety of Arctic marine life. Lit first by the setting sun and later by the stars and northern lights, the mother softly greets each animal they see, until finally the child falls asleep against her tummy. The text says something about each animal's sleep habits: the otter "in his leafy bed," the beluga whale calf on its mother's back, and the puffin in a nest on a cliff. In a sweet gesture, the child feels the baby inside her mother, "asleep, / in a sea of her own quiet dreams." Diaz's soft, stylized illustrations convey the colors of the Arctic world, an amazing range of blues and greens and shaded whites. An unusual bedtime story celebrating a unique part of the world.

Life in the Boreal Forest
Informational picture book

By Brenda Z. Guiberson. Illustrated by Gennady Spirin. Henry Holt & Co.,
    2009. Ages 5–9.
Subject: Taiga ecology

Across a vast stretch of Alaska, Canada, Scandinavia, and Russia the great northern forest is home to a web of interconnected wildlife. Short columns of text introduce the birds and animals of the area as well as the trees and even the lichen that nourish the moose in winter. Guiberson demonstrates their interdependence, the way some animals feed on others, and the effect of periodic population swings. Though the text is lengthy, the language makes it a treat to read aloud. Onomatopoetic words and phrases capture the sounds: the "plish, ploosh" of the diving loon, the "crackle, thwak" as trees tumble, and the "whoom, whoosh" of the dog sled. Spirin's beautiful, detailed paintings invite young readers to pore over this oversized volume to identify the creatures mentioned in the accompanying column of text. Using whites, greens, browns, tans, and occasional spots of red, she demonstrates the changing seasons.

Survival at 40 Below
Informational picture book

By Debbie S. Miller. Illustrated by Jon Van Zyle. Walker & Co., 2010. Ages
    7–12.
Subjects: Cold adaptation, Zoology, Arctic regions

In the Gates of the Arctic National Park and Preserve, animals have special adaptations that allow them to survive eight months of cold, snowy winter.

In an engaging narrative, Miller describes what goes on over a ten-month period. Mentioning a wide variety of species—caribou and Dall sheep, chickadees and jays, squirrels and marmots, frogs and fish, fox and grizzly bears, ptarmigan and hare, musk oxen and wolves, and even the woolly bear caterpillar that reappears in the spring—she covers their preparations, adaptations, and wintertime activities. From protective fur and feathers to hibernation to antifreeze in their tissues, she describes the features that allow them to cope with weather extremes. Acrylic paintings show the landscape in various seasons and the animals in action. A map on the endpapers will help readers locate this frigid world, and the author suggests sources for further reading and surfing.

FORESTS

Over in the Forest: Come and Take a Peek
Informational picture book

By Marianne Collins Berkes. Illustrated by Jill Dubin. Dawn Publications, 2012. Ages 3–8.
Subjects: Stories in rhyme, Forest animals, Animals—infancy, Counting

A temperate deciduous forest is the habitat for this counting book, one of a series of adaptations of "Over in the Meadow," showing animals and their babies. Previous volumes introduced animals of Australia, the Arctic, the rain forest, and a coral reef; the most recent is *Over in a River* (Dawn Publications, 2013). The format is predictable, but appropriate for the audience. Each collage spread includes a numeral, the animal, one to ten babies in an appropriate setting, one to ten footprints, and two verses of the song. Hidden in each background is another forest animal. From one beaver to ten foxes, all animals are identified. More information is provided in extensive back matter, where the author explains that animal baby names, italicized in the text, are correct, as are their actions, though litter sizes may vary. Learning activities and music can enhance the audience experience, and the artist also explains her work.

No Monkeys, No Chocolate
Informational picture book

By Melissa Stewart and Allen M.
   Young. Illustrated by Nicole
   Wong. Charlesbridge, 2013.
   Ages 5–9.
Subjects: Cacao, Cocoa processing,
   Chocolate, Rain forests

Working backwards from chocolate chip cookies and other goodies, expository text, illustrations, and a pair of bookworms providing commentary demonstrate the interrelationships in the rain forest that produce the chocolate we love. Cleverly constructed, the text makes unexpected connections that will keep readers engaged. Midges? Maggots? Lizards? Fungi? The monkeys, who pick the pods from the trees, eat the gooey insides, and spit out the seeds, are the final piece to the cocoa-growing puzzle. Wong's ink-and-watercolor illustrations demonstrate another intriguing fact: cocoa pods grow straight out of the trunk and limbs of the tree. Perspectives vary: she backs off to see two people holding open pods, helpfully cut in two different directions to show the seed arrangement; she focuses in on leafcutter ants busily tearing up the tree's leaves. Light humor and serious science combine to create an appealing demonstration of rain forest connections behind a popular treat.

PRAIRIES AND GRASSLAND

Flying Eagle   *Informational picture book*

By Sudipta Bardhan-Quallen. Illustrated by Deborah Kogan Ray. Charlesbridge, 2009. Ages 7–10.
Subjects: Serengeti (Africa), Tawny eagle

At sunset, a tawny eagle soars over the Serengeti Plain looking for food for its chick. Even the red-orange cover seems to warn readers: this is not a cheerful nature book. The fiery sunset background darkens to deep blue as night comes. The animals the reader sees can be fearsome: hippos and crocodiles with "toothy smiles," "spitting cobras," "roaring lions," and even a human poacher. Others—the zebras, dik diks, and a small hare—are frightened. Written in couplets with a throbbing, trochaic beat and shortened end lines, this description of the Serengeti ecosystem is impressive in both form and content. But the moment when the eagle finally catches and kills a "frantic" weaver bird is jarring. Certainly not a bedtime story, this stark depiction of the world of predator and prey is for readers with strong stomachs who are already familiar with the cycle of life.

Out on the Prairie

Informational picture book

By Donna M. Bateman. Illustrated by Susan
  Swan. Charlesbridge, 2012. Ages 3–8.
Subjects: Animals, Prairie ecology, South
  Dakota, Badlands National Park

"Out on the prairie where the snakeroot greets the sun, / Lived a shaggy mother bison and her little calf One." A skillful adaptation of a traditional rhyme introduces the mixed-grass prairie flora and fauna that can be found in Badlands National Park. Cut-paper art, spreading across two pages, shows each family, from bison and pronghorns to coyotes and toads, all in their natural habitats. An afterword provides more information about the animals and the plants pictured. Appropriately for the young audience, the author concentrates on child-rearing practices. Here's a book with broad appeal: a read-aloud poem for the very young listener plus lots of information for an older child. Bateman used the same approach to celebrate Florida's Okefenokee Swamp in *Over in the Swamp* (Charlesbridge, 2007).

After the Kill   *Informational picture book*

By Darrin P. Lunde. Illustrated by Catherine Stock. Charlesbridge, 2011.
  Ages 7–10.
Subjects: Animals—food, Food chains (Ecology)

This realistic description of predation in the wild is also not for the faint of heart. On Africa's Serengeti Plain, after a lioness kills a zebra, the carcass becomes food not only for the lioness and other members of her pride, but also vultures, hyenas, jackals, and, finally, meat-eating beetles who clean the skeleton, leaving it to dry and turn to dust. The author, a Smithsonian mammologist, minces no words in describing this scene, familiar to those who have visited the area. But he also offers intriguing details about the animals: "White-backed vultures . . . have hooked tongues that keep other vultures from snatching slippery meat out of their mouths." The text is accompanied by notes on the side or below, adding additional information. The illustrations capture the look of the plain and the aggressive energy of the animals, graphically conveying the cycle of life.

DRY PLACES

Survival at 120 Above

Informational picture book

By Debbie S. Miller. Illustrated by
    Jon Van Zyle. Walker & Co.,
    2012. Ages 7–10.
Subjects: Desert animals, Australia,
    Simpson Desert, Desert ecology

In Simpson Desert National Park, in central Australia, the animals have various ways to survive drought and punishing heat, but they take advantage of the water when rain comes. Some animals are nocturnal; others, like the red kangaroos, prefer the dawn and dusk. Sand goannas shelter in burrows. Spadefoot frogs spend months underground. The thorny devil drinks through his feet; the dunnart never drinks at all. Birds like emus and pink-eared ducks come from far away to take advantage of a temporary swamp. The author sets her introduction to this remote part of the world just after rainfall has ended a seven-year drought. Both Van Zyle's paintings and Miller's text are based on journal entries and photographs the Alaskan-based author made during a three-week visit. Pair this with her *Survival at 40 Below* (Walker & Co., 2010, annotated in this chapter) to see the many ways animals have adapted to extreme environments.

Desert Baths   *Informational picture book*

By Darcy Pattison. Illustrated by Kathleen Rietz. Sylvan Dell Publishing, 2012. Ages 5–9.
Subjects: Desert animals, Desert habitat, Baths

In the desert, it's not easy to find water to take a bath. Twelve desert species, from vultures and hummingbirds to coyotes and bobcats, clean themselves in a variety of ways in this natural-world connection to children's own lives. A scaled quail uses ants to clean its feathers, while a desert gecko uses its tongue. The roadrunner takes a dust bath; the desert tortoise waits for rain. The illustrations show animals in their natural habitat and also run through a day and night. Double-page spreads are framed with unlabeled border designs relevant to the ecosystem. Six pages of back matter include facts about the desert habitat, an adaptations matching game, a U.S. map, further information about animal cleaning methods, and instructions for telling time by the sun's position and making a sundial. A useful teaching tool.

Take a Stream Walk

OLD SHOES THAT can get wet are the only special equipment needed for stream-walking. All over the country there are brooks, creeks, and small rivers, often accessible from the road. Be sensible—don't go during a storm or downstream from a dam that regularly opens. Don't wade into water where you can't see the bottom, and remember that the rocks will be slippery. And if you don't want to walk into the water, what can you observe from the sides?

An ocean, lake, or riverside beach is a grand place for construction and artwork. Build sand castles or forts of driftwood. Make decorative arrangements of stones, shells, leaves, and other interesting objects from the shore.

Do you want to explore further? Take a net into the water and see what can be caught. With a little pan or bucket of the same water (a dishpan is especially good) you can keep the creatures long enough to observe them more closely before releasing them back to where they came from.

Learn about dragonflies who reside near wetlands and ponds and report sightings to the Dragonfly Pond Watch Project at the website of the Xerces Society for Invertebrate Conservation (www.xerces.org/dragonfly-migration/pondwatch).

Guess Who's in the Desert   *Informational picture book*

By Charline Profiri. Illustrated by Susan Swan. Rio Chico, 2013. Ages 3–7.
Subject: Desert animals

This introduction to fourteen animals of the southwestern desert is presented in the form of a guessing game. First comes a spread with a rhyming riddle and glimpses of an animal in the illustration. This is followed by a spread with the answer, a clear portrait of that animal, signs of another, and another riddle. Swan's cut-paper and mixed media illustrations show these desert creatures in their native habitat, hidden, at first, as they often would be in the wild. Roadrunner, bighorn sheep, desert tortoise, bobcat, cactus wren, gambel's quail, diamondback rattlesnake, javelina, tarantula, gila monster, elf owl, gray fox, long-tongued bat, and coyote are the animals described, but other animals occasionally appear in the illustrations. The final illustration shows children living in that part of the country who, like readers who don't know the desert that well, will certainly enjoy discovering these often elusive creatures.

WET PLACES

Babies in the Bayou   *Picture book*

By Jim Arnosky. Illustrated by Jim Arnosky. G. P. Putnam's Sons, 2007.
    Ages 4–7.
Subjects: Bayous, Baby animals, Mother and child

From alligators to raccoons, turtles, and wood ducks, there are babies in the bayou whose mothers guard them, shepherd them around, and protect them from danger. Naturalist Arnosky's text has a lovely rhythm and repetition, patterned to encourage reading aloud. One by one, each family is introduced; at the end of its segment, there is a hint, in words or pictures, of the creature to come. The mood is calm and reassuring. In spite of sharp teeth and claws, in spite of lurking enemies, these babies' mothers will keep them safe. In lifelike illustrations of the creatures mentioned in the poem, knowledgeable readers will recognize other birds, animals, plants, and flowers that inhabit southern waterways. This nicely circular description of an ecological chain of connections introduces that world to the youngest readers and listeners.

Coral Reefs

Picture book

By Jason Chin. Illustrated by Jason Chin.
  Roaring Brook Press, 2011. Ages 5–9.
Subjects: Coral reefs and islands, Coral reef
  ecology

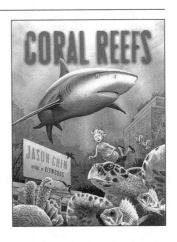

Just reading a book about coral reefs trans-
forms the New York Public Library into a reef
for one reader who explores its nooks and
crannies and meets some amazing inhabitants.
Chin's expository text is set on a background
of detailed watercolors in which the library is transformed, a reef grows,
water pours in, the reader swims delightedly among the fish, and then gradually—as the text compares a reef to a city—returns to reality, sandaled feet
still dripping. The endpapers are filled with sketches of different species of
coral and fish, each labeled with name and size. Further coral reef facts, and
threats, appear in an afterword, and the author includes a note about his
research, which included a trip to Belize. The species shown are all found on
Caribbean reefs. Imaginative children will be as eager to dive in as they were
to climb his *Redwoods* (Roaring Brook Press, 2009, annotated in chapter 8).

Down, Down, Down: *Informational picture book*
A Journey to the Bottom of the Sea

By Steve Jenkins. Illustrated by Steve Jenkins. Houghton Mifflin Harcourt,
  2009. Ages 5–8.
Subjects: Marine animals, Deep-sea animals

Jenkins' cut-and-torn-paper collage illustrations take the reader on an imaginary journey from just above the surface to the depths of the Pacific Ocean.
He presents a wide variety of creatures, from an albatross flying above and
Portuguese man-of-war floating at the surface, through sea turtles, rays, and
vampire squid, familiar and less familiar inhabitants, down to the hag fish
and sea lilies of the "ooze" of the abyssal plain and even deeper, exploring
hydrothermal vents and the Marianas Trench. Each spread shows just a few
creatures, not to scale, but on a background of steadily deepening blue to the
black of the depths. A bar along the right-hand edge indicates the depth, and

a relatively difficult paragraph or two of text adds information. Endnotes provide more detail about these creatures, with silhouettes showing their relative size in comparison to a human body or hand.

Wow! Ocean!
Picture book

By Robert Neubecker. Illustrated by Robert Neubecker. Disney / Hyperion Books, 2011. Ages 3–7.
Subject: Ocean life

Here's a whimsical picture-book puzzle that conveys the excitement of the ocean world, a perfect follow-up to a beach or aquarium visit. The premise is Izzy's family's visit to the seashore. Each spread has a busy illustration filled with color splotches and numerous black-line figures. The captions are simple: "Wow! Beach!" "Wow! Shells!" "Wow! Tide Pool!" "Wow! Turtles!" and so on, but the figures are also inconspicuously labeled. The children encounter some familiar creatures, such as octopus and sharks, and others that will be new. Foldout pages emphasize the spectacle of whales and coral reefs. Izzy and her sister use a variety of equipment for underwater explorations and the dog that joins them grows fins and a tail—this is, after all, fantasy. But for children who enjoy identification there is also plenty of information, and the girls' enthusiasm is irresistible.

Big Belching Bog   *Informational picture book*

By Phyllis Root. Illustrated by Betsy Bowen. University of Minnesota Press, 2010. Ages 5–9.
Subjects: Bog ecology, Bogs, Minnesota

This is a beautiful appreciation of a special place in northwestern Minnesota, a little-known wilderness called the Big Bog, a "big buggy blooming bog of butterflies and burrowers and birds." This mysterious, quiet place holds many secrets: strange, sometimes carnivorous plants; curious, specialized animals; ancient trees; and ghostly trails of long-gone caribou. Root's lyrical text is full of interesting detail and quiet suspense, but also full of alliteration and repetition, a joy to read aloud. A hermit thrush leads the reader into and through the bog in Bowen's bold woodcuts, painted with a dark, shadowy palette, heavy dark lines, and frames. End pages include miniature images of bog plants and animals, encouraging readers to go back to identify details in the pictures and also adding further information including Latin names. A treat for readers everywhere.

Looking Closely Along the Shore *Informational picture book*

By Frank Serafini. Illustrated by Frank Serafini. Kids Can Press, 2008. Ages 4–7.

Subject: Seashore biology

"Look very closely. What do you see? A flower? A fossil? What could it be?" This guessing game asks children to choose what the close-up image, in a small circle on the opposing page, might represent. The next two pages show the big picture, along with two paragraphs of additional information. The riddle is suitable for a young child who has had seashore experience. The explanation is geared to an early elementary school student. Everything pictured can be found somewhere on a North American coast, although not together. The author-photographer's stated intent is to encourage children to look more closely at the natural world. This title is part of a series that also explores the desert, the forest, the pond, the rain forest, and the garden. A drawback to the series is that no locations are given for any of the photographs. Still, the interactive nature of the presentation will appeal.

Pond Walk *Picture book*

By Nancy Elizabeth Wallace. Illustrated by Nancy Elizabeth Wallace. Marshall Cavendish, 2011. Ages 4–8.

Subjects: Pond animals, Pond ecology, Ponds

Buddy and his mother take a walk around the pond, stopping to draw and to identify what they see with a field guide. These nature-walking bears wear human clothes (including backpacks and useful boots). On their expedition they admire whirligig beetles, a frog, cattails, duckweed, water lilies, damselflies, a salamander, water striders, and, finally, a turtle. Wallace captures what young children notice about pond creatures, as well as their special fondness for turtles. Buddy enjoys playing with words and ideas, both in his conversation and in his drawings, which he labels himself. The clean, simple lines of the collage illustrations stand out on the white page backgrounds. The text, mostly dialog, would work well as a read-aloud, the bears' day a fine example for readers to follow. Instructions for making a rock turtle are included. In earlier titles, the two have explored leaves, seeds, shells, and rocks.

Meadowlands: A Wetlands Survival Story

Informational picture book

By Thomas Yezerski. Illustrated by
  Thomas Yezerski. Farrar, Straus,
  Giroux, 2011. Ages 6–10.
Subjects: Wetland ecology, Nature con-
  servation, Hackensack Meadowlands
  (New Jersey), New Jersey

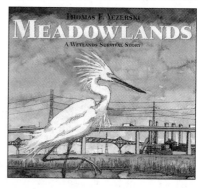

A surprising number of plants and animals can survive and even thrive in urban environments. This charming history of a once-trashed wetlands near New York City documents the destruction and resurrection of a natural area known as the Meadowlands. The text describes human use from as long ago as the time of the Lenni Lenape, the mid-twentieth-century toxic waste-land, and the subsequent development. Ecosystem restoration happened largely naturally in the remaining, protected area of wetlands. The author-illustrator's watercolors show the story, framed with tiny related images in the borders. Clearly identified, these show not only plants and animals to be found in this natural world, but also the works of humans, from bits of trash in the dump to the vehicles that pass by daily. Readers will not need to live in the area to be intrigued by the variety of inhabitants and heartened by the story.

SPECIAL PLACES

Island: A Story of the Galápagos
Informational picture book

By Jason Chin. Illustrated by Jason Chin. Roaring Brook Press, 2012. Ages 4–9.
Subjects: Natural history, Galápagos Islands

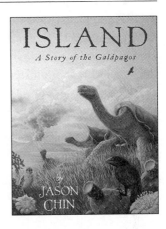

In words and dramatic paintings, Chin offers a scientifically based imagined account of the formation, population, evolution of the plants and animals through natural selection, and the eventual end of an island. In double-page spreads and small boxes, these watercolors demonstrate change. At first the island itself grows. All kinds of animals arrive. Finally, the species themselves are modified: beaks grow, shells change shape, and wings shrink. An epilogue shows the arrival of humans, after six million years. An afterword explains that these pages show Darwin's explorations in the Galápagos chain off the coast of Ecuador. Front endpapers identify thirty-six Galápagos species, each shown in a small sketch. In the back, a map labels the different islands and an inset shows their location in the Western Hemisphere. This is both a simple explanation and vivid demonstration of evolution as a series of gradual changes over a long period of time.

Gopher to the Rescue!
A Volcano Recovery Story

Informational picture book

By Terry Catasús Jennings. Illustrated by Laurie O'Keefe. Sylvan Dell Publishing, 2012. Ages 4–9.
Subjects: Pocket gophers; Saint Helens, Mount (Washington)—eruption, 1980; Volcanoes

After a volcano blows, few animals survive, but some that do make mountain recovery possible. This simple narrative focuses on Gopher, who waited out the eruption deep in his tunnel, and then, through his continued digging, mixed the nutrient-rich ashes with the soil beneath, encouraging new growth. Though told as a story, the science is accurate and the events are based on observations after the 1980 eruption of Mount St. Helens. Many of the realistic double-page illustrations include cutaway underground views, and all emphasize the animal and plant life. Parents of young readers should be forewarned that two animal corpses lie in the background of one early spread showing the devastation. Like other titles by this publisher, this is designed to be both a read-aloud picture book and a spur for classroom discussions, with ample end matter explaining volcanos, tectonic plates, and habitat changes and providing learning activities.

Tree climbing

Chapter 8

Plants and Trees

PLANTS ARE ALL AROUND US. WEEDS SPRING UP THROUGH CRACKS IN CITY pavements; grasses and other ground cover line the sides of the highways. Our supermarkets aisles display potted plants and flowers. Where plants come from and how they grow is usually far clearer to today's children than where their food comes from, because they see plants regularly and planting seeds is still a common childhood experience. You don't need constant access to a garden to sprout an avocado pit in a water glass or put some seeds in a pot on the windowsill. Experiments with growing things are easy to arrange. It's harder, but certainly valuable, to arrange a trip to a community garden or farm.

Climbing trees was once a near-universal childhood experience, too. Safety considerations and the lack of access to good climbing trees has, sadly, made this less common. Even if the children in your care don't have trees to climb, they will surely have trees to investigate. Outdoor educators are fond of tree-hugging—a tactile way to learn about the relative roughness and smoothness of different barks. Early childhood educators and elementary school teachers have children collect leaves both for artwork and for identification.

Perhaps it's the very familiarity of the plant world that makes it a less popular subject in children's books. Or perhaps it's because changes in that world are relatively slow to see. Julie Fogliano captures the seemingly endless wait for seeds to sprout in her charming *And Then It's Spring* (Neal Porter / Roaring Brook Press, 2012, annotated with other books about plants in the home garden in chapter 4). Animals do things from moment to moment; trees and plants take longer, maybe too long for many of us to pay attention. These books will help readers realize that the plant world is constantly changing, too.

Besides the titles in this chapter, there are a number of titles on trees and plants in the poetry chapter.

PLANTS

A Seed Is Sleepy
Informational picture book

By Dianna Hutts Aston. Illustrated by Sylvia
   Long. Chronicle Books, 2007. Ages 5–9.
Subject: Seeds

This follow-up to Aston and Long's award-winning *An Egg Is Quiet* (Chronicle Books, 2006, annotated in chapter 9) looks at the plant world, explaining the many varieties of plant seeds, their appearance, their method of distribution, their composition, and their development. The text is on two levels. For reading aloud, there is a series of descriptive sentences: a seed is sleepy, adventurous, inventive, generous, and more. Each sentence is followed by a very short explanation in a similar script font. Another paragraph, hand-lettered, adds further information for older readers or more patient listeners. Here the author doesn't hesitate to use more scientific words. The careful seed drawings, many highly magnified, and beautiful, accurate illustrations of plants and flowers done with ink and watercolors and set mostly on a white or pale-colored background, deserve lengthy attention. As an extra, readers may want to look for matches in the endpapers.

Growing Patterns: Fibonacci Numbers in Nature
Nonfiction

By Sarah C. Campbell. Illustrated by
   Sarah C. Campbell and Richard P.
   Campbell. Boyds Mills Press, 2010. Ages 5–9.
Subjects: Fibonacci numbers, Mathematics in nature

In the natural world, many flowers and plants with multiple parts arranged around a stem show an intriguing pattern known to ancient mathematicians and called Fibonacci numbers. Here, photographs of flowers arranged in an ever-increasing spiral represent not only the numbers 1, 1, 2, 3, 5, 8, but also a curving line much like the golden ratio. Following a deceptively simple beginning, the authors go on to show how these numbers turn up in pinecone bracts, sunflower heads, and sections of a pineapple skin for the older readers most likely to be curious about the math. Tinted rows and numbers allow for easier counting. Finally, a cutaway of a chambered nautilus shell demonstrates the spiral in the animal world. Not all plants and animals show this pattern; readers are invited to take a closer look outside.

Planting the Wild Garden   *Informational picture book*

By Kathryn Osebold Galbraith. Illustrated by Wendy Anderson Halperin.
   Peachtree, 2011. Ages 4–8.
Subjects: Plants, Seeds—dispersal

Seeds are planted by the wind and rain, the birds and animals, the plants themselves, and even the people passing through, all working together to make the wild garden. This lovely introduction to seed dispersal makes that point through gentle, poetic words and accurate pencil-and-watercolor illustrations, framed close-ups, and meadow landscapes in pastel colors. The narrative opens with a farmer and her boy planting purposely, and then moves on to the role of the wind, the goldfinches, the snapping pods of scotch broom, the rain, and more. Seeds pass through droppings, fall as animals eat, and catch on the coats of people and animals alike. The endpapers have a nice variety of seeds to speculate about and one illustration of a seed growing.

A Leaf Can Be   *Picture book*

By Laura Purdie Salas. Illustrated by Violeta Dabija. Millbrook Press / Lerner, 2012. Ages 5–8.
Subjects: Stories in rhyme, Leaves

"A leaf is a leaf," but it can be so much more. Organized by the changing seasons, a series of rhyming couplets and computer-generated illustrations show all the things leaves can do and ways they can be used. The greens of spring and summer ("Sun taker / Food maker / Tree topper / Rain stopper")

Hands-on with Leaves and Flowers

Make dandelion and fall leaf crowns. Make a hole in the stem of the flower or the base of the leaf and thread the next flower or leaf through until there is a chain long enough to go around the child's head.

Press flowers for later craft work. Use flowers from your garden or from waste places (but not roadsides where others might be enjoying them, too), or use discards from a florist. Place the flowers between sheets of tissue paper and put the flower sandwiches between leaves of a phone book. Put some other heavy books over that. Wait at least two weeks for the flower to dry. If the flower is still sticking to the tissue, wait longer. The flower then can be pasted on to paper and covered with a decoupage glue or laminate or ironed between sheets of wax paper to make pictures or notecards.

Preserve leaves. Sandwich beautiful fall leaves between two sheets of wax paper. Put a cloth on your ironing board to protect it, and have another to put over the wax paper sandwich to protect your iron. Heat the iron to high, but turn the steam off. Press slowly back and forth at first, but when the paper begins to stick, hold the iron in place for four or five seconds. After the sandwich has cooled you can cut around the leaf if you want to use it for further decoration.

Further information at About.com's Gardening site (http://gardening.about.com/od/craftsanddecor/ss/Preserve_Leaves.htm).

give way to the browns of fall ("Pile grower, Hill glow-er") and then back to spring again as the birds begin to use them to make their nests. Some of these concepts may surprise readers. Using a magnifying glass, a girl discovers the prickles on a leaf that raised welts on her skin. A chicken hunts for nearly invisible moths among the brown leaves of fall. An afterword explains some of the author's phrases. A read-aloud celebration of leaves at any time of year.

TREES

Redwoods   *Nonfiction; fantasy*

By Jason Chin. Illustrated by Jason Chin. Flash Point / Roaring Brook
    Press, 2009. Ages 7–10.
Subjects: Redwoods, Giant sequoia

In this interesting combination of fantasy and science fact, an Asian-American boy reading a book about redwoods on the subway imagines it so vividly it comes to life around him. After he finishes his reading—and his fantasy tour to the treetops—he leaves the book on a park bench where a little girl picks it up and begins to have the same experience. The author weaves in many facts about redwoods, ending with an afterword about redwoods in danger. The prose is straightforward exposition, and not especially appealing; the excitement is in the imagery that carries the narrative arc and adds information. The imagination in these detailed watercolors sets this book apart. Details of the boy's real life interrupt but don't stop the vision he sees in his mind as he reads it. Keep an eye out for the flying squirrel.

This Tree Counts!
Picture book

By Alison Formento. Illustrated by Sarah
    Snow. Albert Whitman & Co., 2010. Ages
    3–7.
Subjects: Trees, Schools, Counting

Before Mr. Tate and his ten students plant
new trees behind Oak Lane School, they surround the big old tree that's already there. Ears pressed to the bark, they hear the old oak count the ani-

mals making homes in and around it, from one owl sitting in the branches to ten earthworms munching soil around its roots. The tree washes the air, too, the teacher explains. Students think about other trees they know, and familiar things made from tree wood. Reminded of all that trees can do, this diverse group of students is ready and eager to dig. This simple story makes an important point, but its appeal lies in the counting. The cheerful illustrations reveal a grand variety of creatures: insects, squirrels, and birds. Young readers may want to go out and listen and look themselves. (A revised board book version is annotated in chapter 15.)

Celebritrees: Historic & Famous Trees of the World

Informational picture book

By Margi Preus. Illustrated by Rebecca Gibbon.
    Henry Holt & Co., 2010. Ages 7–10.
Subjects: Trees, Champion trees, Historic trees

Methuselah is a 4,800-year-old bristlecone pine in California; The Tule Tree in Mexico is thought to be the thickest tree in the world, at 177 feet around; today there are trees all over the world grown from seeds that took a trip to the moon in 1971. Here's an intriguing picture book introduction to fourteen trees from around the world so famous for their age, size, or some historic happening that they have acquired names. Each spread features an unusual tree, giving its species, location, size or age, and a short explanation of what makes it special. An afterword offers more about each one and suggests ways children can protect and nurture trees themselves. While the text is instructive, the illustrations are more fanciful than accurate, perhaps to encourage readers to use their imaginations about special trees in their own neighborhoods.

Picture a Tree

Picture book

By Barbara Reid. Illustrated by Barbara Reid. Albert Whitman & Co., 2013.
Ages 2–7.

Subject: Trees

Reid offers readers and listeners an open-ended invitation to looking at trees in a different way. This imaginative celebration of all kinds of trees in all kinds of weather is made even more appealing by her unique illustrations, done with plasticine. There is both astonishing detail and fuel for the imagination. The scenes (which include both trees and people) run chronologically from the bare branches of winter to the colors of spring, the lush greenery of summer, the falling leaves of autumn, back to winter snow. "Every winter tree holds spring, sleeping like a baby," and it's on to spring again. The use of more than a year and the arrival of the baby at the end together emphasize the endless succession of trees and people to love them. The endpapers show forty more small images. An irresistible prompt to tree-themed discussion, unusual artwork, and outside exploration.

Admiring a crab

Chapter 9

Animals

CHILDREN ARE INNATELY CURIOUS ABOUT ANIMALS. AS AN EXHIBIT GUIDE at the National Aquarium in Baltimore, I see hundreds of visiting families each week. If they aren't rushed or tired, the children will spend long periods watching the fish and other creatures in the tanks, and they are captivated by our two exhibits in which animals move about freely. They reach out to the birds and the golden lion tamarins in the rain forest exhibit. I frequently have to remind them that these animals are (at least partially) wild; they are not for petting. Kids love touch tanks and opportunities to hold animals that stay still for them—both their pets and animals from the wild. From reading, viewing, and real-life experience, they also recognize particular animals. There's hardly a child visitor who hasn't been excited to see a clownfish swimming among the tentacles of an anemone, a real-life Nemo from Disney's animated film *Finding Nemo.*

Children don't have to travel far to see animals in the wild as well. Some can be found in their own homes and yards—not only insects and spiders, but also birds. In our yard there are skinks and squirrels and geese, an occasional muskrat or deer, and, rarely, a fox. For a while, raccoons made their home in our attic. We keep wildlife guides and books about animal tracks handy, because we never know what will turn up and we like knowing something about our visitors.

Children also love to learn animal facts. Many young aquarium visitors tell me facts about the animals they see: sharks have to keep swimming to breathe, an octopus squirts ink when it is frightened, a sea star can regenerate an arm that has been cut off. They've learned these facts in their reading and viewing; not all of their facts are absolutely true, but they have stuck in their minds. The books I've selected for this chapter talk about aspects of animals in general: features such as babyhood and body parts, and characteristic behaviors that animals share with each other and with human children. The next two chapters will describe animals in captivity and specific animal groups and species.

BABY ANIMALS

An Egg Is Quiet

Informational picture book

By Dianna Hutts Aston. Illustrated by Sylvia Long. Chronicle Books, 2006. Ages 5–9.
Subjects: Embryology, Eggs

"An egg is quiet. Then, suddenly . . . an egg is noisy!" This beautifully illustrated array of eggs laid by birds, amphibians, reptiles, fish, insects, and even lobsters and crabs is a celebration of their incredible variety and essential similarity. The simple text covers where eggs might be found, their shape, size, texture, appearance, and contents. Elegant ink-and-watercolor illustrations bring the information to life. One spread shows a single sooty tern's egg nestled among many look-alike rocks; another has eggs of sixty different species, and the last shows a similar number of the fully grown creatures. These detailed images are set on a white background with labels that appear hand-drawn and text in a large script font. Endpapers patterned like a scarlet tanager's egg extend the theme and quiet tone. Nature-loving adults will also appreciate this award-winning tribute to the natural world, first in an outstanding series.

Animal Eggs: An Amazing Clutch of Mysteries and Marvels!

Nonfiction

By Dawn Cusick and Joanne O' Sullivan.
EarlyLight Books, 2011. Ages 6–10.
Subjects: Eggs, Baby animals

Who knew there were so many different kinds of animal eggs? More than a hundred examples appear in this intriguing topic book, illustrated with photographs from naturalists and animal researchers. The informational text is organized into sections titled Egg Layers, Egg Shapes and Sizes, Egg Colors, Egg Guarders, Egg Stealers, Egg Shelters, Egg Escapers, Gross or Cool? and Whose Egg Is This? Each page is divided into boxes containing the section title, a short explanation, several photos, and their captions. The photos vary interestingly, and some are even magnified. There are some striking images: baby marine turtles climbing out of their egg-filled nest; snakes with jaws unhinged to swallow eggs whole; a stink bug and her pink jelly bean eggs on the underside of a leaf. A delight for browsers. For naturalists-in-training this could inspire their own egg investigations.

Sisters & Brothers: Sibling Relationships in the Animal World

Informational picture book

By Steve Jenkins and Robin Page. Illustrated by Steve Jenkins. Houghton Mifflin, 2008. Ages 3–7.
Subjects: Baby animals, Brothers and sisters

What a treat to have an animal baby book about siblings! This one has garnered numerous awards. Jenkins' cut-and-torn-paper illustrations accompany concise descriptions of a variety of brother-and-sister relationships across the animal world. Dealing first with numbers—singletons, twins, identical quadruplets, and teeming hordes—the authors go on to describe behaviors. Bears, hyenas, and black widow spiders fight; cheetahs and falcons help each other hone their skills. Some animals live and work together for life; others part company early. Cichlids and myna birds have step-siblings. Images of these animals appear on a white background with a heading, a big label suitable for the youngest reader or listener, and just a paragraph or two of text for the more curious or determined reader. The back matter adds further facts for animal lovers who will surely want to know more.

Guess What Is Growing Inside This Egg

Informational picture book

By Mia Posada. Illustrated by Mia Posada.
   Millbrook Press, 2007. Ages 3–8.
Subjects: Eggs, Baby animals

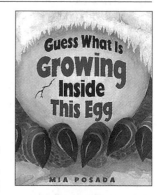

This guessing game for the very young introduces the eggs of penguins, ducks, alligators, spiders, octopus, and sea turtles. The format is simple and repetitive: a couplet or two of description and the title question appear on a double-page spread showing eggs in their nest or natural surroundings and just a small portion of the parent. On the next page, in large print, is the answer plus another paragraph of explanation, on a picture of the emerging tiny creatures—ducklings with their mother, sea turtles aiming for the water, and tiny spiders floating away. The rhyming couplets don't scan well, but the facts are clear and easy to understand and the illustrations are realistic. Simple, straightforward, and effective, this would be a welcome accompaniment to egg-hatching activities as well as an interactive, informative read-aloud.

ANIMAL BEHAVIOR

At This Very Moment   *Informational picture book; Bedtime story*

By Jim Arnosky. Illustrated by Jim Arnosky. Dutton Children's Books,
   2011. Ages 4–8.
Subjects: Stories in rhyme, Nature, Animals—behavior

This appealing bedtime story encourages listeners to think about how animals around the world have gone on with their own lives throughout the day. From dawn to bedtime, Arnosky structures his gentle rhythmical reflection to match the listener's experience, from morning tooth brushing while a "toothy shark" circles a reef to evening dinner while "puffins dine on fresh-caught fish." From mountain cliffs to deserts, swamps, and oceans, there's appropriate variety in his landscapes, and extra animals, too. With its quiet, unforced rhyme and thoughtful pacing, this is a pleasure to read aloud. "Think of all the animals / getting sleepy, too, / who at this very moment / will fall asleep with you." The artist-illustrator has drawn from long nature-watching experience for his accurate portraits; notes on the final endpapers describe his encounters with his subjects. A lovely way to make a sleepy child feel connected to the natural world.

What Happens Next?

Picture book

By Nicola Davies. Illustrated by Marc Bouta-
	vant. Candlewick Press, 2012. Ages 3–7.
Subjects: Animals, Lift-the-flap books, Toy
	and movable books

Flip the flaps to see some surprising animal behaviors in this "What happens next?" guess-ing game. A chameleon's tongue shoots out to capture a grasshopper. A bea-ver makes an underwater door to its lodge, home for its family. A peacock displays to a potential mate. A bee dances to let its relatives know where flowers are. A chimpanzee uses a stick to get termites from a mound. These animals are slightly anthropomorphized; their eyes look at the reader and they have readable emotions. The brightly colored digital illustrations sup-port the information, and the back endpapers include a matching game to reinforce the learning. Best of all, another flap opens to reveal a girl drawing a picture of her own, encouraging young readers and listeners to do some observing and predicting of their own in the natural world.

How Many Ways . . . Can You Catch a Fly?

Informational picture book

By Steve Jenkins and Robin Page. Illustrated by Steve Jenkins. Houghton
	Mifflin, 2008. Ages 5–10.
Subject: Animals

For the nature book browser, this is a fascinating collection of animal solu-tions to familiar problems: finding food and shelter, incubating eggs, and more. After each question, readers can turn the page to find a series of answers. Jenkins' cut-and-torn-paper collages show a wide variety of creatures snaring fish, hatching eggs, using leaves, catching flies, digging holes, or eating clams. An anhinga stabs a fish with its beak; tent bats make their own shelter by biting the ribs of a leaf; and a sea star wraps its arms around a clam to open it enough to inject its stomach. Some animals are familiar and North American; others are less well known. Four pages of back matter give more information about each species including pronunciation for some, where they live, and other distinguishing details, and the authors have provided a bibliography of their sources.

How to Clean a Hippopotamus: A Look at Unusual Animal Partnerships
Informational picture book

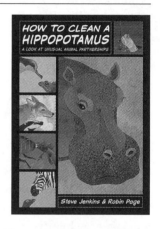

By Steve Jenkins and Robin Page. Illustrated by
    Steve Jenkins. Houghton Mifflin Books for
    Children, 2010. Ages 7–10.
Subjects: Social behavior in animals, Animals—
    communication, Symbiosis

In nature, animals large and small form mutually beneficial partnerships for a variety of reasons. Once again, this experienced husband-and-wife team has found an engaging way to present accurate information about the natural world. This time they illustrate symbiosis with a variety of examples, including giraffes and oxpeckers in Africa, coyotes and badgers in western North America, and tiger sharks and remora in warm ocean waters worldwide. These are presented in comic-book-like layout with small panels, each including a cut-paper illustration and snippets of text. Each page also has a humorous headline: such as "Have beak, will travel," "That tickles!" "Who's in charge here?" The pages aren't numbered, but the end matter includes a small reproduction of each spread with more information about the animals pictured, including size, habitat, and diet. A short bibliography will lead readers to sources for further information.

Time for a Bath   *Informational picture book*

By Steve Jenkins and Robin Page. Illustrated by Steve Jenkins and Robin
   Page. Houghton Mifflin Books for Children, 2011. Ages 5–10.
Subjects: Grooming behavior in animals, Animals

Animals bathe themselves in a variety of ways to keep themselves clean,
to remove parasites, and sometimes even to keep their internal temperatures just right. This fact-filled book describes the bathing habits of fifteen
different species of mammals, birds, lizards, fish, and even ants. Jenkins's
expressive collages offer examples, from a Bengal tiger staring at the reader
to a pair of white-tailed deer, one licking the other's face. A short paragraph
gives the how and why of each animal's bath. Further information about
each creature, including where it can be found, appears in the back matter
next to identifying thumbnails. Part of a series of child-friendly informational titles, which also includes *Time to Eat* and *Time to Sleep* (both Houghton Mifflin, 2011), these should have particular appeal for the reader or
listener who likes to collect animal facts.

Even an Octopus Needs a Home
Informational picture book

By Irene Kelly. Illustrated by Irene Kelly.
   Holiday House, 2011. Ages 5–9.
Subjects: Nests, Animals—habitations

Tree houses, towers, lodges, caves, burrows,
floating and mobile homes, and even bubbles may serve as homes for animals, as
explained in this wide-ranging survey. Organizing her examples by type,
and building on her *Even an Ostrich Needs a Nest* (Holiday House, 2009,
annotated in chapter 11), Kelly shows how a variety of animals find or create spaces for bedding down at night, places for hatching eggs and raising
young, or protective hideaways. With an informal text set in wavy lines
around her detailed illustrations, she explains nest construction and use.
Adults who use this with children need to help them avoid thinking that
animals attach the same values to their homes that we do, but for relatively
young children this is a fine introduction to a grand array of creatures and
their shelters that should make them want to know more.

Look!   *Early reader*

By Ted Lewin. Illustrated by Ted Lewin. Holiday House, 2013. Ages 4–7.
Subjects: Animals, Animal ecology, Africa

"Look! An elephant eats." "Look! Giraffes drink." For fledgling readers, wild-life images are captioned with single lines. These short, accessible sentences accompany Lewin's extraordinary paintings of animals from central and southern Africa. Also pictured are a warthog, a gorilla, wild dogs, zebra, monkeys, hippos, and rhinos, all in natural habitats. The savannah animals are drenched in light; the forest animals peer through leaves and stalks. Hippos splash. The animals' activities parallel those of children: eating, drinking, digging, hiding, listening, running, sitting, napping. Finally, we see the boy reading. These animals are in his imagination, based on the stuffed animals that surround him as he sits with his book, cross-legged on the floor. They are there again on his bed, where he dreams. This tribute to reading and to the natural world is a welcome addition to the author-illustrator's new early reader series.

The Long, Long Journey: The Godwit's Amazing Migration
Informational picture book

By Sandra Markle. Illustrated by Mia
    Posada. Millbrook Press, 2013. Ages 4–9.
Subjects: Bar-tailed godwit, Migration

Continuing to write about the growth of baby animals, Markle here describes the astonishing experience of a bar-tailed godwit chick. From fluffy hatchling on the Alaskan tundra to adulthood on New Zealand's mudflats, she chronicles one female's growth in four short months. This is straightforward nonfiction; the author gives the chick no human characteristics, but readers will easily identify with it just the same, as it huddles in the nest with its brothers and sisters, learns to hunt insects, and avoids predators. While migrating to the Southern Hemisphere, godwits make the longest known nonstop flights of any bird. And so, in mid-October, the young female and others like her set out on a seven-thousand-mile journey. Painted papers and other fluffy materials form the collage illustrations that show the birds against varying backgrounds, including the starry nights and storm clouds they encounter in their flight.

Bird, Butterfly, Eel
Informational picture book

By James Prosek. Illustrated by James Prosek. Simon & Schuster Books for Young Readers, 2009. Ages 5–9.
Subjects: Monarch butterfly, Migration, Barn swallow, Eels

In this handsome introduction to migration and to the life cycles of these species, a barn swallow, monarch butterfly, and eel, living near Long Island Sound on the same New England farm, go their separate ways in the fall. Returning in the spring, the bird, and the young of the butterfly and eel begin the cycle again. Prosek's detailed watercolors emphasize the expanse of the landscape but include interesting additional elements. The reader might imagine observing the natural world along with the cat. Though mentioned only once in the text, it figures prominently in the paintings. In the center of the story, the three different journeys are plotted against a map of the Americas. There is some anthropomorphization and a reassuring but inaccurate statement about a butterfly's life cycle, rectified in the back matter. The author-illustrator also describes his own experience observing monarch butterflies and their milkweed hosts.

Just One Bite: 11 Animals and Their Bites at Life Size!
Informational picture book

By Lola M. Schaefer. Illustrated by Geoff Waring. Chronicle Books, 2010. Ages 4–10.
Subject: Animals—food

Cleverly designed for broad readership, this large square book illustrates in actual size what eleven creatures can eat in the titular "just one bite." The simple text takes a back seat to striking illustrations spreading across two, three, and four foldout pages. A butterfly probes deep into a hibiscus flower. A giraffe's tongue curls around a thorny acacia branch. The focus is the mouths, tongues, and teeth of these animals and their food. The worm, butterfly, frog, octopus, parrot, rabbit, Komodo dragon, snake, bear, giraffe, elephant, and sperm whale are identified generically in the text but more specifically in two pages of back matter which describes mouths and eating habits in more detail. The back matter appears on a trifold page with an optional conclusion: "microorganisms . . . can eat even the largest animal until it becomes part of the earth that feeds us all, large and small."

Predators   *Nonfiction*

By John Seidensticker and Susan Lumpkin. Illustrated with photographs.
    Simon & Schuster Books for Young Readers, 2008. Ages 7–12.
Subject: Predatory animals

Who can resist a book about nature's killers—especially one with a tiger's open mouth embossed on the cover? This splendid introduction to the animal world focuses on creatures at the top of the food chain—cats, bears, dogs and wolves, sharks, crocodilians, and birds of prey. The information is presented in bite-sized chunks on double-page spreads organized into two sections. The first explains the food chain. It describes some predator species of the past and some prey defenses before giving examples of natural weapons, senses, and methods. The second section describes species and habitats more specifically. Two final pages present animal classification. The illustrations are as irresistible as the facts. Through exaggerated focus and perspective, they seem to leap off the paper. One after another, the king species are shown catching and killing their prey. A browser's delight.

ANIMAL BODIES

Best Foot Forward: Exploring Feet, Flippers, and Claws

Informational picture book

By Ingo Arndt. Illustrated by Ingo Arndt. Holiday House, 2013. Ages 3–8.
Subject: Animals—feet

With a simple question and striking photographs of the underside of animal feet, a wildlife photographer introduces the workings of feet that walk, climb, paddle, swim, dig, jump, and do other extraordinary things. "Whose foot is this?" introduces each section. The following pages show the animal and some other animal feet that work similarly and include short explanations. From a tiger's padded and furry paws to a lobster's snapping claws, remarkable close-ups demonstrate similarities and differences among twenty-four different animal feet, flippers, and claws. The author concludes with a photograph of his own foot, connecting these animals with the child reader. A helpful index allows readers to turn back to just the foot they wanted. This topic book is appealing in its simplicity. First published in Germany in 2007, it is the photographer's first children's book in English.

Wings

Informational picture book

By Sneed B. Collard. Illustrated by Robin Brick-man. Charlesbridge, 2008. Ages 3–10.
Subject: Wings, Animals

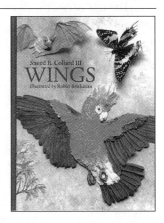

Amazingly realistic, three-dimensional illustrations of a galah cockatoo, leaf-nosed bat, and sunset moth on the cover of this straightforward introduction to the remarkable variety of wings on birds, bats, and some insects will draw readers in. Made of painted and sculpted paper, they show bird feathers and plant tendrils that look almost real. The range of creatures described is impressive; they come from around the world. These examples show that wings come in a variety of shapes, sizes, colors, and numbers. Covered with feathers, scales, or skin, they work in a variety of ways for flying and other tasks. The shape of a curved wing and a diagram of the figure-eight motion of hummingbird and dragonfly wings provide a simple explanation of lift. A glossary and a book and web resource list complete this companion to Collard and Brickman's *Beaks* (Charlesbridge, 2002) and *Teeth* (Charlesbridge, 2008).

Animal Eyes
Nonfiction

By Beth Fielding. Illustrated with photographs.
  EarlyLight Books, 2011. Ages 5–9.
Subjects: Eyes, Animals

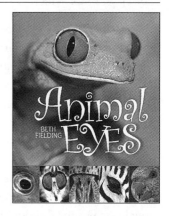

Bulging, staring, hiding, shedding, winking, and blinking—animals have all kinds of eyes. Organizing her intriguing facts by creature, from people to flies, one topic to a spread, Fielding keeps readers connected by making comparisons to human eyes throughout. There is a great deal of information on these pages, but lively design breaks up the text, and the variety of eyes staring out from the many photographs adds to the appeal. She discusses special features like the nictitating membrane of birds, reptiles, and sharks and the tapetum that reflects light from a cat's eyes at night. Specialized words are explained in context and defined in the glossary. Like others in this series (*Animal Baths, Animal Tongues,* and *Animal Colors,* 2009, and *Animal Tails,* 2011, all from EarlyLight Books), this book doesn't provide attribution for the facts or specific identification for every picture, but it is a treat for browsers.

Living Color   *Informational picture book*

By Steve Jenkins. Illustrated by Steve Jenkins. Houghton Mifflin, 2007.
  Ages 4–8.
Subject: Animals—color

Color is the organizing principle for this collection of wondrous animal facts. Red, blue, yellow, green, orange, purple, and pink—Jenkins provides over sixty examples from the animal kingdom and suggests the purpose these bright colors serve in the animals' lives. His colorful cut-paper illustrations pop off clean, white pages, accompanied by paragraphs of text, each offering surprising facts and occasional humor. For the casual browser and animal fact devourer alike, these tidbits provide sustenance. He has chosen examples from around the world, some familiar (like the robin's egg) and some quite exotic (the long-wattled umbrella bird). The range of colors and adaptations described is astonishing. Color-changing animals, the cuttlefish and the chameleon, appear to wrap around page edges. The back matter provides further information about animal color and size, habitat, and diet for each of the species mentioned.

Bones: Skeletons and How They Work

Informational picture book

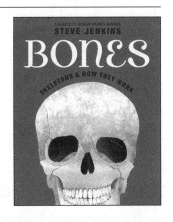

By Steve Jenkins. Illustrated by Steve Jenkins.
    Scholastic Press, 2010. Ages 6–10.
Subjects: Skeleton, Bones

Cut-paper collages also illustrate this introduction to the arrangement and the work of bones in humans and other mammals, birds, reptiles, amphibians, and most fish. Jenkins' intriguing illustrations, slightly textured yellowy-gray bones on solid background, demonstrate the similarities in vertebrate skeletons, showing comparative sizes and adaptations. The scale is usually indicated. The minimal text—simple titles and short paragraphs of explanation—is presented in large, clear type. Humor and questions addressed to the reader add further interest. One double-page spread demonstrates the similarity of the pieces of the arms and hands of humans, moles, spider monkeys, gray whales, turtles, and fruit bats. Another shows symmetry in the skeleton of a bullfrog, and a third illustrates all 206 bones of the human body. Behind a gatefold, the same bones are assembled into a human skeleton. Another foldout shows animal skulls and a human one, at actual size. Irresistible.

Track That Scat!

Informational picture book

By Lisa Morlock. Illustrated by Carrie Anne
    Bradshaw. Sleeping Bear Press, 2012.
    Ages 5–9.
Subjects: Animals—droppings, Animals—
    tracks, Animals—behavior, Stories in
    rhyme

Animal tracks and excrement lead Finn and her basset hound Skeeter to
discover creatures in the wild on their walk through the woods. Playing on
the several uses of the word *scat* and children's natural interest in poop, the
rhyming text and engaging pictures of this story are sure to please. Finn
sets out in her new flowered boots, only to "splat" in rabbit scat, followed
by goose poop, raccoon droppings, and red fox turds. A skunk provides a
"tail-raising funk." Finally, they meet a chickadee, who decorates the top of
her shoe. A cheerful rhyming text chronicles their messy walk, and colorful
double-page spreads show the animals, their tracks, and their droppings.
Each animal's traces (sounds, tracks, and scat) are further described in a
secondary text, set off by a more formal typography. Fun and informative.

Why Are Animals Blue?   *Nonfiction*

By Melissa Stewart. Illustrated with photographs. Enslow Elementary,
    2009. Ages 5–9.
Subject: Animals—color

From great blue heron and blue shark to peacock and blue darner dragonfly,
this simple topic book shows that animals' colors serve to hide them, to warn

Track Some Scat

IN THEIR YARDS and neighborhoods,
children can often find and learn to
identify animal droppings. Even in the
tree lawns, there may be evidence of
dogs whose owners were careless.

In the woods, there are likely to be
deer, fox, rabbit, and raccoon droppings.

In sand and snow they can find and
photograph animal tracks of all sorts.

This is a place where a nature journal
can come in handy as a tool. A ruler
marked off on the cover will allow the
child to measure the tracks he or she
has found.

or surprise predators, to attract mates, and to help them keep an even body temperature. Frankly educational, it begins with a table of contents and short pronouncing glossary of words to know, helpful for beginning readers. These words are boldface the first time they appear in the relatively easy-to-read text. A definition of *animal* and examples of animal colors are given in the opening chapter. Continuing, each double-page spread includes a clear close-up photograph of a creature, a label, and an explanation of the function the blue coloring serves for the species. Finally there's a guessing game. Red, orange, green, yellow, and purple are other colors in the publisher's Rainbow of Animals series.

ANIMALS GENERALLY

Little Kids First Big Book of Animals

Informational picture book

By Catherine D. Hughes. Illustrated with
National Geographic Society (U.S.)
photographs. National Geographic, 2010.
Ages 3–8.

Subject: Animals

Designed for adults to share with children, this reference book and teaching tool has lively graphics and relatively simple text accompanied by National Geographic photographs. It introduces thirty iconic animal species in double-page entries. From grassland and ocean through desert, forest, and polar areas, the organization by biome subtly helps children make the appropriate connection between animals and their environments. Each entry includes fast facts, short paragraphs, info-bits, and a question connecting the animal with young readers' own lives. From cheetah to dolphin, camel, tiger, and penguin, most species are well-known. The author also includes animals that might be in one's own yard like a garden spider or raccoon. In an excellent concluding section of tips for parents, a trip to a zoo is a recommended supplement.

The Animal Book   *Nonfiction*

By Steve Jenkins. Illustrated by Steve Jenkins. Houghton Mifflin Books for
    Children, 2013. Ages 5 and up.
Subject: Animals

This encyclopedic album is the culmination of twenty years of experience in
finding amazing facts and creating realistic cut-and-torn-paper illustrations
of the animal world. Jenkins has chosen more than three hundred creatures,
large and small, exotic and familiar, prehistoric and present-day, for this
demonstration of their astounding diversity. After a section of definitions, he
organizes his examples into chapters on animal families, senses, predators,
defenses, extremes, and the story of life. More animal facts appear in the
final section, which serves both as an index and a quick reference. Most
spreads have an explanatory paragraph and then a number of examples,
each with an animal image and a sentence or two of detail set on white background. Each chapter ends with a chart. Jenkins fills out this appealing celebration with a description of his bookmaking process (also available on his
website). For researchers and browsers alike, a treasure.

What Am I? Where Am I?

Early reader

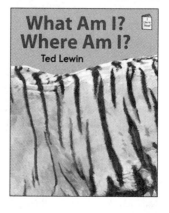

By Ted Lewin. Illustrated by Ted Lewin. Holi-
    day House, 2013. Ages 2–6.
Subjects: Animals, Habitat (Ecology)

Ted Lewin, who has been writing and illustrating beautiful books for children for more than
thirty-five years, has recently turned to the
early reader genre. Here he uses his characteristic light-filled paintings to introduce some
iconic animals in their surroundings through a guessing game. First, a bit of
an image shows through an imagined peephole: "What am I?" Then, the full
animal—lion, reindeer, camel, sea otter, and tiger—with its name and the
question "Where am I?" are shown on a double-page spread, a cutout against
a white background. A third spread shows the animal in its usual habitat—
grassland, tundra, desert, water, forest. Simple words convey an important

concept to fledgling readers who can connect, at the end, with the image of the boy against a "beautiful earth." Prereaders will enjoy the images, too.

Lifetime: The Amazing Numbers in Animal Lives

Informational picture book

By Lola M. Schaefer. Illustrated by Christopher Silas Neal. Chronicle Books, 2013. Ages 5–9.

Subjects: Developmental biology, Life expectancy, Animals

For readers who like numbers and counting, this collection of fascinating animal facts is a welcome surprise, a fresh and original approach to thinking about the natural world. The facts are organized by numbers: from one papery egg sac spun by a cross spider in its lifetime to one thousand baby seahorses. Neal's mixed-media illustrations also show caribou fighting with their antlers (they'll grow and shed ten sets over the years), alpaca being sheered, a woodpecker drilling holes, a rattlesnake, a kangaroo and her fifty joeys, a dolphin's one hundred teeth, a giraffe with spots, an alligator and her eggs, and the nine hundred flowers a giant swallowtail butterfly will visit. Readers who want to can count every one. Older readers may want to go on to the back matter, where each animal is described (including its Latin name), the calculations are explained, and readers are invited to try the math themselves.

National Aquarium, Baltimore, Maryland

Chapter 10

Animals in Captivity

ZOO AND AQUARIUM VISITS ARE A STAPLE OF CHILDHOOD ENTERTAINMENT around the world. But how these institutions keep and display their animals has changed a lot over my lifetime. The Vilas Park Zoo of my childhood in Madison, Wisconsin, had individual cement-floored cages for lions and tigers and bears. You could ride a camel or an elephant. At a zoo in Jakarta that we visited with our children in the 1970s, we were so close to the elephants' small ring that, bored with her sterile surroundings, one reached out over the line and wrapped its trunk around my eight-year-old daughter's upper body. Fortunately, it let go without causing any harm. These were animals whose sole purpose was exhibition: the message was that such creatures are wild, exotic, and should be displayed for human entertainment. Not so today. The Association for Zoos and Aquariums in this country (www.aza.org/StrategicPlan) has become a conservation organization working to help people "respect, value and conserve wildlife and wild places." Conservation and education come before public entertainment. Animals are housed appropriately, cared for carefully, bred, and exchanged with other zoos and aquariums to reduce collection from the wild. Often the zoo or aquarium is connected with a wildlife rescue and rehabilitation facility such as the one in Monterey Bay described in Seababy's story in this chapter. And wildlife rescue efforts have evolved to include cordoning off and protecting wildlife in their natural world, as in turtle-egg watches and seal-sitters guarding wildlife nurseries.

Children, too, capture and care for animals. Fireflies and tadpoles were favorites in my childhood. Even as wildlife access and animal numbers diminish, children can still enjoy catching creatures, following principles that are not too different from those established by the zoo and aquarium association. Catch-and-release and careful care are the keys. A privately sponsored website, www.firefly.org/how-to-catch-fireflies.html, gives excellent instructions for catching fireflies. Suggestions for capturing and raising tadpoles can be found on many websites. Nick Baker's *Bug Zoo* (DK Publishing, 2010), annotated in this chapter, might help you look beyond the usual critters. Who knows—perhaps a child who has caught the animal care bug at home will go on to an adult life working at one of those zoos and aquariums or in a wildlife refuge or natural area.

Slow Down for Manatees   *Picture book*

By Jim Arnosky. Illustrated by Jim Arnosky. G. P. Putnam's Sons, 2010.
   Ages 4–7.
Subjects: Manatees, Wildlife rescue

A manatee injured by a passing boat in the sun-drenched waters of a Florida canal is rescued and removed to a local aquarium. There, visitors could follow her treatment and rejoice when she gave birth to a calf. Naturalist Arnosky bases this fictionalized story on an actual incident, describing it gently and reassuringly for his young readers. He focuses on the experience for the manatee—her wide watery world narrowed to a small tank and then reopened. The book's design supports the subject: a wavy ribbon separates text from pictures that cross the gutter. Two-page spreads show key moments, including the manatees' return to the canal, which now sports a warning sign, "Slow Down! Manatees." Plenty of environmental detail in Arnosky's acrylic paintings offers much for young readers to look for and wonder at in this watery world.

Bug Zoo
Nonfiction

By Nick Baker. Illustrated by Margaret Parrish.
  DK Publishing, 2010. Ages 5–10.
Subjects: Insects—collection and preservation,
  Insect trapping, Science observation, Pets

TV naturalist Nick Baker provides instructions
for capturing and keeping thirteen different
species. He opens with a short chapter on zoo
tools and general techniques, most of which
involve easily obtainable supplies. Then, on double-page spreads that give
the appearance of a notebook, chapter by chapter he introduces each creature. The first spread describes the animal and suggests ways to catch it; the
second gives instructions for constructing housing, feeding, and observing
your creature. There is an extraordinary amount of solid information, but
there's humor and play with words as well: "the louse house," "aphids . . .
the hungry herds," "making an earwiggery." Though researched in England,
Baker makes clear that these creatures—wood lice, slugs, snails, aphids, caterpillars, worms, earwigs, ladybugs, spiders, crickets, katydids, pseudoscor-
pions, mosquito and dragonfly larvae, and backswimmers—can be found
worldwide. Young readers will be intrigued and entranced.

Mossy   *Picture book*

By Jan Brett. Illustrated by Jan Brett. G. P. Putnam's Sons, 2012. Ages 4–8.
Subjects: Turtles, Museums

When Mossy, an eastern box turtle whose back sprouts moss and a flower
garden, is collected for Dr. Carolina's museum, she spends an unhappy year
in a fancy viewing pavilion before being returned to Lilypad Pond and the
waiting Scoot. Brett celebrates old-fashioned natural history museums by
filling the intricately illustrated pages and their margins with the kinds of
things that were admired and collected: shells and beetles, butterflies and
moths, fossils and beautiful rocks, seeds and flowers and feathers. In this
slower-moving, Edwardian setting, people travel by horse and buggy. Dr.
Carolina's niece, Tory, who realizes the turtle's unhappiness, wears a sailor

shirt, pleated skirt, and lace-up boots. Artists named Flora and Fauna memorialize Mossy in a painting so the real turtle can be returned to her home. The endpapers are filled with different mosses. Extraordinary to look at and satisfying to hear.

A Little Book of Sloth

Informational picture book

By Lucy Cooke. Illustrated by Lucy Cooke.
    Margaret K. McElderry Books / Simon &
    Schuster, 2013. Ages 6–10.
Subject: Costa Rica, Sloths, Baby animals

Cuteness reigns in the *Aviarios del Caribe* sloth sanctuary in Costa Rica. This humorous photo essay introduces a number of rescued two- and three-toed sloths now living in a sanctuary founded by Judy Arroyo. The baby sloths are the stars here. Photographs show these slow-moving Xenarthrans wearing onesies crafted from old socks, peering out of baskets and bins, hugging each other and their personal stuffed toys, hanging upside down, and climbing down a "poo pole" (a device designed for toilet training). While chattily introducing the sloths and imagining what might be going on in their heads, the author also describes sloth habits and behavior both in the sanctuary and in the wild. The text is long for a read-aloud but the illustrations are irresistible. The author's message is clear: "Just chill." The sloth lifestyle rules!

Winter's Tail: How One Little Dolphin Learned to Swim Again

Informational picture book

By Juliana Hatkoff, Isabella Hatkoff, and Craig Hatkoff. Scholastic Press,
    2009. Ages 8–12.
Subjects: Dolphins, Tail surgery, Artificial limbs, Clearwater Marine Aquarium (Clearwater, Florida)

Badly entangled in a crab trap rope, a baby Atlantic bottlenose dolphin is rescued and rehabilitated in Florida, and provided with a prosthetic tail that allows her to swim normally. Illustrated with photographs, including

Go to the Zoo! Visit an Aquarium!

MOST PEOPLE IN the United States live not too far from a zoo or aquarium, or both. These public attractions have a long history. In the U.S., New York's Central Park Zoo was established in 1850, before the Civil War. An aquarium was opened in Boston in 1859. But today's zoos are quite different. In most zoos, animals are no longer taught to do tricks and perform for the human visitors. The animal housing often provides a visitor with a sense of its native habitat, as well. Sometimes both animals and visitors are enclosed, as in aviaries and replicated environments. Zoos and aquariums are often the only place a child or adult can get to see a particular animal species. Take advantage of that opportunity, often.

Some tips for a successful zoo or aquarium visit:

- **Plan for short sessions.** If you won't be back to that zoo again, at least plan to break up your visit with frequent rests and eating breaks.
- **Stop when the kids are tired.** It isn't worth it to go through the displays with a child who is melting down.
- **Focus your visit.** Prepare by checking the institution's website to see what the highlights are, where to find the creatures you most want to see, and when it will be less crowded.

remarkable pictures of the actual rescue, this heartwarming tale highlights the work of the Clearwater Marine Aquarium and Kevin Carroll of Hanger Prosthetic and Orthotics. Woven through the story are details of dolphin life, both in the wild and in aquariums. But this is as much a story of healing as it is a story of an animal. The human connection is clear. An extensive endnote provides further information about Winter's journey, the aquarium, bottlenose dolphins, dolphin training, and the rehabilitative company. Readers who enjoy stories about rescued baby animals will enjoy others by the Hatkoffs, beginning with *Owen & Mzee* (Scholastic, 2006).

Dogs and Cats
Informational picture book

By Steve Jenkins. Illustrated by Steve Jenkins. Houghton Mifflin, 2007.
Ages 7–10.
Subjects: Dogs, Cats, Pets

Jenkins introduces these familiar pet families as two books packaged in one. Open from the cover with the appealing kitten and you see a book about cats, with tiny thumbnails reminding you that you can turn it over to read something similar about dogs. Open from the cover with the dog, and you find the same format for that species. In either case, he includes equivalent descriptions. Each topical double-page spread includes several paragraphs of text, a large illustration, and smaller ones, with captions including even more information. Jenkins's collages, on a plain white background, highlight the colors and shapes of each breed, showing typical poses and significant details effectively. Young readers, curious about these common pets, will surely find the format intriguing and the parallels eye opening. Text-heavy for reading aloud, this is, nonetheless, a book that can be appreciated by prereaders for its pictures alone.

Saving Yasha:
The Incredible True Story
of an Adopted Moon Bear
Informational picture book

By Lia Kvatum. Illustrated by Liya
    Pokrovskaya. National Geographic,
    2012. Ages 5–9.
Subjects: Wildlife rescue, Orphaned
    animals, Asiatic black bear

Yasha, an orphaned moon bear cub, was rescued by a pair of scientists and raised and observed with two others in a natural setting for more than two years. He was successfully returned to the wild after proving his ability to survive in the Russian wilderness, climbing trees, swimming in the river, and even escaping a tiger. This heartwarming story is told in a straightforward fashion with just a bit of imagining his human-like feelings. It's illustrated with irresistible photographs by the scientists. Woven into the narrative is information about Asiatic black bear life and something of the scientists' work. The useful back matter includes a map, further facts about the species, and suggestions for learning more.

Seababy: A Little Otter Returns Home

Picture book

By Ellen Levine. Illustrated by Jon Van
    Zyle. Walker & Co., 2012. Ages 4–8.
Subjects: Sea otter, Baby animals, Wildlife
    rescue, Monterey Bay Aquarium

Separated from his mother at a very early age, a baby otter is rescued and
cared for by humans and an otter foster mother who teaches him the skills
he needs to survive on his own in the wild. Dedicated, in part, to adoptive
moms everywhere, this sweet story of animal rescue is based on the
work of the Monterey Bay Aquarium, cited in the back matter. The text
focuses tightly on the pup, imagining how he experienced this rescue, how
he remembered his mother feeding him and the smell of the sea, and how he
felt happy meeting his new mom and again, after his release, when he found
a new group of otters to live and play with. Van Zyle's paintings have the
same otter-world focus, which will draw young readers in. Web links to the
aquarium are provided for those who want to know more.

How Many Baby Pandas?   *Informational picture book*

By Sandra Markle. Illustrated by Walker & Co., 2009. Ages 5–9.
Subjects: Giant panda, Baby animals, Counting

Baby pandas, most from China's Wolong Giant Panda Breeding Center, are
shown from birth through cubhood in this introduction to this endangered
species, which could also serve as a counting book. Beginning with the first-
page question, "How many baby pandas have just been born?" and an illustration of the tiny pink, almost unrecognizable newborn, each left-hand page
shows more and more pandas growing and developing. At six, pandas are
shown on both pages as "three on the playground . . . plus three in the
yard." The counting continues to eight; a final page shows the sixteen born
in one banner year at the breeding center. This title complements Ryder's
Panda Kindergarten (Collins, 2009, annotated in this chapter); its text is more
difficult and more detailed. The strength of this book is its developmental approach, which will intrigue elementary school readers, and the nearly
irresistible photographs.

Pierre the Penguin: A True Story

Informational picture book

By Jean Marzollo. Illustrated by Laura
   Regan. Sleeping Bear Press / Gale,
   2010. Ages 4–7.
Subject: African penguin

When a penguin loses the feathers that
protect him from the chilly water, a biologist in the San Francisco museum where
he is housed makes him a wet suit from neoprene, like the one she wears.
A straightforward, simple text in rhyming couplets tells this satisfying true
story chronologically, focusing entirely on Pierre, the penguin, and his
keeper, Pam. No more than a few lines per page are set on large-scale realistic paintings, double-page spreads. An opening spread shows the museum's
African hall, with the penguin exhibit at the end, but quickly the viewer
moves inside the penguins' world. Readers and listeners will learn intriguing details of museum work, like the secret door behind the exhibit through
which Pam enters to feed the penguins twice a day. A series of questions
and answers about the story and a link to a webcam conclude this heartwarming tale.

Leopard & Silkie: One Boy's Quest to Save the Seal Pups

Informational picture book

By Brenda Peterson. Illustrated by Robin Lindsey. Christy Ottaviano Books
   / Henry Holt & Co., 2012. Ages 4–8.
Subjects: Seals (Animals), Conservation, Wildlife rescue

On the shores of Seattle's Salish Sea, human seal sitters like young Miles
protect harbor seal pups who rest on the beach during the day while their
mothers fish offshore. Profusely illustrated with appealing photographs, this
describes the first few months of one such pup, called Leopard. Miles uses
yellow warning tape to keep crowds at a safe distance and builds a floating
platform for the seals to rest offshore. Silkie, a slightly older pup, comes to
keep Leopard company after his mother leaves, teaching it to fish and hide
in the kelp forests offshore. An afterword describes the work of Seal Sitters,
an organization of volunteers who help keep crowds and dogs away from the

young pups as they rest on the beaches. A few facts about harbor seals are woven into the narrative, but the focus of this encouraging story is the kid-friendly human-animal connection.

Parrots over Puerto Rico
Informational picture book

By Susan L. Roth. Illustrated by Cindy
   Trumbore. Lee & Low, 2013. Ages
   8–12.
Subjects: Puerto Rican parrot, Conservation, Endangered species, Natural
   history, Puerto Rico

Puerto Rican parrots, endangered to the point of near-extinction, are slowly making a comeback thanks to a recovery program started back in 1968. There are now two breeding aviaries in forests where the parrots once flourished in the wild, and free-flying parrots in both places. Released captive-bred parrots are now doing well in both forests, though they have yet to breed there. This piece of environmental good news has been presented strikingly in a picture book opening vertically, as if the reader were looking up into the treetops where the birds live. The text combines two thousand years of human history on that island with the history of the parrots, showing how that history contributed to their gradual demise and, now, return. The illustrations, fabric and paper collage, appear three-dimensional; their texture makes you want to stroke these birds. For older readers and listeners, ready to cope with the bad news turned good.

Panda Kindergarten   *Informational picture book*

By Joanne Ryder. Illustrated by Katherine Feng. Collins, 2009. Ages 5–9.
Subjects: China, Giant panda

Irresistible photographs of sixteen baby pandas (and some mothers) introduce the Wolong Nature Reserve's project for raising and training cubs of this endangered Chinese species in this alternative version of that story. With no more than a paragraph of simple text on a page, Ryder explains that these black-and-white bears often have twins but can only rear one. The center steps in, making sure that both get time with the mother and ample food. They provide a "kindergarten" where cubs can learn to interact and try new things. Restoring some bears to the wild is their eventual goal. The photographer, a tour escort for the center, finds the most appealing moments: a cub searches for its mother's nipple; another is fed with a bottle; a group explores a giant wooden play structure, later curling up for a nap. (Pandas from this facility, destroyed in China's 2008 earthquake, are currently housed elsewhere, but the work continues.)

Alex the Parrot: No Ordinary Bird

Informational picture book

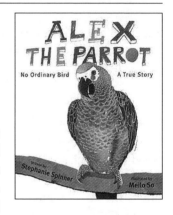

By Stephanie Spinner. Illustrated by Meilo So.
  Alfred A. Knopf, 2012. Ages 6–10.
Subject: African gray parrot

In the pet store, Alex looked just like all the other African gray parrots. But as his owner and trainer, Irene Pepperberg, worked with him, he became famous and changed public and scientific beliefs about animal communication and understanding. In his relatively short life, Alex learned to speak clearly, to count, and to combine words to get his meaning across. Tested along with nursery school students on words, shapes, numbers, and colors he did as well as three-and-a-half-year olds; in another testing he was found to be as smart as a five-year-old child. Spinner's conversational narrative weaves in information about other animals, but Alex is her focus. Long for reading aloud, this has the look of a picture book, with its appealing watercolors, but the heft of a chapter book. Either way, it is a fascinating story with lots of kid appeal.

Friends   *Informational picture book*

By Catherine Thimmesh. Illustrated with photographs. Houghton Mifflin,
    2011. Ages 5–8.
Subjects: Friendship, Animal behavior

This sweet celebration of friendships that cross boundaries introduces twelve
examples of surprising animal pairings. Most, but not all, are between young
ones in captivity in places like zoos and wildlife refuges. A poetic text reminds
us that "A friend comforts . . . connects . . . snuggles . . . helps . . . plays . . .
protects"; ". . . deep where it counts, / one knows a true friend." The author
invites young readers to connect animal behavior with their own feelings
through irresistible images—striking close-up photographs of cross-species
friends. An orangutan and Siberian tiger cuddle on the cover; a giraffe and
ostrich nuzzle; a polar bear and a chained sled dog play. Some of these cou-
ples would even be predator and prey in the wild, but their need for comfort
and companionship took precedence, at least for a while. Along with the
poem, Thimmesh provides a short explanation of each picture identifying
what, where, and how the encounters began.

Chapter 11

Bird watching at Hawk Mountain, Pennsylvania

More Animals

PERCHED ON A ROCK AT HAWK MOUNTAIN, IN PENNSYLVANIA, THIS EIGHT- year-old is watching for hawks flying south through a corridor over the Appalachian Mountains. Perhaps seventy-five thousand people come every year to this sanctuary, which is one of the best places in northeastern North America to watch the autumn hawk migration. Families and school groups return year after year. This is not like watching an animal on a screen. There's some scrambling around on rocks, wind and weather to contend with, and the possibility on a given day that no hawks will appear. But the site is predictable enough and both comfortable and challenging enough to provide an exciting natural experience for adults and children alike.

Hawk Mountain is just one of thousands of places around the country that offer children an opportunity to connect with the natural world and to experience some natural wonders. The National Wildlife Federation's website has a map of wildlife viewing opportunities in your own area—local, state, and national parks and refuges and special events (www.nwf.org/NatureFind .aspx). The site also provides a place where young wildlife observers can record what they see.

There are loads of titles written for young people about animals in our world, both familiar animals and unusual ones. I have been able to be especially selective, choosing books that stand out particularly for their approach, their accuracy, and their appeal. For easier browsing, I've organized this list roughly by types of animals.

INSECTS AND SPIDERS

Insects in general

Busy Builders   *Informational picture book*

By Roxie Munro. Illustrated by Roxie Munro. Marshall Cavendish, 2012.
   Ages 4–9.
Subjects: Insects—habitations, Bees

For listeners who like their facts straight up, this oversized introduction to insect and spider constructions will be a treat. Much enlarged, each of nine creatures—honeybee, red harvester ant, organ-pipe mud dauber, garden orb spider, Australian weaver ant, leafcutter bee, pine processionary caterpillar, African termite, and paper hornet—appears against a white background along with a simple text: "This is an [name]." "Where does it live?" On the next spread, detailed ink paintings show the animal's nest or web with insets showing what's inside. Alongside is a straightforward, fairly extensive description. The language is reasonably simple, with unfamiliar words defined in context. The single lengthy paragraph may look daunting to a young reader, but it's ideal for an adult to read aloud. The author describes how the construction is made and how it is used, and she includes Latin names for each species.

Bug Shots: The Good, the Bad, and the Bugly   *Nonfiction*

By Alexandra Siy. Illustrated by Dennis Kunkel. Holiday House, 2011. Ages
   8–12.
Subjects: Insects, Photomicrography

Is being a bug a crime? That's the question the author and illustrator attempt to answer in this lighthearted, detective-themed introduction to insects. Siy opens with some general definitions and descriptions. Her survey covers true bugs, beetles, butterflies and moths, bees, ants, wasps, and true flies. In lively, informal prose spiced with humor, she describes some typical insect behavior, pointing out the harm they do but also the good. Kunkel's stunning photographs, taken with a scanning electron microscope, are colored to highlight important structures. Many of the creatures described are not also shown as we would see them, but the back matter includes many resources for further study. Young readers who want to collect bugs on their own are encouraged to do so with a digital camera.

Insect Detective

Informational picture book

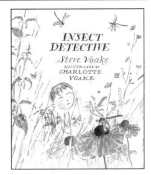

By Steve Voake. Illustrated by Charlotte Voake.
    Candlewick Press, 2010. Ages 3–7.
Subjects: Insects, Garden animals

"LISTEN—over by the fence. Can you hear a scratching sound?" Here's a gentle invitation to step outside and explore, looking for insects that camouflage themselves, hide, or fly over a pond. The text is organized by the kind of insect described and is presented on two levels. In large type is a suggestion: "Lift up a stone and you might see an earwig scuttle out." Additional facts are added in a smaller font. The author includes details that intrigue young listeners, but along the way he makes the major points: insects have six legs and three body parts, they begin as eggs, and most undergo metamorphosis. His calm text is accompanied by ink-and-watercolor sketches, beginning with the insect-filled meadow on the end covers, just right for an identification game. This inviting, intriguing introduction would be an appropriate read-aloud for a young child curious about the world.

Bugs by the Numbers: Facts and Figures for Multiple Types of Bugbeasties

Informational picture book

By Sharon Werner and Sarah Nelson Forss. Illustrated by Sharon Werner
    and Sarah Nelson Forss. Blue Apple Books, 2011. Ages 8–12.
Subjects: Insects, Counting

The wonder here is twofold: the art, which uses relevant numbers to illustrate twenty-three different kinds of creepy-crawlies, from ants to earthworms, and the statistics about these creatures. Some are simple and instructive: ants, like many insects, have three body parts: head, thorax, and abdomen. Some are appealingly gross: a cockroach can live 168 hours without its head. And some are simply astounding: There are over 300,000 species of beetles on the planet. Attractively designed and printed on heavy-duty paper, this oversize book includes foldout pages that reveal even more. Behind the chrysalis is a butterfly. Chan's megastick, the longest stick insect in the world, stretches for twenty-two inches. Behind a wooden wall are 2,500 termites. This companion to the authors' *Alphabeasties* (Blue Apple, 2009) is sure to wow young fans of facts and figures.

Ladybugs

Bug Life

Informational picture book

By Lynette Evans. Illustrated by Francesca
    D'Ottavi. Insight Editions, 2013.
    Ages 4–7.
Subject: Ladybugs

Seven-spotted ladybugs, beloved of gardeners and children everywhere, are the subject of this striking picture book. With bold, colorful illustrations and a conversational text, this is an intriguing introduction. Almost photographic in their detail, close-up, hyperrealistic images done from an insect's perspective show these beetles and their prey larger than life. One spread shows the ladybug's "paper-thin back wings" and raised "fiery-red front wings, ready for takeoff." In another, she chomps on "sugary aphid bugs." In the foreground, more two-inch aphids wait on a thorny stem. The story-telling narrative text describes the insect's body features, feeding, defense, egg-laying, and the development of its larva and pupa. Ladybug-egg-shaped sidebars include occasional additional information. A companion to the author and illustrator's *Bee Life* (Insight Editions, 2013), this would also be an appealing read-aloud.

Citizen Science with Insects

LOOK FOR LADYBUGS yourself. Find them, photograph them, and upload your images to a citizen science project. Help the Lost Ladybug Project (www.lostladybug.org) document the changing patterns of ladybugs.

Use cookies to attract ants. Send specimens to the School of Ants (www.schoolofants.org). The researchers running this project are investigating different ant species across the country, especially in urban areas.

This project is particularly good for families because it doesn't require travel or a long-term commitment.

Butterflies and Moths of North America is another website that collects photographs and will make identifications for you (www.butter fliesandmoths.org). This program, which began with the U.S. Geological Survey and other institutions, is now supported by advertising on the website.

Ladybugs

Informational picture book

By Gail Gibbons. Illustrated by Gail Gibbons.
Holiday House, 2012. Ages 4–7.
Subject: Ladybugs

Just the facts, capably organized and clearly stated, simply but with appropriate vocabulary. Gibbons introduces ladybugs, describes their bodies, and shows, with a general map, where they live on six continents. In more detail she outlines the four stages of their life and goes on to describe predators and defenses, what these beetles do in winter, and their use in agriculture. She concludes with an explanation of the discovery that pesticide use harmed ladybugs and their use today to help protect crops. A final page of fast facts suggests two websites for further research. The oversized text is set on equally informative ink-and-watercolor illustrations showing these insects much larger than life. (An early inset shows the actual size.) Labels are used where necessary, and some words are defined in asides. By a prolific author and illustrator, this is a go-to resource for a curious child.

Scorpions

Scorpions! Strange and Wonderful

Nonfiction

By Laurence Pringle. Illustrated by Meryl Henderson. Boyds Mills Press,
2013. Ages 7–10.

Subject: Scorpions

A yellow desert scorpion capturing a lizard is the opening scene in this introduction to a species traditionally associated with evil and death: scorpions.
The latest in a series of collaborations between a prolific author and skillful
wildlife illustrator, this highlights the amazing variety among that family of
arachnids. Pringle explains something of their history, their physical features, their habits and habitats. True scorpions have a poisonous stinger and
can live almost anywhere. Scorpion babies, born alive, actually remain with
their mothers until after their first molt, but after that, the smaller scorpions
become any bigger scorpion's prey. Pringle's Strange and Wonderful series
also includes titles on frogs, cicadas, crocodilians, penguins, snakes, whales,
crows, sharks, and bats. All provide solid information and intriguing facts for
middle-grade readers.

Beetles

The Beetle Book

Informational picture book

By Steve Jenkins. Illustrated by Steve Jenkins. Houghton Mifflin Books for Children, 2012. Ages 3–10.

Subject: Beetles

One out of every four kinds of plants and animals in our world is a beetle. Jenkins takes
full advantage of their astonishing variety in

this appealing album. Topic by topic, he introduces seventy-seven beetle
species. His beetles are illustrated with torn-and-cut-paper collages set on a
white background. Short paragraphs accompany the images, set in a text

that could have been hand-lettered. Some beetles are shown life-size; others are oversize and frankly frightening. They're colorful, intricate, and recognizable. Silhouettes on each spread show the actual size of the beetles described on the two pages. In the back is a list of the common and Latin names for all his beetles, where they might generally be found, and the size if it is not already given. From very young children fascinated by the large images to budding middle-grade entomologists, this should have wide appeal.

Bees

In the Trees, Honey Bees

Informational picture book

By Lori Mortensen. Illustrated by Cris Arbo.
    Dawn Publications, 2009. Ages 4–7.
Subjects: Bee culture, Honeybees, Stories in
    rhyme

From "Morning light, / Warm and bright." to "Chilly night, / Cluster tight." simple rhyming couplets and photo-realistic full-bleed illustrations introduce the lives and work of honey bees to the youngest readers and listeners. At the bottom of each spread, a short paragraph of explanation adds information. This cheerful introduction contains no hint of current honeybee issues, but it will give younger children a beginning understanding of what bees do. Detailed paintings show close-ups of the inside of a hive where worker bees dance a wiggle dance, bring pollen back to the hive, and care for their queen, and nurse bees feed larvae in the combs. Two double-page spreads show bees collecting nectar and pollen, others back off to show the garden of a farm where the honeybees live in a tree. A "bear attack" adds humor. An afterword adds more facts and offers suggestions for further learning.

Caterpillars, Butterflies, and Moths

Caterpillars   *Nonfiction*

By Marilyn Singer. Illustrated with photographs. EarlyLight Books, 2012.
   Ages 7–10.
Subjects: Caterpillars, Butterflies

Organized with a catchy poem, this introduction to caterpillars displays the
larvae of sixty different species of butterflies and moths. This surprisingly
informative survey is illustrated with clear, close-up photographs of an
astounding variety of caterpillars—spotted and striped, smooth and hairy, in
groups and on their own. Carefully shown and explained, too, are cocoons
and chrysalises, and some of the beautiful winged creatures that emerge. A
pop quiz and matching exercise at the end provide an opportunity for readers to review, and there is a final page about caterpillar anatomy. Glossary,
suggestions for further research in books and on the Web, a list of scientific
and common names, and an index complete the package of this exemplary
introduction to a vast field that should spur young readers to look more
closely themselves.

Butterflies   *Nonfiction*

By Seymour Simon. Illustrated with photographs. Collins, 2011. Ages 7–10.
Subject: Butterflies

This general introduction to butterflies and moths—Lepidoptera—describes
their four-stage life cycles, their body parts, and their appearance, and presents a few families common in the United States. Designed for comfortable
nonfiction readers and illustrated with beautifully reproduced stock photographs, this is not a field guide. Many of the images aren't even labeled. But
Simon encourages readers to go outside and look at these beautiful creatures
and keep their own records. He suggests some other attributes a curious
observer might notice. Do they appear in a group or singly? Do they seem
to have a favorite flower? He uses appropriate technical vocabulary and
defines it in an appended glossary. While the photographs are not as striking
as those of researcher Darlyne Murawski or nature photographer Nic Bishop,
the clarity of Simon's writing makes this, like his many other titles, a natural
choice for readers seeking a broad overview.

A Butterfly Is Patient

Informational picture book

By Dianna Hutts Aston. Illustrated by Sylvia Long. Chronicle Books, 2011.
   Ages 5–10.
Subject: Butterflies

In the same gentle, imaginative way they described eggs and seeds in earlier titles, Aston and Long here introduce butterflies. The endpapers show butterfly scales, highly magnified. On the next two pages is a display of more than thirty colorful caterpillars, carefully labeled in hand-lettering. At the end is a similar display of butterflies (not all the same species). Two levels of narrative provide simple descriptors followed by a bit of information about the butterfly life cycle with examples from different species. A butterfly is patient, creative, helpful, protective, poisonous, spectacular, thirsty, big and tiny, scaly, a traveler, magical, and not a moth. The nicely rounded narrative arc begins and ends with the patient egg. The finely detailed, accurate watercolor illustrations sometimes show both butterfly and caterpillar; though close-ups, they often they include something of the insect's habitat. For readers and viewers alike, a wondrous celebration.

Monarch and Milkweed

Informational picture book

By Helen Frost. Illustrated by Leonid Gore.
   Atheneum Books for Young Readers, 2008.
   Ages 3–10.
Subjects: Monarch butterfly, Life cycles

Simple poetic lines describe the relationship between monarch and milkweed showing changes in both over time. "Rain comes / snow comes, rain comes again. / Sun warms the earth. / Earth warms the seed, / and under the dirt, it opens." A milkweed grows. A north-flying butterfly passes by and lays an egg. A caterpillar hatches, eats its leaves, forms a chrysalis, and breaks out as a butterfly that will fly to Mexico in the fall. At the same time, the milkweed seeds develop and float out from the pod to a new place. This title about the often-studied butterfly is unusual in giving equal attention to the host plant. The illustrations show both, close-up and from a distance in a natural setting. The endpapers, redrawn from Monarch Watch maps, show the migration path, and an author's note makes clear that it takes several generations of butterflies to complete each northward journey.

Spiders

Sneaky, Spinning Baby Spiders   *Informational picture book*

By Sandra Markle. Illustrated with photographs. Walker & Co., 2008.
   Ages 5–9.
Subjects: Baby animals, Spiders

As she has done previously in *Tough, Toothy Baby Sharks* (2007) and *Slippery, Slimy Baby Frogs* (2006), also from Walker, Markle draws child readers into learning about a species by focusing on its young. In this appealing introduction to spiders she discusses how spiderlings are born, how their mothers feed and care for them, and the kinds of changes that happen as they grow up. She discusses species, ranging from the black-and-yellow garden spider, found in temperate North America, to the garden-orb web spider of New Zealand, where she used to live. A map shows where each spider was photographed and also serves as an index. Unfamiliar terms are defined in context. Striking photographs, some close-up and even magnified, come from a variety of sources. Readers intrigued by this sample may want to go on to other books in her Arachnid World series.

Up, Up, and Away
Informational picture book

By Ginger Wadsworth. Illustrated by Patricia
   Wynne. Charlesbridge, 2009. Ages 4–7.
Subject: Spiders

From egg sac to egg-laying and a new generation, the life of a garden spider is chronicled
here. Most of this story follows a "sister spi-

der" whose efforts to escape her hungry siblings and a variety of predators are shown close-up. But the illustrator also zooms out to show the broad landscape and sky through which the baby spiders soar, carried by their own silk threads. The illustrations are done with a draftsman's care, and the text, set in short phrases accessible for early readers, employs a lively language, good for reading aloud. There is a bit of anthropomorphism as Spider "decides to stay" in her new farm home, but for the most part the author sticks to description that can come from careful observation, even including the death that comes at the end of a spider's year, just as in E. B. White's *Charlotte's Web* (Harper & Bros., 1952).

See also references to insects, specific insects, and spiders in the index.

SEA CREATURES

Star of the Sea: A Day in the Life of a Starfish

Informational picture book

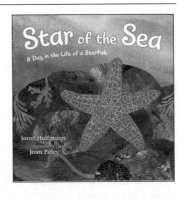

By Janet Halfmann. Illustrated by Joan Paley. Henry Holt & Co., 2011. Ages 5–8.
Subject: Starfish

An ochre sea star comes to shore at high tide, making her way slowly on hundreds of tiny tube feet. She tips over and rights herself, feeds, and has an encounter with a seagull that leaves her one ray short but still able to return to the sea where she will rest and regrow the lost arm. This story of a remarkable creature, common along the rocky Pacific shoreline, is gently told and beautifully illustrated with collages of hand-painted papers. The author explains how the tube feet work and mentions some of the other creatures feeding at the tidal edge. But it is the sea star's eating method that will capture readers. After pulling apart a mussel's two shells slightly, she "extends her stomach right out of her mouth—and into the tiny crack." The back matter adds further scientific facts for older readers and their curious parents.

Seahorses

Informational picture book

By Jennifer Keats Curtis. Illustrated by
    Chad Wallace. Henry Holt & Co., 2012.
    Ages 5–9.
Subject: Seahorses

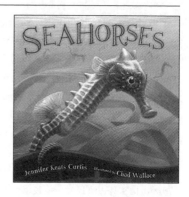

With a gentle, lyrical text and dreamy pictures, this topic book describes a seahorse's life from birth as one of three hundred "small fry" through fatherhood. Digitally created artwork shows rounded seahorses floating in a blue-green sea and hiding among fronds of grass. As the seahorse matures, the background colors change, allowing readers to see the color changes in courting seahorses. After an interval of dancing, male and female bond, the two entwined in a symbolic heart shape. Mating is described explicitly, and appropriately, since this fish stands out in the animal kingdom because the male gestates the eggs and gives birth. The text also describes their locomotion and their eating habits. The text description is based on behavior of the mustang, or lined seahorse, which lives along the Atlantic Coast but is diminishing in the wild; readers are more likely to see these intriguing fish in an aquarium.

Sharks

Nonfiction

By Beverly McMillan and John A. Musick. Illustrated with photographs.
    Simon & Schuster Books for Young Readers, 2008. Ages 7–12.
Subject: Sharks

The first section of this striking introduction to an ocean superpredator describes its physical characteristics, history, life, and relationships with other animals and human beings. The second focuses more closely on seven specific species. The jazzy design and eye-catching illustrations of the Insiders series are perfectly suited for this topic. Sharks lunge out from the page, jaws agape; cutaways show their internal organs; a time line charts the evolution of sharks and bony fish over millions of years; and a map plots their migrations in the world's oceans. The information is delivered in single paragraphs, one describing the main subject of the double-page spread and the others as picture captions. This reading isn't easy, but the reader drawn in by the astonishing (sometimes scary) graphics will be likely to puzzle it out or insist that an adult provide the explanations.

Dolphin Baby!
Informational picture book

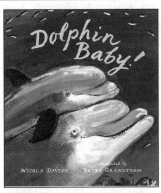

By Nicola Davies. Illustrated by Brita Granström. Candlewick Press, 2012. Ages 3–8.
Subjects: Dolphins, Baby animals

Tail first, a dolphin calf pops out of its mother into the water. Immediately he swims to the surface to take his first breath. Davies' simple story of Dolphin and Mom describes the calf's first six months, nursing, playing, learning to understand and communicate with dolphin clicks and whistles, and catching his first fish. A sentence or two in smaller, italic type adds a second level of information for older readers and listeners. Beginning on the endpapers, realistic acrylic paintings emphasize the blues and greens of the water and shades of pink and orange in the sky. This is a handsome book, sure to make young listeners admirers of these engaging mammals. But it is informative as well. There is even an index of the behaviors described: breathing, clicking, diving, following, hunting, playing, suckling, swimming, and whistling. Irresistible.

TURTLES, SNAKES, LIZARDS, AND FROGS

Turtle, Turtle, Watch Out!   *Informational picture book*

By April Pulley Sayre. Illustrated by Annie Patterson. Charlesbridge, 2010.
Ages 5–9.
Subject: Sea turtles

Repeating the title as a refrain, the narrator describes the life of a sea turtle from egg to egg-laying motherhood, pointing out the many predators and hazards she may meet along the way and the many hands that help her. Turtle's story is straightforward, told as a series of suspenseful encounters and escapes. Night herons, cats and raccoons, cars on the beach, and bright lights in the wrong direction are threats to the hatchling; gulls, sharks, plastic bags masquerading as jellyfish, and a shrimper's net are hazards in the water. The illustrations emphasize the blueness of the nocturnal and underwater worlds. Brown baby Turtle, realistically depicted and gradually increasing in size, stands out. Structure and language lend themselves well to reading aloud. This attractive reillustration of a title first published in 2000 is an ideal introduction to sea turtle life, so dependent today on the helping hands of humans.

Crocodile Safari

Informational picture book

By Jim Arnosky. Illustrated by Jim
   Arnosky. Scholastic Press, 2009.
   Ages 7–10.
Subjects: Crocodiles, Reptiles,
   Everglades (Florida)

Survivors from the age of dinosaurs, crocodiles live all over the world, some two thousand here in the United States. Having researched their alligator cousins, naturalist Arnosky and his wife decide to canoe through southern Florida mangrove swamps to photograph, paint, and count crocodiles for themselves. Opening with an introduction to these large wild reptiles, Arnosky explains how to distinguish the two. (When its mouth is closed, a crocodile's teeth still show.) Along the way he weaves in information about their characteristics, their lives, and the habitat they share with other dangerous animals and plants. Detailed paintings show crocs close-up along with some of their neighbors. Their softly colored backgrounds vary, as does the changing light in the swamps. Like any good naturalist, Arnosky includes details of time, weather, and tide for each picture. Slightly menacing and wonderfully informative, this includes a DVD and a song.

At Home with the Gopher Tortoise: The Story of a Keystone Species

Informational picture book

By Madeleine Dunphy. Illustrated by Michael Rothman. Web of Life Children's Books, 2010. Ages 5–9.

Subjects: Gopher tortoise, Turtles, Keystone species

The burrows made by gopher tortoises in southeastern U.S. forests provide homes for an astonishing variety of wildlife. Spread by spread, Dunphy's straightforward exposition describes the tortoise and its many neighbors—skunks, lizards and skinks, mice, owls and other birds, toads, insects, snakes, and even a bobcat. Rothman's acrylic paintings look like photographs. They show their subjects not only on the forest floor, but also deep inside the burrows and sometimes even in cutaway. Some illustrations show animals with babies; one shows a skunk with a lizard in its mouth. Through pictures and text, this description of a not-well-known animal introduces the concept of a keystone species. More than 360 species depend on the gopher tortoise's burrows for shelter from weather and forest fires, nesting, and protection from predators. This is an appealing and convincing demonstration of the interconnectedness of life in an ecosystem.

A Place for Turtles

Informational picture book

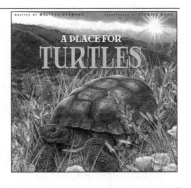

By Melissa Stewart. Illustrated by Higgins Bond. Peachtree, 2013. Ages 5–9.

Subjects: Turtles, Conservation

Turtles are an important part of the natural world that people protect in various ways. This introduction to the species is part of the publisher's A Place for . . . series, which concentrates on environmental support. After a quick introduction, Stewart describes twelve species that might be found in this country, from the tiny Blanding's turtle to the lumbering desert tortoises. Endpaper maps locate the species. Bond's realistic paintings show each in its natural habitat. Two narratives accompany these spreads. The first, suitable for reading aloud, describes a particular danger a turtle might face in the modern world—like fishing nets, busy highways, and collection for pet stores and food—and what has been done to help them.

Text boxes provide a bit more information about the turtle pictured. The emphasis is positive, reinforced by the paintings that show people studying, admiring, and helping turtles in a variety of ways.

The Voyage of Turtle Rex   *Informational picture book*

By Kurt Cyrus. Illustrated by Kurt Cyrus. Harcourt Children's Books, 2011.
    Ages 5–8.
Subjects: Sea turtles, Stories in rhyme, Marine animals, Prehistoric animals

Centuries ago, a tiny sea turtle hatched on a primeval beach, scrambled to the ocean, and sheltered in a seaweed bed. There she grew to a gargantuan size, becoming a two-ton archelon who returned to her home beach to continue the cycle. Carefully crafted rhyming couplets carry the story slowly across oversize pages of striking illustrations. Tiny turtles in the green water are surrounded by toothy prehistoric fish. Pterosaurs fly overhead. Threatened by an even larger mosasaur, the archelon buries herself in the sand. The size of these long-gone creatures is conveyed by the vast spaces and oversized paintings, but the modern-day connection is clear: "Gone is that sea and the creatures it knew. / Archelon. Mosasaur. Pterosaur, too. / Gone is the plesiosaur's clam-cracking smile . . . / but full-body helmets are still in style." Fans of prehistoric animals will want to hear this engaging read-aloud over and over.

Awesome Snake Science!
40 Activities for Learning About Snakes
Nonfiction

By Cindy Blobaum. Illustrated with photographs. Chicago Review Press,
    2012. Ages 7–12.
Subject: Snakes—experiments

What child could resist making virtual viper venom? Emphasizing careful observation and note-taking, this collection of activities doesn't require live snakes but does provide a good foundation for budding ophiologists. (Herpetologists study reptiles and amphibians generally. Ophiologists study snakes specifically.) A longtime snake enthusiast designed these projects and tested them with children. They make use of common household items. Some are time-consuming; others can be done in a single afternoon or classroom period. Diagrams, directions, and instructions for record-keeping are clear. Readers are invited to investigate snake body size, shape, and structure, adaptations, senses, offensive and defensive mechanisms. Sidebars provide human connections, facts about specific species, and nuggets of snake science. The author also suggests ways to see live snakes and intriguing videos on the Internet. A glossary, list of further resources, teacher's guide, extensive bibliography, and detailed index complete this package of hands-on projects that will delight young researchers.

Sneed B. Collard III's Most Fun Book Ever About Lizards
Nonfiction

By Sneed B. Collard. Illustrated with
    photographs. Charlesbridge, 2012.
    Ages 8–12.
Subjects: Lizards, Lizards as pets

Readers may be surprised by the wealth
of information presented here in Collard's breezy, conversational style. He introduces his readers to these common reptiles through Joe Lizard, a western fence lizard, a typical example. He goes on to describe some lizard stars: Komodo dragons, Gila monsters, chameleons, and iguanas. A chapter on eating is followed by one on being eaten. He also covers temperature regulation, mating, and family life. He makes sure to include atypical examples: lizards that walk on water, glide, swim, or tunnel underground. Strongly preferring observation of lizards in the wild, he also offers suggestions for those who really, really want to keep them as pets. Plentifully illustrated with photographs, many by the author, this humorous introduction might lead to true lizard love.

Black Spiny-Tailed Iguana: Lizard Lightning!   *Nonfiction*

By Natalie Lunis. Illustrated with photographs. Bearport Publishing, 2011.
    Ages 6–9.
Subjects: Lizards, Iguana (Genus)

Animal speed records always appeal. This title, featuring an unusual Central American lizard, now occasionally found in Florida, is part of a series of topic books about fast animals. Each includes clearly presented information alongside well-reproduced color photographs. The information includes the animal's natural range and habitat, behavior, predators and prey (the lizard eats mostly plants), and physical features, including those that help it be so speedy. The text on each spread is presented in a few short narrative paragraphs with supplemental facts inside a stopwatch symbol. There's a map and a chart, an index, a link to web resources, and a helpful photo glossary for appropriate vocabulary (bolded and explained in the text). Other animals in the series include the California sea lion, cheetah, greyhound, killer whale, peregrine falcon, and pronghorn antelope. Designed for school use, this series will also appeal to fact-loving readers who enjoy superlatives.

Born to Be Giants:
How Baby Dinosaurs Grew
to Rule the World

Informational picture book

By Lita Judge. Illustrated by Lita Judge.
    Flash Point / Roaring Brook Press, 2010.
    Ages 7–10.
Subjects: Baby animals, Dinosaurs

Baby animals are a perennial fascination—even baby dinosaurs. New scientific discoveries and clues from modern animals suggest how dinosaur babies grew and were cared for from egg to nestling to adult. Judge provides a relatively simple and engaging overview. She uses and defines—in context and in a glossary—scientific terms such as *paleontologist, altricial,* and *precocial,* and she makes clear the difference between speculation and scientific findings. At one point she describes the discovery of thousands of closely packed fossilized eggs, some still with dinosaur embryos inside. "A herd of Saltasaurus mothers must have gathered by the riverbank to bury the eggs in the sand." Watercolor illustrations show large-eyed dinosaur babies, sometimes in comparison to their enormous parents. The end matter includes further description of the eight species described and much more for those who wish to explore further.

Frogs! Strange and Wonderful *Informational picture book*

By Laurence Pringle. Illustrated by Meryl Henderson. Boyds Mills Press, 2012. Ages 6–10.
Subjects: Frogs, Amphibians

From the opening invitation to make a sound like a frog, through the double-page seek-and-find puzzle demonstrating frog camouflage, to the author's note describing his own experiences, this is an appealing introduction to frogs from around the world. Accurate watercolor illustrations nicely aligned to the text show over eighty species of frogs and toads, some in close-up to emphasize particular features and others in context. Pringle's smoothly readable narrative is full of interesting facts. He makes clear that generalizations don't work: these species are full of exceptions. Varied in color and size; in egg-laying and child-rearing habits; and in habitat, locomotion, and eating habits, frogs are astonishingly diverse. For readers who enjoyed the photographs in Bishop's *Frogs* (Scholastic, 2008, annotated in chapter 6) or the paintings in Guiberson's *Frog Song* (Henry Holt & Co., 2013, annotated next), this is a different, more wide-ranging approach. The author ends with frogs as food, frogs as part of food webs, and current threats.

Frog Song *Informational picture book*

By Brenda Z. Guiberson. Illustrated by Gennady Spirin. Henry Holt & Co., 2013. Ages 4–9.
Subjects: Frogs—behavior, Frogs—vocalization

"Frogs have a song" Guiberson writes. From the "PSSST-PSSST" of the strawberry poison dart frog in the rain forest to the "BRACKBRACK!" of the wood frog in a bog, she introduces readers to both songs and singers on beautifully designed double-page spreads. Short paragraphs about each of eleven frogs from around the world illustrate the varied ways frogs get the moisture necessary to keep themselves and their eggs and tadpoles alive. Spirin's detailed paintings, in a realistic palette of greens and browns, show frogs in their surroundings, looking ready to leap at the reader. Finally, "A frog song is a celebration of clean water, plants, and insects to eat." This message is followed by two pages of fast facts about the species described, illustrated with thumbnails but no maps. There's also a reminder that frogs today are in trouble, and a bibliography that includes both children's and adult books and websites.

Hip-Pocket Papa

Informational picture book

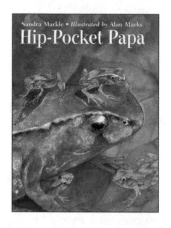

By Sandra Markle. Illustrated by Alan Marks.
    Charlesbridge, 2010. Ages 5–8.
Subjects: Frogs—behavior, Assa darlingtoni,
    Hip-pocket frog

In the tiny Australian hip-pocket frog species, fathers do the child-rearing. In this large-format picture book, beautifully illustrated in double-page spreads, Markle follows a father frog through the process, from guarding his eggs to watching his froglets crawl away. Although male and female guard their "pearl-like eggs" together, the female leaves after they hatch. The tadpoles "wiggle" up the male's legs to pockets on his hips. For nearly thirty days, with his developing tadpoles safely hidden, the male travels the temperate rain forest floor, searching for water and food and avoiding his natural enemies. Other creatures from this Australian environment, antechinus, quoll, currawong, and more, may be unfamiliar to American readers, but who they are is clear from the illustrations, and they are described more fully in an animal glossary at the end, where silhouettes show the animals at half their actual size. An excellent read-aloud and introduction to an unfamiliar world.

See also references to turtles, snakes, lizards, and frogs in the index.

BIRDS

Bird Talk: What Birds Are Saying and Why

Informational picture book

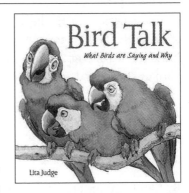

By Lita Judge. Illustrated by Lita Judge.
  Roaring Brook Press, 2012. Ages 5–9.
Subjects: Birds—behavior, Animal communication, Birdsongs

Lively, well-chosen examples show how birds from around the world communicate to attract attention, to find and help their chicks, to avoid predation, and to mimic other species. Using their voices, gestures, and physical features, they send clear messages that Judge translates for us in words and pictures. With pencil and watercolors, she gives us birds with personality—we can almost understand them ourselves. Her engaging text is thoughtfully organized. Each point is clearly stated and followed by several examples. The balanced design includes plenty of white space with the short paragraphs of text less prominent than the illustrations. Further information about the twenty-eight species described can be found at the end, in the order in which they appear. The author, pictured as a child with a bird on her shoulder, describes her own childhood experiences in an endnote that invites readers and listeners to discover bird communication for themselves.

Even an Ostrich Needs a Nest: Where Birds Begin

Informational picture book

By Irene Kelly. Illustrated by Irene Kelly. Holiday House, 2009. Ages 5–9.
Subjects: Birds, Nests

From emperor penguins and others that make no nest at all to the complicated courting constructions of bowerbirds, this appealing title introduces the astonishing variety of methods birds use to keep their eggs warm around the world. The focus is mainly on different nest-building materials and techniques. Curiously, although the birds range from American dipper to yellow-rumped thornbill of Australia, the ostrich isn't one of them. This probably won't worry readers, who will pore over the detailed drawings and the text, which looks like hand-printed notes. One to three birds are shown on a page; a final map gives a general idea of where they might be found in the world. Small sketches show birds, nests, and some surprising materials such as clothespins, dollar bills, and trash bags. Young readers are encouraged to offer feathers, bits of yarn or string, and animal fur for birds in their own neighborhoods.

The Blues Go Birding Across America

Informational picture book

By Carol Malnor and Sandy Ferguson
    Fuller. Illustrated by Louise Schroeder.
    Dawn Publications, 2010. Ages 5–9.
Subjects: Birds, Bird-watching

Looking for a new song to perform, an imagined band of five bluebirds travel across America listening and looking at sixteen different bird species. From the bald eagle in Alaska and black-footed albatross flying over Hawaii to feeder birds in Ohio and American robins on the White House lawn in Washington, D.C., these entertaining songbirds find iconic species all over the country. While the narrative chronicles the birds' adventures, text boxes offer observations (the birds each keep a notebook), a pseudo-field guide adds information, and bird-watching expert Eggbert adds birding tips. In cartoons drawn on top of realistic illustrations of the birds they spot, the five birders converse and joke in speech bubbles. They even get in a plug for citizen science. Both entertaining and informative, this is the first in a series that also includes *The Blues Go Birding at Wild America's Shores* (2010) and *The Blues Go Extreme Birding* (2011) from the same publisher.

Hatch!   *Informational picture book*

By Roxie Munro. Illustrated by Roxie Munro. Marshall Cavendish, 2011.
    Ages 5–10.
Subjects: Birds—eggs, Birds—behavior

Guess whose eggs these are and learn about nine bird species and the animals that share their habitats. This oversized book offers a nature guessing

Do Some Bird-Watching

FOOD WILL ATTRACT birds to your windows or yard. Make a feeder from an old soda bottle or milk carton, or simply scatter birdseed on a tray. Store-bought feeders can be simple or fancy. The important thing is to hang the feeder where the birds and not the squirrels and other hungry creatures will get it— unless you want to feed them, too.

There are many ways to participate as a citizen-scientist-birdwatcher.

eBird (http://ebird.org/content/ebird), a program of Cornell University's Lab of Ornithology and the National Audubon Society, collects bird sightings from all over. No expertise is necessary.

Cornell University's Ornithology Lab sponsors many citizen science programs, some of which are described in chapter 16.

One such program, Celebrate Urban Birds (http://celebrateurbanbirds.org), offers suggestions for making a welcoming area for birds in a city apartment and for bird-related art projects, as well as another place to record sightings.

Another Cornell program, YardMap (www.yardmap.org), which is funded by the National Science Foundation, helps people map their own yards and gardens, track the birds, and learn how to attract more birds.

game. A double-page spread shows an egg or eggs in their usual clutch with a description of where a bird can be found, what its nest is like, how its eggs are cared for, plus some other clues. The next page shows the bird in its customary environment, with other species, and adds further information. Munro's selection includes a wide variety of birds and habitats and plenty of surprises. Orioles like to sit on anthills. Mallards can sleep on the water with one eye open. A cactus wren never drinks. The India ink outlines in her accurate illustrations make the creatures easy to see, even in their busy surroundings. Suggestions for books and websites for further learning and a list of "fun bird words" complete the package.

Birds of a Feather
Informational picture book

By Francesco Pittau. Illustrated by Bernadette Gervais. Chronicle Books, 2012. Ages 4–8.

Subjects: Birds, Lift-the-flap books, Toy and movable books

Lift the flaps to find pop-up birds and bird facts in this oversized volume that children might read most comfortably on a coffee table. This hands-on experience provides silhouettes, detailed portraits, eggs, feathers, puzzles, peek-a-boo glimpses of various bird features, as well as short paragraphs on a variety of birds. Originally published in France, the book includes birds from around the world. Familiar U.S. birds such as cardinals and mallard ducks are outnumbered by exotic species such as cockatoos and European bee-eaters. The eggs concealing the pop-up birds are recognizable and vary in size, though they are not specifically life-size. (That of the domestic chicken is noticeably too large.) A mix-and-match puzzle allows readers to arrange and rearrange flaps to reveal six different bird species. Entertaining and reasonably informative.

A Place for Birds

Informational picture book

By Melissa Stewart. Illustrated by Higgins
    Bond. Peachtree, 2009. Ages 6–10.
Subjects: Birds, Conservation

This unusually positive approach to environmental issues describes how eleven bird species thrive in their particular environments, how those environments have changed, and what humans are doing to protect and encourage them. Stewart uses a two-level text, combining a general statement about bird and human behavior and a sidebar about each species. Piping plover, for example, nest directly on the beach, so people are fencing off areas where nests have been found. Some birds are well known—eastern bluebird, northern cardinal, bald eagle, and spotted owl. Others are unusual—Hawaii's crested honeycreeper, Florida scrub jays, common murre. Acrylic paintings show birds in their habitat. These finely detailed illustrations make the birds easy to identify and show nests and eggs or chicks as well. Range maps on the endpapers include thumbnails of the birds described. Finally, the author suggests things young people can do to help birds flourish, and why they should do so.

Seabird in the Forest:
The Mystery of the
Marbled Murrelet

Informational picture book

By Joan Dunning. Illustrated by Joan Dunning.
    Boyds Mills Press, 2011. Ages 5–9.
Subjects: Birds—nests, Marbled murrelet,
    Seabirds

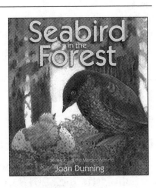

A seabird mystery was solved in 1974, when researchers discovered that marbled murrelets nest in old-growth trees far from the ocean where these curious birds are usually seen. Mates for life, the pair fly far inland. Choosing the same tree, often a redwood, year after year, the female lays a single egg on a branch. Hidden from other forest creatures by its down camouflage, the hatched chick spends a month mostly own its own, waiting for a parent to arrive with fish. In this oversized picture book the story of one such chick runs beneath atmospheric paintings supporting the mood of mystery. These illustrations include close-ups of the adult birds and their chick as well as landscapes suggesting their contrasting worlds. Text boxes add further information about this unusual life cycle and the Pacific Northwest ecosystem that supports it.

As the Crow Flies   *Picture book*

By Sheila Keenan. Illustrated by Kevin Duggan. Feiwel & Friends, 2012.
    Ages 4–7.
Subject: Crows, Stories in rhyme

Do you ever think about the crows watching you? You will after reading this crow's description of the lives of urban crows. Short rhyming couplets reveal that crows are stealing food from people and animals alike, feeding on roadkill when the traffic allows, leaving messy tracks and splotches, and gathering in great numbers to roost in the winter. The realistic illustrations portray the actions described, sometimes looking at the crow and sometimes looking down on the world from a bird's-eye view. Panels show the sequence of events. The unusual emphasis on urban birds makes this a particularly valuable selection for city-dwelling children who may not realize that wildlife is all around. Based on actual observations of crow behavior by the husband-and-wife team who created this book.

Lucky Ducklings
Picture book

By Eva Moore. Illustrated by Nancy
 Carpenter. Orchard Books /
 Scholastic Inc., 2013. Ages 3–7.
Subjects: Ducks, Baby animals, Rescues

Five little ducklings, following their mother, fall through the grate into a storm sewer and are rescued by townspeople. Then, "Fireman Dennis knew just what to do." Clearly familiar with Robert McCloskey's *Make Way for Ducklings* (Viking, 1941), he held up his hand to stop traffic so the mother duck could cross the street and return to her family. The homage to that children's classic begins with the cover illustration showing Pippin, Bippin, Tippin, Dippin, and Little Joe in line behind their mother. Inside, their peaceful pond is nicely contrasted with the busy town, where interesting food can be found in the trash cans but danger lurks. The story moves in episodes from accident to rescue attempts to success, and the storyteller adds suspense by suggesting that it could have ended at several points along the way. This satisfying survival story is based on a true incident in Montauk, New York.

Vulture View
Informational picture book

By April Pulley Sayre. Illustrated by Steve Jenkins. Henry Holt & Co., 2007.
 Ages 4–7.
Subject: Turkey vulture

This playful, poetic introduction to carrion-eating turkey vultures would be a delight to read aloud to a group of preschool children. "Wings stretch wide / to catch a ride / on warming air. / Going where?" Flying high, the vultures turn up their noses at the live animals they see; they look for foods that "REEK." After dining on a "stinky dead deer," the vulture washes and preens, soars high in the sky again, coming to rest in the evening to sleep in groups, "like families." The simple text works for beginning readers, too. There are just three big ideas: the flying, eating, and sleeping habits of these distinctive birds. Jenkins's cut-paper collages on solid backgrounds show well at a distance, highlighting the black birds' purple-red faces, heavy gray beaks, and white wing edges. Sources for more information are given in the end matter, and they will be welcomed.

Pale Male: Citizen Hawk of New York City
Informational picture book

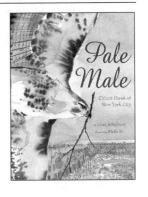

By Janet Schulman. Illustrated by Meilo So. Alfred
   A. Knopf, 2008. Ages 7–12.
Subjects: Red-tailed hawk, New York (City)

When a pale red-tailed hawk finds a home near the roof of a fancy New York apartment house, the building's human occupants try to evict it. Bird-lovers watching from Central Park and all over the country rally successfully in his support. Happily, Pale Male has now raised numerous families; some descendants have chosen to nest in the city as well. Two things distinguish this version of his highly publicized story: the extensive bird-watching detail and the way Schulman uses the example of one bird to present a larger environmental issue to middle-grade readers: how can humans and animals occupy the same area? So's beautiful illustrations demonstrate the variety of bird and human life that can be found in and around Central Park, an oasis in the middle of the city. Fledgling bird-watchers can find all kinds of identifiable birds. Pair with other titles about this saga, including Winter's *The Tale of Pale Male* (Harcourt, 2007) and McCarthy's *City Hawk* (Simon & Schuster, 2007).

Loon   *Informational picture book*

By Susan Vande Griek. Illustrated by Karen Reczuch. Groundwood Books /
   House of Anansi Press, 2011. Ages 4–7.
Subject: Common loon

A gentle prose poem and realistic paintings chronicle the early lives of a pair of loon siblings. Their story begins with the two speckled eggs shown in the nest on the front endpapers, follows the chicks as they grow and learn through the summer, and mentions the adolescent years they spend in more southern oceans before returning to start families of their own. While the poet sometimes imagines human motivations for her avian subjects, her facts are accurate. Repeat readers can use the thumbnails on the closing endpapers to identify white-tailed deer, beaver, yellow perch, and more, which also appear in Reczuch's beautiful textured acrylic paintings. This warm appreciation is a Canadian import. Its appeal is not limited to children who live where these iconic birds can be heard.

Fly, Chick, Fly!

Picture book

By Jeanne Willis. Illustrated by Tony Ross.
    Andersen Press USA: Distributed by Lerner,
    2012. Ages 3–7.
Subjects: Owls, Baby animals, Flight

When the third of three barn owl chicks hesitates to fly, its parents provide encouragement. In this gentle read-aloud, a rhythmic, repetitive text and realistic pictures work together to tell the story of a child's first steps toward independence. The parent owls, rendered in pastels on a textured surface, look on lovingly as the last chick hatches. Who can resist their heart-shaped faces? Time passes and the seasons change. Though its siblings have flown successfully, the third chick worries and clings desperately to a branch. Finally, she flies. But that's not the end. "Snow came. Crow came. Spring came. / But what became of this last chick?" Soon she'll be encouraging young of her own. In this gentle story for an anxious child, the birds have human emotions, but there's a surprising amount of realism.

See also references to birds in the index. There are also several titles in the
    poetry chapter.

MAMMALS

A Platypus' World

Informational picture book

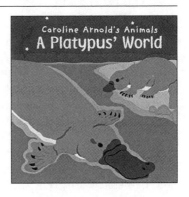

By Caroline Arnold. Illustrated by Caroline
    Arnold. Picture Window Books, 2008.
    Ages 5–8.
Subjects: Animals, Baby animals, Platypus,
    Australia

This appealing introduction to the Australian egg-laying mammal follows a female
platypus into the water, where she hunts for food, and into a new land
burrow, where she lays eggs and raises a pair of babies. The straightforward narrative is ideal for reading aloud. Simple cut-paper illustrations fill
the double-page spreads, their dark, shadowy colors reflecting the animal's
nocturnal world. Other animals in the pictures are identified in text boxes.
Caroline Arnold's Animals series includes titles about other Australian animals as well as some more familiar ones. All feature an opening of fast facts
and a gentle story focused on child-rearing. Each ends with a map, fun facts,
glossary, index, and suggested books and websites for further research. Each
acknowledges the advice of experts. Carefully researched and attractively
presented, they provide exactly the kind of information young readers want
to know, nicely connected to their universal interest in animal babies.

Desert Elephants   *Informational picture book*

By Helen Cowcher. Illustrated by Helen Cowcher. Farrar, Straus, Giroux,
    2011. Ages 5–9.
Subjects: Elephants, Migration, Desert ecology, Human-animal relation-
    ships, Mali

In the Sahel, south of Africa's Sahara Desert, around 550 elephants make a
three-hundred-mile circular migration in search of water each year. On the
way, they all stop at a hidden forest lake and later pass through a narrow
pathway between desert cliffs known as the Elephants' Doorway. They can
sense rain from miles away. Dogon, Fulani, and Tuareg peoples live in this

Mammals in Your Backyard

SQUIRRELS MIGHT BE the most common wild mammal regularly seen in the United States. Visitors from abroad are often intrigued by animals many of us don't notice or even consider pests.

Encourage children to observe these animals carefully. How do they communicate? Can you recognize different calls? What do they eat? Do they leave traces? Where are their nests? (In my neighborhood they are big leafy constructions high in the trees, and the nipped-off branches that didn't make it into nests lie everywhere.) Where there is room to run and play, children can be squirrels, chasing each other, and then curling up together in their nests.

Citizen scientists are studying squirrels, too. The University of Illinois at Chicago and the Peggy Notebaert Nature Museum have jointly sponsored a squirrel study which, though focused particularly on squirrels of Chicago, encourages contributions from observers all over the country (www.project squirrel.org).

Other projects in California and South Carolina are collecting data from those areas. Look on the Web to see if there are researchers in your area.

area, maintaining the elephants' freedom to make this traditional journey. The author-illustrator tells this story of human-animal interactions through words and watercolor paintings showing the animals on their journey, tourists coming to admire them, and tribesmen and women using desert radio to communicate, among other subjects. A map on the endpapers shows their route through Mali and Burkina Faso, but there is no larger map of Africa or the world to put this in context for young American readers and listeners. Parents can help.

Tracks of a Panda   *Informational picture book*

By Nick Dowson. Illustrated by Yu Rong. Candlewick Press, 2007. Ages 5–9.

Subject: Pandas, Baby animals, Parental behavior in animals

This appealing introduction to the likable Chinese bear follows a panda baby and its mother from birth through several years as the two find food, move to a more productive location, and move again to avoid approaching humans. Brush-and-watercolor paintings on double-page spreads, done in a

Chinese style, close in enough to show details of panda paws and claws, and back off to show the landscape. Information is given on two levels: fast facts are set off in a smaller font from that of the imagined story of their journeys. The presentation of this small, square book is attractive as well: brown endpapers have a bamboo design; there's a traditional landscape on the back cover, and a charming mother and baby on the front. This has been reissued in paperback as part of the publisher's extensive Read and Wonder series.

Beavers
Informational picture book

By Gail Gibbons. Illustrated by Gail Gibbons. Holiday House, 2013. Ages
  4–8.
Subject: Beavers

The author and illustrator of over 170 books for children on an amazing variety of subjects, Gibbons's picture books are characterized by well-organized information and carefully labeled illustrations. This introduction to a fascinating dam-building mammal is no different. Beavers are rodents, like squirrels and rats. Their front teeth keep growing throughout their lives. This allows these dam-building animals to cut down trees and trim branches as well as gnaw on the bark and twigs that make up part of their diet. Gibbons's pen-and-ink and watercolor illustrations show beaver families hard at work. They show both dam and lodge construction, as well as the animal's physical features and its surroundings. In one, a mother nurses her kits, others show the kits at play and, soon, at work themselves. For reading aloud and reading alone, a solid introduction.

Ice Bears
Informational picture books

By Brenda Z. Guiberson. Illustrated by Ilya Spirin. Henry Holt & Co., 2008. Ages 4–9.
Subject: Polar bear, Arctic regions, Parental behavior in animals, Baby animals

During their first year twin ice bear cubs learn about their tundra world, waiting through a long lean summer until the ice returns and they can

ICE BEARS
Brenda Z. Guiberson • *illustrated by* Ilya Spirin

fatten up on seals. Words and sharply detailed watercolor illustrations combine to give a sense of the Arctic environment, the brief spring and summer of birds and bees, flowers and mosquito hordes, and the animals around them. Onomatopoetic words in italics describe sounds the cubs might hear: the "Slurpslurp" of their nursing, the "Chuffchuff" of their mother's warning when a male threatens them, "Crunch, crik!" as the ice breaks up. Interesting small details of polar bear behavior are included. Young readers and listeners will enjoy the story, whose sobering message is contained in the back matter, an "Arctic Ice Report" noting the effects of global warming and the melting of polar ice on the bears and other animals who share the world.

What to Expect When You're Expecting Joeys: A Guide for Marsupial Parents (and Curious Kids)

Informational picture book

By Bridget Heos. Illustrated by
    Stéphane Jorisch. Millbrook Press /
    Lerner, 2012. Ages 6–11.
Subjects: Baby animals, Marsupials

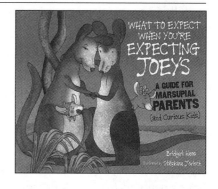

This tongue-in-cheek introduction to the animal group that includes opossums, kangaroos, koalas, and even Tasmanian devils is framed as questions and answers for expectant parents. The process is unique among mammals, with tiny, tiny "pinkies" spending time in their mother's pouch (or a belly fold) where they nurse and develop further before emerging, but the author goes on to describe childhood as well. Painted pen-and-ink sketches of fond parents and their offspring add to the humor. There is just enough information about where these animals live and what they eat to make readers want to learn more. A glossary and suggestions for further reading and websites add to the information value of this appealing, offbeat approach to learning about the natural world that targets exactly the stage young readers most want to know about. They may also enjoy *What to Expect When You're Expecting Larvae* (2011) and *What to Expect When You're Expecting Hatchlings* (2012), also from Millbrook Press.

Ape
Informational picture book

By Martin Jenkins. Illustrated by Vicky White. Candlewick Press, 2007.
Ages 5–9.
Subject: Apes

This beautiful introduction to four rare great apes species—orangutan, chimp, bonobo, and gorilla—reminds readers of their similarities to a fifth, much more common species, human beings. One member of each species stands for the whole: "Orangutan swings with her baby." "Gorilla lounges, chewing on bamboo stems and chomping on leaves." In a few sentences, the author describes common behaviors children will understand. Captions offer a bit more detail. What distinguishes this oversized album are the striking pencil-and-oil illustrations by a talented former zookeeper. These realistic, expressive close-ups show the animals in action. The book concludes with the gentle reminder that humans have taken up so much space in the world that there is little room left for other great apes. A map of the Eastern Hemisphere shows where these four species live in a band across central Africa and on the islands of Sumatra and Borneo.

Hello, Bumblebee Bat
Informational picture book; Early reader

By Darrin P. Lunde. Illustrated by Patricia Wynne. Charlesbridge, 2007.
Ages 4–7.
Subjects: Bumblebee bat, Bats

No larger than a bumblebee, the world's smallest bat is only an inch long. This endangered species from Thailand flies at dawn and dusk, eats insects, and folds its wings to sleep hanging upside down in its cave. With brown fur, a pig nose, and long, pointy ears, this tiny creature looks anything but fierce in Wynne's illustrations, which give the animal a cheerful smile and show its diminutive size by including other creatures. The format is predictable and reassuring. A simple question such as "Bumblebee Bat, how do you see at night?" and the bat's first-person answer appear in large white text on a dark blue left-hand page. Finally, the words "Good Night, Bumblebee Bat!" appear on a double-page spread showing bat and siblings asleep in a cave. This easy reader would also be a perfect bedtime book for a preschool naturalist.

Monkey Colors

Early reader

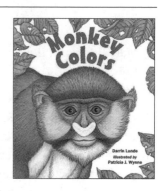

By Darrin P. Lunde. Illustrated by Patricia
  Wynne. Charlesbridge, 2012. Ages 4–7.
Subject: Monkeys—color

For the beginning reader, this is an inviting
exploration of color in the monkey world. The
fact that "monkeys come in many colors" is
repeated like a refrain and demonstrated by the
descriptions of twelve monkey species. Four have fur in a single color: yellow, red, brown, orange. Four have colorful features or stripes, and four have colors that vary. Each is shown in a watercolor-and-ink illustration that includes a tiny label and, usually, a pictorial suggestion of the animal's habitat. The book's format also allows for an identification game, showing the different monkeys in groups, as you might see them in a museum (though not in the real world). A simple but effective way of marveling at nature's variety.

Race the Wild Wind:
A Story of the Sable Island Horses

Picture book

By Sandra Markle. Illustrated by Layne Johnson. Walker, Bloomsbury, 2011.
  Ages 5–9.
Subjects: Wild horses, Nova Scotia, Canada

Wild horses have considerable appeal, and those of Sable Island, off the coast of Nova Scotia, may be unfamiliar to U.S. readers. Markle imagines the story of the horses that first came to that island, dropped from a schooner off shore to swim to the beach and make new lives. She focuses on a young stallion, bred to be a race horse, who becomes leader of his own band, fathering children, fighting with other stallions, and racing away from violent storms. Dramatic oil paintings show the horses in the surf and on the sand, and the island in winter and summer, good weather and bad. Though fictional, the story is based on fact, and the author concludes with a short description of the island's horses today, some amazing horse facts, and suggestions for further research.

Snow School

Informational picture book

By Sandra Markle. Illustrated by Alan Marks. Charlesbridge, 2013.
Ages 4–7.
Subjects: Baby animals, Learning in animals, Snow leopard

"Snow leopards are amazing!" writes the author in a note at the end of this charming story of a snow leopard family. For more than a year, a pair of cubs follow their mother, learning important lessons before they can hunt independently in their rugged mountain home in Pakistan. Readers and listeners can't help but learn with these appealing youngsters. "Be quiet when you go hunting." "Always find shelter from a storm." "Staying safe is more important than having a full stomach." These are wild animals and the illustrator shows them in action—playing, sleeping, on the prowl, and with a discreetly bleeding kill. The author, who often researches in the field for her animal stories, here relies on experts who have made the difficult journey to the snow leopard's world and on films. In an afterword she provides links to some of those videos.

The Chiru of High Tibet: A True Story

Informational picture book

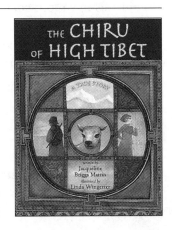

By Jacqueline Briggs Martin. Illustrated by
Linda S. Wingerter. Houghton Mifflin Books
for Children, 2010. Ages 5–10.
Subjects: Chiru; Antelopes; China; Tibet;
Schaller, George B.; Travel; Endangered
species

In the high northern plains of Tibet, antelope-like creatures called chiru were hunted almost to extinction for their valuable soft wool. Naturalist George Schaller first took up their cause. He hoped to find their remote calving grounds and then ask the Chinese government to protect the area, but the trip was too difficult. Later, four experienced trekkers did make their way across the plains, through mountains and a canyon to discover this secret place. Martin spins the tale of their journey in lyrical prose, emphasizing its length, its difficulty, and the distinct possibility it would be fruitless. Her circular narrative begins and ends with description: "There is a place so cold, it takes the fleece of five sheep to keep one person warm . . ." A map sets the story geographically, and some photographs from the expedition conclude this story of survival in a remote part of the world.

Skunks   *Nonfiction*

By Adrienne Mason. Illustrated by Nancy Gray Ogle. Kids Can Press, 2006.
   Ages 5–9.
Subject: Skunks

Spread by spread, this topic book introduces a species more often smelled than seen in North America. Striped skunks and their relatives are nocturnal mammals distinguished by their defensive weapon: a strong-smelling oil spray. All four native species are shown. The text, accessible to beginning readers, describes their habitat, behavior, child-rearing, and relationship to human beings. Illustrations also include signs (tracks and diggings) and a spread showing skunks of the world. Realistic, finely detailed paintings show the animals in various contexts: on a meadow, in the woods, curled up in an underground den in winter, facing a fox, and even with kits. These images emphasize the skunk's claws. Though small, this animal is formidable. With a table of contents, glossary, and index, this topic book, part of the publisher's long-standing Wildlife Series, demonstrates the conventions of nonfiction exposition through a subject endlessly fascinating to young naturalists.

Polar Bears   *Informational picture book*

By Mark Newman. Illustrated by Mark Newman. Henry Holt & Co., 2011.
   Ages 4–8.
Subject: Polar bears

A simple text and stunning photographs introduce the largest bears in the world to young readers. It is the wildlife photographer's images that make this title stand out among many about these iconic bears. There's the irresistible cub face on the cover, the determined bear on an ice floe, the patient hunter with its head in a seal hole, the gaping, hungry mouth, and the surprisingly sleek swimmer. These pictures demonstrate Newman's love for these creatures as well as his remarkable photographic skills. Beautifully designed, with a text on two levels clearly supported by the images, this book conveys a clear sense of how dependent the bears' lives are on their habitat. By the time readers reach the last page and learn about their threatened status, they will already be fans, eager to help preserve the species. A note about the photographer's methods is also included.

Armadillo Trail: The Northward Journey of the Armadillo

Informational picture book

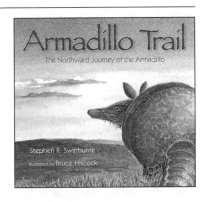

By Stephen R. Swinburne. Illustrated by Bruce Hiscock. Boyds Mills Press, 2009. Ages 7–10.

Subjects: Migration, Armadillos

A mini armored truck, a nine-banded armadillo, born in a cozy den in Texas, grows up to wander north all the way to Kansas, mirroring the journey many have taken in the northward expansion of this species. Swinburne uses the story of one armadillo to introduce these curious animals, relatives of sloths and anteaters who have a protective shell with bands in the middle allowing them to bend. The traveler's story is illustrated with watercolors, often showing the slow-moving animal in an expanse of southwestern landscape. One startling picture shows her leaping two feet in the air as a red pickup narrowly misses her on a road where she was eating a dead opossum. Armadillo babies are usually quadruplets. Parents planning to share this story should know that one of this armadillo's siblings is eaten by a farm dog early on—a realistic but possibly upsetting event.

Yosemite's Songster: One Coyote's Story   *Picture book*

By Ginger Wadsworth. Illustrated by Daniel San Souci. Yosemite Conservancy, 2013. Ages 4–8.

Subjects: Coyotes, Yosemite National Park

Both Yosemite National Park and its coyotes are celebrated in this tender story. After a frightening avalanche separates a coyote and her mate, she spends thirty-six hours watching and waiting for his return. For readers who aren't bothered by the scary opening, this would be an appealing, gentle read. The author and illustrator have filled the pages with details of the coyote's daily life and the sights and sounds of the park. People are everywhere, but few notice the coyote who prowls at night, hunts for mice in the tall grasses in the daytime, and stalks the river's shore until, finally, her mate answers her call. Framed watercolor paintings accompany the lyrical prose, showing the coyotes as well as other animals, park scenes, and dramatic vistas. While the author and illustrator give this pair no human characteristics, readers and listeners will surely add the relief they feel when they are reunited.

AND THREE BOOKS ABOUT WOLVES

The Wolves Are Back
Informational picture book

By Jean Craighead George. Illustrated
    by Wendell Minor. Dutton Chil-
    dren's Books, 2008. Ages 5–10.
Subjects: Yellowstone National Park,
    Wolves, Endangered species,
    Wildlife reintroduction

The successful reestablishment of wolves in Yellowstone National Park is a welcome piece of environmental good news three noted children's nature writers have publicized. George's version introduces a single wolf pup, demonstrating its role in the ecosystem through its daily activities. Then she flashes back to the time when there were no wolves. Her gentle, lyrical prose uses variations on a repeated refrain, "the wolves were gone" and "the wolves were back." The repetition supports reading aloud and remembering; the underlying information is all true. Wendell Minor's lushly detailed, expressive paintings show individual species—moose, ravens, vesper sparrows, buffalo, beaver, badger, bear, and more—in the context of the spectacle of that vast wilderness. This is a book for reading aloud and reading alone, one that can be returned to again and again.

Family Pack
Informational picture book

By Sandra Markle. Illustrated by Alan Marks.
  Charlesbridge, 2011. Ages 4–10.
Subjects: Wolves, Hunting, Survival, Yellowstone
  National Park

To tell the story of wolf resettlement in Yellowstone
National Park, longtime collaborators Markle and
Marks also focus on a single individual, a young
gray wolf. Basing their narrative on actual fact, they imagine the early years
of the wolf that scientists called Female 7. Taken from her family pack in
Canada to be resettled in Yellowstone, she sets off on her own, learning her
new surroundings and developing her hunting skills before finding a mate
(Male 2) and making a family pack of her own, the first naturally formed
pack in Yellowstone Park in over sixty years. Her story is sweet, gently told,
and beautifully illustrated with watercolor, pen-and-ink paintings showing
the wolf in a variety of poses, the natural scenery of Yellowstone park, and
the changing seasons. This would be a good title to begin exploring this popular ecological success story.

When the Wolves Returned: Restoring Nature's Balance in Yellowstone
Informational picture book

By Dorothy Hinshaw Patent. Illustrated by Dan Hartman and Cassie
  Hartman. Walker & Co. Distributed to the trade by Macmillan, 2008.
  Ages 6–10.
Subjects: Wildlife reintroduction, Wolves, Conservation, Yellowstone
  National Park

When Yellowstone National Park was established over a hundred years ago,
the geologic wonders were the attraction. It didn't seem unreasonable to
eradicate wolves in favor of elk and deer. But with wolves removed, the balance of nature was disturbed. Thanks to their reintroduction in the 1990s,
that balance is being restored. Patent's approach to this piece of good news

meets children's informational needs on two levels. On the left-hand page, short, simple sentences describe the issue and the outcomes. On the right, these ideas are developed more fully. The striking modern photographs along with pictures from the past give the book the look of a photo album. Patent gives detailed examples of the effects of the reintroduction on different parts of the ecosystem, emphasizing its complexity. This well-designed and thoughtfully organized informational book makes an interesting comparison with the other two titles described here.

See also references to mammals in the index.

An orangutan in Sabah

Chapter 12

Poetry

YOUNG CHILDREN ENJOY THE SOUND OF WORDS AS MUCH AS THE SENSE.
Both rhythm and rhyme appeal. Indeed, stories in rhyme are so common
that they are a genre subject heading for library catalogs. In the books in this
section, the writers have used not just rhyme and comfortable, memorable,
singable rhythm, but imagery as well. "Poetry is language compressed, an
intensification of language" poet Alice Schertle writes.[1] Not only does the
poet use fewer words—as does the author of a picture book—these words do
double or triple duty. They say one thing (or maybe two) and hint at more.
They make pictures in the minds of readers and listeners that go far beyond
the words and even pictures on the page, although a good illustrator can
sometimes support the imagery.

When I evaluate poetry books, I read the poetry aloud. The sound matters.
It makes the difference between poetry and verse. Verse—in the rhyming
couplets of greeting cards and in many, many children's books—comes out
in a boring sing-song. Poetry has subtle variations in rhythm, line length,
and punctuation, encouraging the reader-aloud to provide expression. When

careful word choice and placement are combined with fresh and original images, the result is poetry.

One nice thing about poetry is that, often, there's a selection from which to choose. You might want to read, or even learn, one poem a day. You can skip around in a book, finding sounds and subjects that particularly appeal. Books in this chapter are organized under subjects that correspond with the organization of the rest of the book: animals, plants and forests, the natural world, some special times and places, and play. They convey similar information, but in a special way.

ANIMALS

In the Wild

Informational picture book

By David Elliott. Illustrated by Holly Meade.
   Candlewick Press, 2010. Ages 3–8.
Subjects: Poetry, Animals, Wildlife

Fourteen poems about iconic animals have been beautifully illustrated with painted woodcuts in this splendid, oversized volume. From the fearsome jaguar on the cover to the polar bear "disappearing / in the snow" on the last page, memorable images accompany short, playful poems that beg to be read aloud or even memorized. Most of the animals stare directly at the reader from an appropriate natural background: the panda in bamboo, the orangutan from a perch in the jungle, the sloth clinging to a tree. A kangaroo bounces "Boing! Boing! Boing!" across the outback. A wolf howls at the moon. There are some not-so-subtle environmental messages: we're reminded that the buffalo "once was sixty-million strong" and there's that disappearing bear, but there's also a friendly connection to the orangutan: "How nice to have someone like you / sitting in our family tree." Simply wonderful.

What's for Dinner? Quirky, Squirmy   *Poetry*
Poems from the Animal World

By Katherine B. Hauth. Illustrated by David Clark. Charlesbridge, 2011.
  Ages 7–12.
Subjects: Predation (Biology), Animals—food, Food chains (Ecology)

The title poem from this engaging collection of twenty-nine poems concludes: ". . . finding food / is not a joke. / Living things must eat / or croak."
Filled with curious creatures and little-known facts, this book is a more-
than-just-palatable way to introduce natural history facts and concepts.
From dermestid beetles (used by museums to clean skeletons) to sloths and
polar bears, the poet has celebrated animals big and small, from around the
world. Along with food capture and eating habits, she covers predator-prey
relationships and peaceful, productive coexistence. The collection concludes
with a vocabulary poem, "Eating Words," and further information about
the web of life and the animals described as well as suggestions for further
reading. Humorous ink-and-watercolor cartoons show animals with human
expressions, a contrast to the accurate, if sometimes whimsical, text.

National Geographic Book of Animal Poetry: *Poetry*
200 Poems with Photographs That Squeak,
Soar, and Roar!

Edited by J. Patrick Lewis. Illustrated with National Geographic Society
  (U.S.) photographs. National Geographic, 2012. Ages 5–12.
Subject: Animals

Two hundred poems, selected by the U.S. children's poet laureate and set
on beautifully reproduced color photographs, celebrate the "variety, beauty,
and strangeness of the animal world" (p. 2). This oversized volume is organized into sections grouped by characteristic (quiet, winged, strange) rather
than animal family. There are almost as many different animal subjects
as there are poems. Ranging widely in style, mood, and approach, Lewis's
choices come from a broad range of writers for children and adults and
include a number of old favorites, as well as some new ones. The discreetly
labeled photographs are mostly images submitted to National Geographic
My Shot, the magazine's online photo community. The editor concludes with

suggestions for young readers about writing poems about animals and an extensive bibliography of resources modeling various forms. This is a splendid collection for any nature library.

The Cuckoo's Haiku   *Poetry*

By Michael J. Rosen. Illustrated by Stanley Fellows. Candlewick Press, 2009. Ages 7–10.
Subjects: Birds, Haiku (American)

Twenty-four haiku, organized by season, describe familiar birds of the eastern and central United States. Extra handwritten notes and detailed watercolors turn this poetry collection into a nature notebook and beginner's field guide. This gem rewards the kind of patient, careful attention birdwatching requires. Fellows's accurate illustrations, in watercolor and pencil, show birds where you might see them. Turkeys wander off into the woods; purple finches cluster around a feeder. The script of the notes is lovely to look at but spidery and not easy to read. Some poems reflect the Ohio poet's personal experience; others describe the bird or its actions: "twittering at dusk / chimney swifts sail above the / citronella glow." This is a book for adults to share with young children just beginning to appreciate the pleasures of bird-watching as well as for older readers who can do it on their own.

Where Else in the Wild?
More Camouflaged Creatures
Concealed—and Revealed
Poetry

By David M. Schwartz and Yael Schy. Illustrated by Dwight Kuhn. Tricycle Press, 2009. Ages 5–10.
Subjects: Animals, Camouflage (Biology), Puzzles

Poems and photo puzzles are the ingredients for this intriguing demonstration of animal camouflage. Eleven species, insects (from inchworms to ambush bugs) and vertebrates (from scorpion fish to white-footed mouse and snowshoe hare), are shown concealed in their environment, sometimes singly, and sometimes with others of their kind. A poem on the left-hand page gives a clue to the animal; lift the flap on the right-hand page and the animals are revealed, with the background faded out. On the reverse of the flap is a page of information about the animal, including both habits and habitats. The full-color photographs are remarkable; even a sharp-eyed adult may have trouble with finding some creatures. The poems, in a variety of forms, are fun to read aloud and would be easy to memorize. This is equally as engaging and challenging as the trio's first collection, *Where in the Wild* (Tricycle Press, 2007).

A Strange Place to Call Home: The World's Most Dangerous Habitats & the Animals That Call Them Home
Poetry

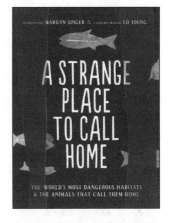

By Marilyn Singer. Illustrated by Ed Young.
   Chronicle Books, 2012. Ages 5–12.
Subjects: Animals, Animals—habitations

Everyone loves a survivor. Here, fourteen poems and striking collage illustrations celebrate animals that thrive in unlikely places. From Humboldt penguins on the coasts of Chile and Peru to the foxes in our cities and suburbs, a variety of creatures take advantage of environments that might seem hostile. Internal rhyme and alliteration as well as thoughtful word choice make these poems a delight to read and read aloud. Their varied forms, and more about each species, are described in the back matter. But what really makes this book stand out are Young's collages. Cut, torn, painted, and textured papers and photos layered across the double-page spreads make intriguing images of the animals in their worlds. Designed more to inspire than to inform, this beautiful combination of words and pictures will surely make readers and listeners want to know more.

An Egret's Day

Poetry

By Jane Yolen. Illustrated by Jason Stemple. Wordsong, 2009. Ages 7–11.
Subjects: Herons, Birds

From sunrise to evening roost, poems and photographs describe the appearance and the activities of a great egret. Another in a sporadic series of mother-son combinations of poetry and clear crisp pictures of the natural world, this one also answers factual questions about this striking bird. The poems are short, appealing to young readers, and done in a variety of forms. Yolen uses lively language and wide-ranging imagery to convey both information and appreciation. Stemple's photographs show egrets in the natural world, from a distance and up close. With a variety of angles and lighting, they demonstrate how cooperative this bird can be for photographers: "As conscious of his beauty / As any Hollywood star, / The egret poses. // He supposes / Your camera is not very far / And that you will do your duty." An ideal springboard for young nature enthusiasts with cameras of their own.

Birds of a Feather: Poems   *Poetry*

By Jane Yolen. Illustrated by Jason Stemple. Wordsong, 2011. Ages 8–11.
Subject: Birds

Yolen and her photographer son Stemple, frequent collaborators, here offer a new collection of fourteen poems in varied forms. These are accompanied by short informational paragraphs about each species and set on striking photos of bird species that might be found in the eastern United States. The range is wide, including familiar feeder birds, birds of ponds and shores, and birds children are more likely to have read about than seen. Sharp focus and careful composition make these birds the center of attention, but the poetry is enjoyable, too, highlighting birds' looks and actions both. A kingfisher has a "blue Mohawk." "Turning terns are all returning / There upon the shore. " A three-stanza haiku matches the pattern of the mockingbird's song. This is a nice companion to earlier titles: *A Mirror to Nature* (Wordsong, 2009) and *An Egret's Day* (annotated above).

PLANTS AND FORESTS

Poetrees

Informational picture book

By Douglas Florian. Illustrated by Douglas
Florian. Beach Lane Books, 2010. Ages
6–10.

Subjects: Trees, Poetry

The sideways cover shows how this unusual book must be turned so that the trees pictured can stretch up to their full height. Eighteen poems describe interesting trees from around the world, as well as their seeds, roots, rings, leaves, and bark. Some species will be familiar: oak, giant sequoias, paper birch, and weeping willow. Others, like the baobab, scribbly gum, and monkey puzzle may be new and intriguing. As always, Florian makes use of a variety of poetic forms and arrangements of letters and words on a page. Puns abound. "The bark's a thing to bark about." A Japanese cedar seed is "ex-seed-ingly small." The book ends with a "Glossatree" providing more information about the subject of every poem. All this is illustrated in Florian's characteristic scribbly style. This playful poetry collection is a delight to the eye and the ear.

Winter Trees

Informational picture book

By Carole Gerber. Illustrated by Leslie Evans. Charlesbridge, 2008. Ages 5–9.
Subjects: Poetry, Trees, Trees in winter, Stories in rhyme, Seasons

Walking in a snowy winter woods, a boy and a dog identify seven common eastern North American trees through their shape, bark, twigs, buds, and occasionally needles and leftover leaves. "They stand distinct as skeletons. / We clearly see the form of each: / the egg shape of the maple tree; / the taller oval of the beech . . ." The quiet tone of this rhyming celebration of winter is supported by its clean, simple illustrations. Sugar maple, American beech, paper birch, yellow poplar, bur oak, Eastern hemlock, and white spruce are the trees shown, their heavy lines contrasting with the white space of the snow. A single four-line poem appears on each double-page spread; both text and appearance are suitable for the early elementary school reader, but the book could be read aloud to even younger children, even as a soothing bedtime story. Back matter adds further information.

Seeds, Bees, Butterflies, and More! Poems for Two Voices

Informational picture book

By Carole Gerber. Illustrated by Eugene Yelchin. Henry Holt & Co., 2013. Ages 4–8.

Subjects: Poetry, Plants

Eighteen poems, written for paired first-person voices, introduce processes of plant biology. Personified plants and animals describe seed distribution; plant germination; and the roles of roots, sunlight, and pollinators. Other creatures are connected to this world: bees, worms, snails, ladybugs, and monarch butterflies in three stages. Bright, colorful paintings on double-page spreads illustrate each topic. A child blows a dandelion seed; two children observe seedlings indoors. Birds eat fruit, passing the seeds. Cockleburs stick to a dog's tail. A hungry rabbit waits for a green sprout. Designed to be read aloud or even learned, these poems have short lines, comfortable rhyme, and interesting language. In the text, the two voice parts are distinguished by spacing on the page as well as by color. The possibilities for performance add savor to this taste of plant biology.

THE NATURAL WORLD

Outside Your Window: A First Book of Nature

Poetry

By Nicola Davies. Illustrated by Mark Hearld. Candlewick Press, 2012. Ages 3–8.

Subjects: Nature, Seasons

This grandly illustrated album of original poetry celebrates nature in all its variety. Over three hundred poems, organized by season, describe both small things and large. There is the natural world of the farm ("Five Reasons to Keep Chickens"), of the beach ("Tide Pooling"), and of the yard ("Dandelions"). Mostly free verse, the poems are simple and relatively short. Some, like "Pond Dipping," are instructive, others descriptive. Originally published in England, the book deals with some creatures that may not be familiar to American readers, but the images are clear. Spiderlings leave "a sea of silver." In the snow "you can hear the quiet, / as if every sound had been wrapped up and put away." Davies includes instructions for saving seeds and for making suet cakes for the birds and berry crumble for humans. Hearld's dramatic illustrations spread across the oversize pages, creating varied colors and textures with paint and collage and even some woodcuts.

Bees, Snails, & Peacock Tails: Patterns & Shapes . . . Naturally
Informational picture book

By Betsy Franco. Illustrated by Steve Jenkins. Margaret K. McElderry Books, 2008. Ages 4–7.
Subjects: Nature, Poetry

This introduction to the mathematical shapes and patterns that appear in nature is made particularly appealing by Jenkins's illustrations. From the hexagons inside a beehive to the spiral of a top shell sea snail, his cut-paper collages almost pop out from the page. He uses bright colors, intricate shapes, and textured papers to show details like the fuzz on a bee or a piece of seaweed. The simple text is written in rhyming couplets, occasionally missing a beat. Reading aloud takes practice. "New Angles on Animals" at the end adds just a bit more information about each creature. The point here is not the animals, but the demonstration of line, shape, and symmetry in the natural world, which might encourage young readers and listeners to look for patterns and forms in nature.

Step Gently Out   *Poetry*

By Helen Frost. Illustrated by Rick Lieder. Candlewick Press, 2012. Ages 2–7.
Subjects: Insects, Nature, Photographs

Frost's gentle poem about looking closely at nature has been stunningly illustrated with close-up photographs of insects and a spider. The animals are identified and described in the back matter. The pace of her text is measured. It slows the reader down to look carefully—as you want children to look when they are outside. Only the insects—honeybee, praying mantis, caterpillar, ants, cricket, moth, yellow jacket, firefly, katydid, and damselfly—are distinguishable in these images; the backgrounds are almost completely out of focus. A single exception is the orb-weaving spider, where what is obvious in the picture is the web, "splashed with morning dew." You have to look very closely to see the spider. Suffused with a sense of mystery and discovery, this is a perfect book to increase a child's sense of the wondrous creatures that "in song and dance / and stillness, / . . . share the world / with you."

What in the Wild? Mysteries of Nature Concealed . . . and Revealed: Ear-Tickling Poems
Poetry

By David M. Schwartz and Yael Schy.
    Illustrated by Dwight Kuhn. Tricycle
    Press, 2010. Ages 5–10.
Subjects: Animals, Puzzles

For nature explorers, this third in a series of puzzle-poem books offers photographs of mysteries in the natural world matched with a poem with a hint, and a hidden answer. Kuhn's close-up photographs show curious bubbles, balls, holes, and tunnel tops that serve as nests, home for developing larvae, and the residue of eating for ten different creatures. Some poems are perfect for reading aloud. "Skittery, scattery, / Gathery, chattery / Stashing my treasures / where no one can see" describes a grey squirrel. Others depend on their look on the printed page: the wavery lines of an earthworm's "Lumpy Mounds," and the filled circle of the owl's "Regurgitate" are appropriately shaped. Behind the flap there are photographs of the animal creator (sometimes both larva and adult), and a page of discussion adds information. With *Where in the Wild* (Tricycle Press, 2007) and *Where Else in the Wild* (2009, annotated earlier in this chapter), this offers an intriguing series.

Ubiquitous: Celebrating Nature's Survivors

Informational picture book

By Joyce Sidman. Illustrated by Beckie Prange. Houghton Mifflin Books for
   Children, 2010. Ages 8–12.

Subjects: Poetry, Biology, Nature

This celebration of life forms that have survived and flourished on our planet
combines poems in a variety of forms, expository informational paragraphs,
and intriguing, beautiful illustrations. Striking endpapers show a curved and
coiled time line, conveying a sense of the vast stretch of time that passed
after the formation of the earth before the first appearance of life, as bacte-
ria, and the even longer time span before the far more recent development
of mollusks, lichens, sharks, beetles, diatoms, geckos, ants, grasses, squirrels,
crows, dandelions, coyotes, and, finally, humans. Sidman has arranged her
poems in the order in which each species appeared and has carefully matched
form to subject. Her explanations are equally interesting, and the many
sources for her information are detailed in an author's note that stresses the
changing nature of scientific fact. A complex subject portrayed in an amazingly accessible way.

Swirl by Swirl: Spirals in Nature

Informational picture book; Bedtime story

By Joyce Sidman. Illustrated by Beth Krom-
   mes. Houghton Mifflin Harcourt, 2011.
   Ages 2–7.

Subjects: Poetry, Spirals, Mathematics

Scratchboard illustrations and a simple text
demonstrate that in the natural world, spiral
shapes can be snuggly and strong, useful,
graceful, and beautiful. Unusually, author and illustrator worked together to
produce this stunning shape book. A poetic text explains what spirals are;
the illustrations—black and white, shaded with color—demonstrate with
examples from throughout the natural world. Some are surprising: the defensive shape of a ram's horn, the swirl of a whirlpool. Though the narrative
might have ended with spiral galaxies, instead it returns to the snuggle that

opens the text. Squirrel and mouse curl up in their nests. That last page, with stars, swirling clouds, and sleeping animals makes an ideal ending to a realistic bedtime story. From the endpapers on, all illustrations are full of curved images. Small print labels identify interesting creatures. This is a book that will make you look at the world differently.

SOME SPECIAL TIMES AND PLACES

Animal Poems of the Iguazú: Poems
Poetry

By Francisco X. Alarcón. Illustrated by Maya Christina Gonzalez. Children's Book Press, 2008. Ages 5–12.

Subjetcs: Iguazú Falls (Argentina and Brazil), Rain forests, Animals, Nature, Bilingual books

The wonders of Iguazú National Park, a dazzling waterfall in the rain forest on the borders of Argentina, Brazil, and Paraguay, are celebrated in these twenty-six bilingual poems. Toucans, caimans, coatis, jaguars, monkeys, and more speak in their own voices, first in Spanish and then in an English translation by the Chicano author, conveying "the green voice / of the rainforest." There is some gentle humor: the hummingbird poem plays with its Spanish name, *picaflor;* and both monkeys and giant ants comment on the tourists. Gonzalez painted and cut paper for illustrations that reflect the poet's description: "in this paradise / of plants and animals / . . . every day / offers more colors / than the rainbow." With their curving shapes and varied colors, they convey the abundance of the region.

At the Sea Floor Café: Odd Ocean Critter Poems   *Poetry*

By Leslie Bulion. Illustrated by Leslie Evans. Peachtree Publishers, 2011. Ages 8–14.

Subjects: Marine animals, Humorous poetry

Opening with an invitation to "Dive in!" these eighteen poems invite readers to explore ocean wonders. From snapping shrimp to the Osedax worm that digests whalebones on the ocean floor and the ROVs that allow humans to explore that previously inaccessible world, these poems and accompanying informational text and block print illustrations make an appealing package. The poet has used a variety of forms, explained in the back matter, to craft poems notable for their language as well as their curious subjects. One piece calls for two voices, a leopard sea cucumber and an emperor shrimp. Shape poems introduce the violet snail and a swarm of krill. These poems lend themselves to reading aloud, and many are short and catchy enough to be memorized. Illustrated with block prints, this looks like a collection for young readers, but the sophisticated language and information make it suitable even for middle school.

Water Sings Blue: Ocean Poems   *Poetry*

By Kate Coombs. Illustrated by Meilo So. Chronicle Books, 2012. Ages 4–8.
Subjects: Ocean, Fish, Seashore

Coombs invites young readers into the ocean world with twenty-three short poems. Opening with "Song of the Boat" and ending with "Tideline," what she chooses to describe may surprise you. Her repetition, rhythm, rhymes, and alliteration combine with some unexpected imagery to make verses that read aloud well and stay with the listener. Allusive watercolor illustrations show tiny finds in the sand and broad seascapes, shells and coral, birds and surprising fish, jellies, sea turtles, and even a large blotch of octopus ink. A series of interesting wave patterns support "What the Waves Say." Turning the book sideways, the "Blue Whale" dives down to the "Shipwreck." There's even a poem about driftwood. A fine reminder of days at the beach.

In the Sea
Poetry

By David Elliott. Illustrated by Holly Meade.
    Candlewick Press, 2012. Ages 3–7.
Subject: Marine animals

Seventeen short poems celebrate sea creatures, from dainty sea horse to singing blue whale. The verse works. It reads aloud smoothly, with thoughtful rhymes and pleas-

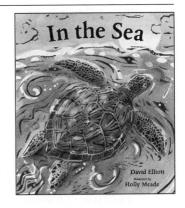

ant rhythms. It tells readers something important about the creature described, and it leaves a memorable image. Best of all, it is accompanied by beautiful watercolored woodblock illustrations, perfectly matched to the subjects. The colors of sand and sea are realistic and the creatures recognizable. These images show off animals like the toothy, ferocious moray eel, elegant orca, leaping dolphin, and spinning chambered nautilus. The sea turtle on the cover is shown inside, having arrived thirty years later on the beach where she was born. This companion volume to *In the Wild* (2010) (annotated in this chapter) and *On the Farm* (Candlewick Press, 2008) will provoke a similar sense of wonder for listeners and emerging readers alike.

Dark Emperor & Other Poems of the Night

Poetry

By Joyce Sidman. Illustrated by Rick Allen. Houghton Mifflin Harcourt, 2010. Ages 6–10.

Subjects: Night, Forest animals

Beginning and ending with spreads showing the woodland at sunset and dawn, this beautiful combination of poetry, facts, and art celebrates the night world. After an opening welcome song, each of Sidman's poems introduces a different creature. Great horned owls, spiders, crickets, and bats are familiar, but some are unusual—like the snail, primrose moth, and wandering eft. "I am a baby porcupette" describes the life of a young porcupine, left on the ground while its mother sleeps in trees during the day; they're reunited at night. Intriguingly, Sidman also describes the nocturnal activities of mushrooms and oak trees. These twelve poems vary in style and form; all work well for reading aloud. Careful observers will find even more creatures hiding in the intricate illustrations, painted linoleum block prints. Raccoons appear in several pictures and are introduced in the explanations. Playful, appealing, and informative nighttime reading.

Out of This World: Poems and Facts About Space

Informational picture book

By Amy E. Sklansky. Illustrated by
    Stacey Schuett. Alfred A. Knopf, 2012.
    Ages 5–9.
Subjects: Poetry, Outer space

"Astronaut footprints / mark the Moon's dusty surface, / lasting mementos."
Twenty short poems for young readers, illustrations ranging from photographs and early scientific drawings to paintings showing children as astronauts, and sidebars with supporting information introduce space travel and astronomy. The range of poetry is wide and includes both rhyme and free verse. One poem describes wishing on a star, another explains the sun as "fusion profusion," a third describes astronauts practicing for zero gravity. There is an acrostic about the moon and a shape poem about the universe. Each is set on a painting or digitally combined image. The informational text, vetted by an astronomer, appears in white on black along the sides of each illustration, adding to the nighttime, space exploration feel of this pleasing collection.

Forest Has a Song: Poems   *Poetry*

By Amy Ludwig VanDerwater. Illustrated by Robbin Gourley. Clarion
    Books, 2013. Ages 5–10.
Subject: Nature

This former elementary school teacher crafts poetry with staying power. Her collection of twenty-six poems about exploring the woods includes images that will linger in the reader's memory. On wintergreen: "One bit of winter / lingers in a summer leaf." Walking on moss: "toe-by-toe I squish across." These are memories, perhaps, of a series of forest visits over different times of the year. Watercolor illustrations show a young girl, sometimes with her family, and vignettes of the plants and animals she describes. There are fiddleheads, lichens, a cardinal, a squirrel. She imagines herself inside an animal's head: an owl worries about its first flight. She listens to the voices of snowflakes. She and a friend enjoy a puffball. She warns readers about poison ivy. Close observation of the natural world, thoughtful expression, and careful structure make this a collection to return to again and again.

Slither Slide, What's Outside?   *Picture book*

By Nora Hilb. Illustrated with photographs by Simon and Sheryl Shapiro. Annick Press, 2012. Ages 2–5.
Subjects: Poetry, Seasons, Nature, Play

This suggestive concept book could be a springboard for any number of imitations. Photographs of the natural world are paired with illustrations of a diverse group of children as they play, pretend, and participate in connected activities. Each illustration is explained by a poem: a rhyming couplet set as three lines, plus a final word. "Bouncing and bounding / right over the log. / Long legs are leaping—it must be a frog. / CROAK!" Whether slithering like an earthworm or making a star with friends, these actions look like fun, and are good prompts for an active read-aloud session or later games. The poems are organized through the seasons, from spring tree-planting to gliding on the winter ice. One slightly less playful note is the truck plowing a snow-covered road; at least one child has abandoned his shovel for making a snowman. Overall, an encouragement for creative nature-related play.

A Stick Is an Excellent Thing: Poems Celebrating Outdoor Play
Poetry

By Marilyn Singer. Illustrated by LeUyen Pham. Clarion Books / Houghton Mifflin Harcourt, 2012. Ages 4–8.
Subject: Play

From early morning solo ball-play to late-night stargazing, eighteen short poems celebrate summer play. There are skateboard

races, sprinklers to run through, hills to roll down, and bubbles to blow. Hopscotch, jacks, and hide-and-seek can be played with friends; swinging and catching fireflies can be done on your own. This is really a fine collection of suggestions of things to do outdoors, on city sidewalks and suburban lawns, in parks, and in the countryside. The equipment is simple and familiar; no electronics are required, but imagination helps. "Soup, soup, we're making soup / with grass and stones and mud (one scoop)." The poetry is well-written and varied, with interesting language play. The lively illustrations, drawn in pencil and ink and digitally colored, show a diverse, active group of children readers just might want to join.

NOTE

1. Alice Schertle, "Up the Bookcase to Poetry," in *A Family of Readers*, ed. Roger Sutton and Martha Parravano (Somerville, MA: Candlewick Press, 2010), 228.

Orb-weaving spider
and Galapagos hawk (Ecuador)

Chapter 13

Biography

THIS GROUP OF BOOKS DESCRIBES THE LIVES OR SOME PERIOD IN THE LIVES of men and women who are noted for observing, exploring, and preserving the natural world. Darwin's investigations were the earliest among those treated here. On his trips to the Galápagos he was functioning as a naturalist, looking at the landscape as well as its plants and animals—all the wildlife and its connections, just as more recent naturalists have done. Some of the naturalists whose biographies are annotated in this chapter are famous for studies of a particular species, but most of them have spent their lives describing the web of life in some portion of the natural world.

Biographies for young readers introduce them to a person. They can't cover whole lives in detail, but instead they often choose just a few moments in a person's life to exemplify what that person's life meant. A vivid description of an incident or a few incidents can give a sense of who the person was and why he or she might be important to the reader today. Much will be left out, of course. This is representation, not a summary. When choosing a biography, it's important to think about that selection. Do the moments the author chose accurately convey the subject's life and importance? It's just as important that the story be told in an appealing manner. A straightforward encyclopedia entry can give the facts, but vivid and telling details can provide context, feeling, and atmosphere. Humor makes a story more engaging. The illustrations can add enormously to the sense of time and place.

Readers who are already interested in the natural world can benefit from exposure to the lives of people who made that study their career. But these books also have interest for children who want to know more about a particular habitat or species and the people who first opened eyes and doors to those areas.

Into the Deep: The Life of Naturalist and Explorer William Beebe

Informational picture book; Biography

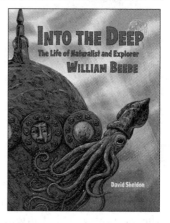

By David Sheldon. Illustrated by David Sheldon. Charlesbridge, 2009. Ages 5–9.
Subjects: Beebe, William, 1877–1962; Zoologists; Explorers

Famous deep-sea diver William Beebe began as a bird collector, but decided he'd rather study them in the wild. A trip to the Galápagos Islands ignited his interest in sea life and prompted the record-breaking dive for which he's most known today. A colleague, Otis Barton, invented a diving vessel they called a bathysphere in which they descended over three thousand feet in 1934, seeing things no one had seen before. Acrylic paintings capture the feeling of their dive. In dim blue light the two men peer out from the capsule. From outside, the tiny vessel is surrounded by toothy animals and mysterious dots of light in the inky deep-sea blackness. This picture book biography is illustrated with images of plants and animals in all kinds of environments, conveying this early ecologist's excitement about the natural world as well as his passion to share his interest.

Rachel Carson and Her Book That Changed the World

Biography

By Laurie Lawlor. Illustrated by Laura
    Beingessner. Holiday House, 2012.
    Ages 7–10.

Subjects: Carson, Rachel, 1907–1964;
    Women; Biologists; Environmentalists

Naturalist and writer from a very early age, Rachel Carson published several
well-known books about the natural world, culminating in the best-selling
and world-changing *Silent Spring*. This picture book biography stresses her
connection with nature, opening with an iconic scene in which the young
Rachel follows a yellowthroat to its nest and takes a picture. It tells how she
cared for other family members much of her life, including adopting a five-
year-old nephew, Roger. The illustrations show Carson at home and at work
and also enjoying the natural world, especially on the Maine coast. There are
a few anachronisms in the pictures, but the narrative smoothly tells Carson's
story, right up to her early death. The back matter explains what happened
after the book's appearance in 1962 and includes excellent source notes.

The Fantastic Undersea Life of Jacques Cousteau

Informational picture book; Biography

By Dan Yaccarino. Illustrated by Dan Yaccarino. Alfred A. Knopf, 2009.
    Ages 5–9.

Subjects: Cousteau, Jacques, 1910–1997; Oceanographers

From a sickly boyhood in which swimming was therapeutic, Jacques Cousteau grew up to become a man who loved the sea, exploring it extensively,
inventing new tools and equipment, and sharing his discoveries through
books, films, and TV. With a simple text, no more than a paragraph a page,
Yaccarino highlights the oceanographer's career, ending with his realization
of threats to his beloved underwater world and his founding of the Cousteau
Society. Appropriate quotations from his writings appear in bubbles on occasional pages. There is much to look at in the stylized illustrations: cartoon-
like drawings of the scrawny, tinkering boy as well as Cousteau and his
crew; double-page underwater spreads; a busy set of lights, cameras, and

equipment; and, over and over, the variety of creatures he encountered in the underwater world. A bibliography and chronological list of events complete this enthusiastic introduction to this renowned scientist.

Darwin

Informational picture book; Biography

By Alice B. McGinty. Illustrated by Mary Azarian.
   Houghton Mifflin Harcourt, 2009. Ages 8–12.
Subjects: Darwin, Charles, 1809–1882; Naturalists

Looking at this beautifully illustrated biography of the noted naturalist, one might almost imagine opening one of Darwin's own leather-bound journals. Inside, a clear conversational narrative describes his life from childhood through his famous Beagle voyage, to his years of work on his theory of natural selection and then to his eventual success. The text is accompanied by detailed woodcut illustrations, hand-tinted with watercolors, as well as quotations from the naturalist's own writings, presented in script on scraps of yellowed paper. From the fossil on the title page to the Galápagos finch on the closing copyright page, illustrative vignettes sprinkled around the text add to the story. The author emphasizes Darwin's passion for collecting and experimentation. She addresses, but doesn't dwell on, his hesitations to publish his controversial ideas, so at odds with church teachings. From the many Darwin titles published to mark his anniversary, this one is particularly appealing.

Life in the Ocean: *Informational picture book; Biography*
The Story of Sylvia Earle

By Claire A. Nivola. Illustrated by Claire A. Nivola. Frances Foster Books /
   Farrar Straus Giroux, 2012. Ages 5–10.
Subjects: Earle, Sylvia A., 1935–; Marine biologists; Explorers

Oceanographer Sylvia Earle has spent more than seven thousand hours underwater exploring the "blue heart of the planet," staying longer and going deeper than ever before to discover the wonders of that relatively unknown world. Neither a formal biography nor a scientific description, this celebrates the wonder of Earle's engagement with the natural world, as a child and as an adult. Nivola's colorful and intricately detailed illustrations show the different kinds of equipment she used, as well as the creatures she sees and hears. One striking image shows a tiny Earle, wearing scuba equipment, being observed by a huge humpback whale. Another spread makes the ocean depths look like nighttime stars. An introduction stresses the importance of the ocean and an author's note, surrounded by labeled portraits of beautiful sea creatures, discusses modern-day threats. As a show-and-tell or read-alone, this has appeal for a wide age range.

Me . . . Jane

Picture book; Biography

By Patrick McDonnell. Illustrated by
    Patrick McDonnell. Little, Brown, 2011.
    Ages 3–7.
Subjects: Goodall, Jane, 1934–; Childhood
    and youth; Primatologists; England

Jane and her stuffed chimpanzee watched animals and plants in her backyard and learned about them in books. She dreamed of growing up to watch animals in Africa . . . and she did. Only at the end of this wonderfully paced story does the author-illustrator reveals his subject, with a touching photograph of Jane Goodall and a live chimpanzee. Ink-and-watercolor cartoons are supplemented by some of Goodall's own work. The reader seems to be looking back into her life and memories. Ornamental engravings underlie a simple text on the opposing pages. These images support the story's old-fashioned feel. Even though only a few scenes are shown, the reader feels connected to this famous scientist. An author's note and message from Goodall at the end will help children understand how important she has been in our world. Pair this with Winter's *The Watcher* (Schwartz & Wade Books, 2011, annotated below) as complementary approaches to a wondrous life.

The Watcher: Jane
Goodall's Life with the Chimps

Informational picture book; Biography

By Jeanette Winter. Illustrated by Jeanette Winter. Schwartz & Wade
 Books, 2011. Ages 4–8.
Subjects: Goodall, Jane, 1934–; Primatologists; England; Chimpanzees;
 Tanzania

From childhood, Jane Goodall loved to watch animals, both in her yard
and in the wild. She grew up to have the patience to watch chimpanzees in
Tanzania and the ability to speak for them. There, she documented behavior
that had never been seen before. The illustrations, done with acrylic paint
and pen, are clean and sharp-edged, flat with no shadows. The pictures of
the naturalist's childhood are displayed in a box, with just a bit of the illustration escaping into the complementary-colored page background. When
she gets to Tanzania, these pictures open into double-page spreads that show
a grand variety of chimpanzee behavior. Still, there's a quiet tone to both
words and pictures, appropriate to her activity. This "brave woman who
wasn't afraid to do something that had never been done before" provides an
extraordinary example for young readers and listeners.

In the Belly of an Ox: The Unexpected
Photographic Adventures of Richard
and Cherry Kearton

Informational picture book

By Rebecca Bond. Illustrated by Rebecca Bond. Houghton Mifflin Books for
 Children, 2009. Ages 5–9.
Subjects: Kearton, Cherry, 1871–1940; Kearton, Richard, 1862–1928; Wild-
 life photographers; Great Britain; Wildlife photography; Bird-watching

Missing the Yorkshire countryside of their late nineteenth-century childhood, the Kearton brothers often returned there from London, where they
worked, to photograph birds' nests in the early mornings. Constructing ever
more elaborate hides and traveling around the country, they produced, in
1895, the first photographic guide to nests, eggs, and birds in their natural
surroundings. This biographical vignette is gently told in short lines that are
a pleasure to read aloud. Bond makes particularly effective use of watercolors to show the expanses of countryside and adding details with pen and
brown ink. This is a charming glimpse into that world. The contrast between

the busy, built-up city and the countryside will help readers understand the pull of the Yorkshire moors, full of fascinating living things to study. Two pages at the end show a selection of photographs taken by these two remarkable naturalists.

The Goose Man:
The Story of Konrad Lorenz

Informational picture book; Biography

By Elaine Greenstein. Illustrated by Elaine
    Greenstein. Clarion Books, 2009. Ages 5–9.
Subjects: Lorenz, Konrad, 1903–1989;
    Ethologists; Biography; Geese

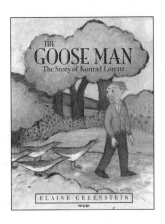

A childhood fascination with ducks and geese serves as the opening hook for a biography of Konrad Lorenz, the Nobel Prize–winning scientist whose studies of his pet goose, Martina, and other animals, led to important new findings about animal behavior. Summarizing the life and work of this famous ethologist in language appropriate to young readers, Greenstein uses simple sentences, with plenty of repetition. She introduces the ideas of imprinting and instinct but does not use those exact words except in a note at the end. Her illustrations feature a pastel palette, simple composition, flattened perspective, and primitive style, adding a childlike effect. For the beginning reader, they offer clues to the text, demonstrating the story being told. The author's focus on Lorenz's pets makes this scientific biography accessible for the intended audience.

Summer Birds: The
Butterflies of Maria Merian

Informational picture book; Biography

By Margarita Engle. Illustrated by Julie Paschkis. Henry Holt & Co., 2010.
    Ages 5–8.
Subjects: Merian, Maria Sibylla, 1647–1717; Caterpillars; Butterflies—meta-
    morphosis

In medieval Europe, butterflies were thought to come from mud. In this imagined first-person account, thirteen-year-old Maria Merian describes how she captured and observed them, painting their life cycles from caterpillar through chrysalis to beautiful "summer birds," and dispelled the mystery around their metamorphosis. An afterword gives more information about this seventeenth-century naturalist, a woman ahead of her time. The bright colors, curving lines, and fanciful detail of the illustrator's paintings are particularly well suited for a book demonstrating the movement from a view of nature as mysterious, magical, and possibly evil toward appreciation and more modern understanding. At first, her images show whimsical butterflies hatching in mud or being created by odd, unsettling beings; later, they become more accurate. This is basic science fact and science history in a delightful, appealing combination.

John Muir: America's First Environmentalist

Informational picture book; Biography

By Kathryn Lasky. Illustrated by Stanley
    Fellows. Candlewick Press, 2006.
    Ages 7–10.
Subjects: Muir, John, 1838–1914;
    Naturalists; Conservationists

Nineteenth-century environmentalist John
Muir was instrumental in preserving the
natural world of this country, promoting the establishment of national parks and the founding of the Sierra Club. In her chronologically organized biography, Lasky emphasizes Muir's impressive travels, often on foot. From Scotland to Wisconsin to Canada during the Civil War, from Florida, California, Alaska, and back to California's Yosemite, he explored the countryside. He experimented with inventions, wrote up his observations, and convinced movers and shakers to set up measures to protect the wilderness. The straightforward text is presented on a background of paintings showing the boy and the gradually aging man, often in his beloved natural world. Double page spreads demonstrate the glory of northern lights in Wisconsin, the magnitude of the Sierra peaks, the danger of a narrow ice bridge across a glacial crevasse in Alaska, as well as the comforts of camp and dog. Beautiful.

For the Birds: The Life of Roger Tory Peterson

Informational picture book; Biography

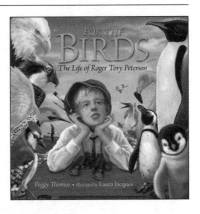

By Peggy Thomas. Illustrated by
Laura Jacques. Calkins Creek, 2011.
Ages 7–10.

Subjects: Peterson, Roger Tory; Ornithologists; Naturalists; Bird-watching

The love of nature comes naturally to some children. Roger Tory Peterson was such a child. His classmates called him "Professor Nuts," but they recognized his abilities and a teacher encouraged his interests. Peterson invented a system for identifying birds by their "uniform" and, as a young adult, wrote the first modern field guide. This picture book biography tells his story in some detail and illustrates it with hyperrealistic paintings, sketches, and bird silhouettes that would make a grand identification game. The author uses language appropriate to her subject, describing Peterson's "prominent beak," his "leaving the nest," and the "flock of friends" who completed his final field guide revision. The endpapers include some of Peterson's own sketches and a "topography of a birder" done as if it were a page in a field guide. A graceful, loving, and inspiring description of an extraordinary naturalist.

Down the Colorado: John Wesley Powell, the One-Armed Explorer

Informational picture book; Biography

By Deborah Kogan Ray. Illustrated by Deborah Kogan Ray. Francis Foster
Books / Farrar, Straus, Giroux, 2007. Ages 8–12.

Subjects: Powell, John Wesley, 1834–1902; Explorers—West (U.S.); Colorado River (Colorado-Mexico)—discovery and exploration; West (U.S.)—discovery and exploration

In spite of losing an arm in the Civil War, Powell continued his lifetime passion to explore the natural world, most notably leading an expedition down the Colorado River, the first ever recorded to pass through the Grand Canyon. This picture-book biography is notable for its well-crafted story.

After briefly covering his childhood and Civil War service, the author concentrates on that expedition, emphasizing its danger and difficulty. The suspense is heightened by the use of double-page spreads where the reader sees small boats and churning rapids and, worse, Powell clinging to the rock face high above the river. Ray's dramatic paintings make liberal use of shades of brown and red; their colors blend into the yellowed paper of the text pages. Organized chronologically and topically, the text is lengthy for a picture book and suitable for middle-grade readers, who will appreciate the map and time line.

The Camping Trip That Changed America: Theodore Roosevelt, John Muir, and Our National Parks
Informational picture book; Biography

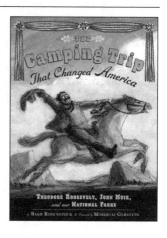

By Barbara Rosenstock. Illustrated by Mordicai
    Gerstein. Dial Books for Young Readers,
    2012. Ages 7–10.
Subjects: Roosevelt, Theodore, 1858–1919;
    California; Muir, John, 1838–1914;
    Yosemite National Park (California)—
    history; National parks and reserves—
    United States history; Environmentalism—United States history;
    Environmental protection

After reading John Muir's book about vanishing forests, Teddy Roosevelt, already president of the United States, asked the famous naturalist to take him camping in Yosemite. The result was a splendid trip, imagined here, that prompted the president to push for laws that would save the wilderness. Details of the camping trip include the first night's luxury—for Roosevelt— and subsequent roughing it, a bear story (no grizzlies roam the area now), the glacial origins of the Yosemite Valley, a snowstorm, and a horseback ride into the scenic valley under towering sequoias. (Turn the book sideways to see how tall.) Gerstein's appealing illustrations have plenty of humor, and some are recreated from photographs. This book captures a moment that was emblematic of who the two men were and important to the development of our national park system.

Strange Creatures:
The Story of Walter Rothschild
and His Museum

Informational picture book; Biography

By Lita Judge. Illustrated by Lita Judge. Disney / Hyperion, 2011.
  Ages 5–9.
Subjects: Rothschild, Lionel Walter Rothschild, Baron, 1868–1937;
  Zoologists

For young animal collectors, Walter Rothschild's life must seem a dream.
A shy child who had trouble speaking, this son of Queen Victoria's banker
was passionately interested in animals, beginning a collection of exotic creatures while still a child, and growing up to use his family's fortune to collect around the world, studying unknown species, and establishing a still-
standing museum. Some invented dialog helps the author connect this biography to a child reader's world, but it is her lighthearted illustrations that
bring it to life. Seussian animal faces peer from the endpapers. A formally
dressed small boy explores the family's acres of gardens on his velocipede.
Toward the end, in top hat and tails and wearing a monocle, the now-grown
Lord Rothschild rides a tortoise. An author's note tells us that animal science
is pursued differently these days, but it certainly looks like he had fun!

If You Spent a Day
with Thoreau at Walden Pond

Informational picture book

By Robert Burleigh. Illustrated by Wendell Minor. Henry Holt & Co., 2012.
  Ages 5–9.
Subject: Thoreau, Henry David, 1817–1862

This charming picture book introduces the ideas for which Thoreau is most
famous through a child reader's imagined visit to nineteenth-century philos-
opher. Endpapers set the stage with an artistic map of Walden Pond, showing some of its highlights. Burleigh draws readers in by addressing them
directly. If you met Thoreau in his tiny cabin, he would lead you through
a day of out-of-doors wonders. There is rowing on the pond, wading in
the water, weeding the bean patch, following a fox, listening to birds, and
watching an ant war. There are appealing tastes as well as sights and sounds:
fresh cold water and huckleberries and homemade bread. This trip back in

time is further brought to life by expressive paintings, showing the visitor in modern clothes exploring Thoreau's natural world from early morning until dusk. Who could resist this invitation?

Examining a beach treasure

Chapter 14

Children's Songs
and Traditional Tales

THE TITLES IN THIS SHORT SECTION RANGE FROM TRADITIONAL CHILDREN'S songs and stories to folk tales and biblical teachings. There is quite a long tradition of turning fables, folklore, and songs into children's books, but these stood out for their use of particular, identifiable settings. Some are realistic: Pinkney's animals could leap right out of the pages. Some, like DePaola's Mexico and the Kuru Art Project's Botswana, are more abstract. But all convey a sense of a particular natural place.

There are some special considerations for evaluating these kinds of books. Traditional stories come from somewhere. There should be notes that indicate where the author got the text and how (or at least whether) he or she has adapted it. Illustrator notes matter, too. Why did the illustrator set this story in this particular time or place? If a song book includes music, has it been written out accurately in a way that could be played (or at least the melody picked out) and sung?

From lullabies and familiar stories to original folklore, these are a reminder that traditional material can often be presented in fresh and original ways.

Let the Whole Earth Sing Praise   *Picture book*

By Tomie DePaola. Illustrated by Tomie DePaola. G. P. Putnam's Sons, 2011. Ages 3–7.

Subjects: Creation, Biblical teaching, Nature, Religion

Following the biblical order of creation, DePaola offers a hymn of praise joyfully illustrated with folk art–inspired designs on tea-stained paper. Like his earlier *The Song of Francis* (Putnam, 2009) this reworks Old Testament scripture, here, the *Benedicite* from the Book of Daniel and Psalm 148 (*Laudate*). The stylized imagery "echoes the beautiful folk art embroideries and naive designs of the Otomi people from the mountain villages around San Pablito in Puebla, Mexico," the author explains. Hand-lettered, with each line large on a double-page spread, the text is surrounded by designs representing the content. From sun and stars through lightning and clouds, fruitful trees, whales, birds, and "all people, / young and old," it reminds readers to "bless and praise God." The abstract art is allusive, not representational, but delightful small details contribute to the sense of playful celebration.

All Things Bright and Beautiful
Picture book; Songs

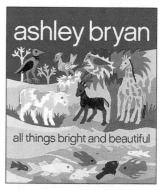

By Ashley Bryan and Cecil Frances Alexander. Illustrated by Ashley Bryan. Atheneum Books for Young Readers, 2010. Ages 2–8.

Subjects: Children's poetry, English, Christianity, Nature, Hymns, Creation

Bryan's exuberant illustrations—cut-paper collages featuring hundreds of animals, people of all sizes and colors, landscapes, and glorious, sun-filled skies—give new life to a familiar hymn. Swirling, curving shapes make a backdrop for a lavish garden, an ocean full of sea creatures, even a book from which sprouts a savannah. "Each little flower that opens, / Each little bird that sings, / He made their glowing colors, / He made their tiny wings." The human figures celebrate; the birds do seem to sing. God's hands—with at least ten different flesh tones—illustrate the final line: "The Lord God made them all." Appended is a short biography of the poetess, Cecil Alexander, and music and words for singing. The endpapers feature Bryan's mother's sewing scissors, used to make these stunning images. Though the poem comes from Christian tradition, this wonderful combination of old and new has relevance for many faiths.

Mouse & Lion

Picture book; Fable

By Rand Burkert. Illustrated by Nancy Ekholm Burkert. Scholastic, 2011. Ages 3–8.
Subjects: Folklore, Lion, Mice

A glorious retelling of Aesop's fable, lushly presented with Nancy Burkert's intricate drawings, setting the story in the Aha Hills on the border of Botswana and Namibia in southern Africa. These extraordinary illustrations use soft colors and emphasize the space around the animals as well as the details of their bodies and coloration. Both landscapes and close-ups emphasize this distinctive habitat. These illustrations are complementary to Jerry Pinkney's version, described below, which was set in the Serengeti Plain two thousand miles northeast. But, while Pinkney's is near wordless, Rand's retelling employs terrific language. Mouse is the star of this version. "At sunrise, Mouse hopped out of his nest and sniffed. . . . He found Lion in a sorry tangle, panting beneath the baobab tree." There are good author's and illustrator's notes and information about the research.

The Lion & the Mouse   *Picture book; Fable*

By Jerry Pinkney and Aesop. Illustrated by Jerry Pinkney. Little, Brown, 2009. Ages 3–8.
Subjects: Folklore, Lion, Mice, Cooperation, Stories without words

In his Caldecott Medal–winning rendition of the familiar fable, Pinkney uses only animal sounds and his amazing ability to make animals come alive on a page. There are double-page spreads for the lordly lion free on the Serengeti plain and smaller pictures for the mouse (especially at home with her many babies) and for the lion after it gets trapped. On the boards under the paper cover, the lion and mouse share space in a rebus title on the front, while a large group of African savannah animals pose together on the back, in a scene reminiscent of Edward Hicks's "Peaceable Kingdom." Even prereaders can follow the story and admire the tiny details of the animals' world: butterflies on blades of grass and the onlooking birds and baboons. The endpapers show the amazing Serengeti wildlife on the front, and the lion and mouse families together on the back. It will make you want to be there.

The Tortoise & the Hare   *Picture book; Fable*

By Jerry Pinkney. Illustrated by Jerry Pinkney. Little, Brown, 2013. Ages 3–8. *Subjects:* Folklore, American Southwest, Animals

Pinkney continues his pattern of connecting traditional children's stories with the natural world, setting a near-wordless version of this Aesop's fable in the American Southwest. These lively pages are filled with recognizable animals, clothed just enough to be seen against a desert background. Endpapers set the stage: a dry landscape with flowering cactus plants and a weatherbeaten farm. The hare challenges the tortoise on the title page; a gray fox officiates. A toad keeps the tortoise company, but a variety of animals cheer them along. But there's the farmer's tempting garden; the hare stops for a snack and falls asleep. The steady tortoise tumbles down a hill to end up ahead at the finish line. Satisfyingly, the hare ties the winner's kerchief on his victorious friend. The words "slow" and "slow and steady" repeat themselves; this book's audience will want to take it slowly, too, to enjoy every detail.

Rainbow Crow / Nagweyaabi-Aandeg
Folklore

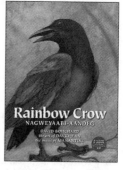

By David Bouchard. Illustrated by David Jean. Red
  Deer Press, 2012. Ages 7–11.
Subjects: Lenape Indians, Fire, Crows, Bilingual
  books

In words, pictures, and an audio CD, a Métis storyteller tells how Little Crow brought the gift of fire "before two-leggeds walked on Mother Earth." In doing so, he sacrificed his colors and beautiful song for the shiny black feathers and croak we know. Origin stories remind us that humans have always wondered at the natural world. This one is told in the style of Bouchard's Lenape grandmother and in several languages—English and Ojibwe in the edition described here, and English, Ojibwe, and French, with musical accompaniment, on the included CD. Lifelike animal portraits painted on traditional drumheads illustrate the story. The Creator who provides the gift for animals suffering from winter's cold is depicted as Native American. The unhurried narrative can be appreciated by very young listeners as well as middle-grade children able to read the text.

There Was a Tree

Picture book; Songs

By Rachel Isadora. Illustrated by Rachel Isadora. Nancy Paulsen Books / Penguin Group, 2012. Ages 3–7.

Subjects: Nature, Rebuses, African wildlife, Savannah

The green grass grows all around in the African savannah in this version of the cumulative song. A superb starling is the bird in its speckled egg in the nest on the tree. Among the bright oranges and greens of the grassland worlds are animals that live there: lions, vervet monkeys, giraffes, elephants, rhinoceroses, gemsboks, zebras, and wildebeests. Finally, two children stand under the acacia tree in the sunset. Painted and collage illustrations are framed in kente cloth and geometric designs. Using rebuses as well as words, the author turns the lyrics into a game for near-readers. Sheet music and the text are appended for those who want to be able to sing along. Plenty of picture books use this familiar folk song, but the setting and the participation possibilities make this one distinctive.

Twinkle, Twinkle, Little Star   *Picture book; Songs*

By Jane Cabrera. Illustrated by Jane Cabrera. Holiday House, 2012. Ages 3–6.

Subjects: Nursery rhymes, Poetry, Lullabies, Stars, Animals

As part of her long series of illustrated nursery rhymes and songs, Cabrera expands and illustrates "Twinkle, Twinkle" with parent-and-child pairs of animals in their expected habitats all over the world. Unlike Jerry Pinkney's version (2011, annotated next), which imagines a chipmunk's adventures and uses several of the original verses, Cabrera adapts the first verse to meet the experiences of a variety of animals. Deer see it "peeking through the silent trees," whales from the water, kangaroos find it "smiling down on desert dry," and for polar bears on ice floes it is "lighting up the cold night sky." She uses different verbs, too: "sparkle," "flicker," "shimmer," and "glisten." The familiar song becomes a celebration of animals in the natural world, concluding with a blonde mother and child. Music and chords appear on the endpaper, for those who wish to sing the song.

Twinkle, Twinkle, Little Star   *Picture book*

By Jane Taylor. Illustrated by Jerry Pinkney. Little, Brown, 2011. Ages 3–6.
Subjects: Nursery rhymes, Stars, Poetry, Lullabies, Chipmunk

A chipmunk's journey through the twilight world and the dream world illustrates the familiar nursery song. Stars are everywhere in this imaginative recreation, from the morning glories that surround the chipmunk's hole on the title page to the night sky on the back endpapers. Following a starry dandelion seed, the chipmunk explores his world, ending up in an empty robin's nest. From there, he ventures into dreamland, sailing a boat into the night sky, landing on a lily pad, and sinking under the water of a stream, only to emerge on a swan that flies him to the moon. The details of the chipmunk's natural world are lovingly rendered by this accomplished illustrator who did much of his observation from his own Westchester, New York, studio window. The chipmunk's sense of wonder at the world around him can't help but arouse the same feeling in the reader.

Ostrich and Lark
Picture book

By Marilyn Nelson. Illustrated by Kuru Art
    Project. Boyds Mills Press, 2012. Ages 4–7.
Subject: Ostriches, Larks, Botswana,
    Southern Africa

Lark and other veld creatures sing every day, while ostrich stays quiet. But one evening he finally finds his booming voice. This original folktale by an award-winning poet is illustrated with naïve paintings by six San artists Nelson met on a trip to Botswana, in southern Africa. More evocative than meaningful, the narrative celebrates the natural world of their homeland, the glaring sun, the termite castle, the acacia trees, and the many different creatures—plant eaters, meat eaters, insects, and birds. "Every day, all day, / over the cicada's drone, / a drizzle of buzzings fell, / and a downpour of birdsong." The muted greens and reds of the background, the edges with a zig-zag pattern on the side frames, and the gently curved lines, dots, and stripes all evoke that part of the world and complement the story line.

Story time

Chapter 15

Books for Babies
and Toddlers

IT'S NEVER TOO EARLY TO BEGIN SHARING BOOKS WITH CHILDREN. THE TWO-
month-old baby in the photograph at the beginning of this chapter already
seems to be looking as well as listening. And the comfortable cuddling that
goes along with this experience makes it extra special.

Books for babies and toddlers have specific characteristics: a tight focus,
clear, easy to recognize illustrations, and simple language. Many of the
books annotated in previous chapters have those qualities and can be shared
with very young children who will enjoy the illustrations and the sound of
well-chosen words. Home, babies and families, and, a little later, friendship
are themes that work well. This chapter lists titles I thought had particular
appeal for children age three and under, but they might also work well for
older children. (Some make excellent beginning readers.) They have bold
illustrations, often including faces. They may inspire actions or choral repetition; toddlers love to follow a story with their whole body. I have included

a group of counting books because counting begins very early even if number-to-object correspondence takes longer.

Some of the titles have been republished recently as board books, and I have mentioned where others come in that practical format as well. The advantage of a board book is obvious: even toddlers can handle and enjoy it in their own ways. However, converting a picture book to a board book can have disadvantages, too. It often involves combining some pages and dropping some pictures. The original shape and size will have been reduced, and pages may feel cramped or crowded. Such changes make the story less effective. Accordingly, I have only recommended board books when I have seen them in that format and think they work.

COUNTING BOOKS

One Gorilla: A Counting Book
Counting book

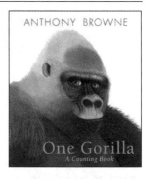

By Anthony Browne. Illustrated by Anthony
    Browne. Candlewick Press, 2013. Ages 2–7.
Subjects: Primates, Animals

From one gorilla to ten lemurs and on to the artist himself, realistic and detailed primate portraits
demonstrate the variety of their facial features
and expressions, hair, and skin color. This oversized and beautifully presented album is both a counting book and an introduction to primates: apes,
monkeys of several kinds, lemurs, and the human family. Browne's carefully
crafted portraits show familiar facial expressions and seem to endow his
subjects with personality. A red-haired orangutan looks fondly at her child;
a chimpanzee parent poses with twins. As the groups get larger and larger,
the variety of faces looks very much like a group family portrait, with some
members already distracted and bored. A striking and surprising counting
book with a clear final message: "All primates. / All one family. / All my
family . . . / and yours!"

This Tree, 1, 2, 3

Board book; Counting book

By Alison Formento. Illustrated by Sarah Snow. Albert Whitman & Co.,
2011. Ages 0–3.

Subjects: Trees, Schools

An abridged version of *This Tree Counts!* (2010, annotated in chapter 8), this
board book retains the best parts—the counting and the cheerful pictures of
creatures that live on and around the tree. From one owl sitting in the
branches to ten earthworms munching soil around its roots, a tall tree counts
the animals that make a home in and around it for a group of children and
one adult who stand listening. Colorfully illustrated with collage and paint,
the images are clear and recognizable. The tree bark is realistic. The spiders,
caterpillars, flies, and ladybugs all look like themselves. There are squirrels
and robins, too. Simple, short sentences and phrases describe actions and
sounds: ants march, crickets chirp. Appealing and appropriate for the age
group.

Ten Little Caterpillars

Counting book

By Bill Martin. Illustrated by Lois Ehlert. Beach
Lane Books, 2011. Ages 2–7.

Subjects: Stories in rhyme, Caterpillars, Insects

This oversized counting book introduces ten
different caterpillars, each on its own expedition. The last one finds just the right spot to
rest until it becomes a butterfly. Ehlert's strik-

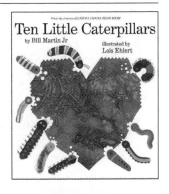

ing cut-paper-and-watercolor images on an expanse of white almost pop off
the page. Though stylized, these illustrations are surprisingly realistic. The
monarch caterpillar has been "carried off to school" in a jar with milkweed
leaves. The back matter identifies each caterpillar, describing their usual
food and showing the resulting butterfly or moth. The large type and simple
sentences suit the youngest readers. From mourning cloak to tiger swallowtail, the species described can be found across North America.

BABY ANIMALS

Where Is Baby?   *Informational picture book*

By Kathryn Osebold Galbraith. Illustrated by John Butler. Peachtree, 2013.
   Ages 2–5.
Subjects: Baby animals, Animals—defenses

Human and animal babies are alike in that they know how to hide, and their
mothers know where to find them. A simple, single line of text is set on each
double-page illustration, close-ups of wide-eyed baby animals, not at all hidden, but in their appropriate environments. These meticulously rendered,
visually appealing paintings are done with soft colors and subtle textures.
The animals include baby deer, rabbits, robins, leopards, river otters, polar
bears, elephants, prairie dogs, wolves, bats, ostriches, and a small child who
shares his living space with a dog, kitten, cat, and playful, loving mother. A
foldout page comes as a surprise at the end, and is followed by end matter:
a repetition of the animal pictures and a paragraph of further information
about each one, including what it's called and an interesting fact about its
infancy. Sure to prompt a peek-a-boo game in listeners.

Little White Rabbit
Picture book

By Kevin Henkes. Illustrated by Kevin Henkes.
   Greenwillow Books, 2011. Ages 2–7.
Subjects: Rabbits, Baby animals

Henkes is a master of representing the interests and concerns of a small child, usually in
the form of animals. Here, little white rabbit
explores the world wondering what it would be like to be different—green,
tall, solid, or able to fly—but when he comes home he knows who loves
him. This satisfyingly circular story of exploring the world outdoors is spring
green on the paper cover, but the boards are a surprising pink. The pastel palette makes it a perfect spring book. The rounded shapes are gentle,
even with their solid outlines, and show well to a small group when read
aloud. Listeners will want to act out the things rabbit sees: fluttering but-

terfly wings, stretching tall as a tree, and staying still as a rock. Little white rabbit's curiosity is contagious.

My First Day   *Informational picture book*

By Steve Jenkins and Robin Page. Illustrated by Steve Jenkins. Houghton Mifflin, 2013. Ages 2–7.

Subject: Baby animals

How can anyone resist an array of animal babies? Here, twenty-two adorable little ones describe what they did on their very first day of life. From the kicking kiwi to the snuggling polar bear, each page or spread shows a different species. The focus is on the baby; sometimes parents or parts of parents are also visible against a plain background whose color may suggest the animal's environment. A short, read-aloud text describes the animal's initial abilities and level of parental care. There are familiar species, like giraffes and zebras, and unusual ones like tapir and megapodes (chicken-like birds from Australia). Each illustration includes a label. The pictures are reproduced in thumbnails in the back matter along with further information about where the animal can be found, how big it grows, and other behaviors. A treat to share with even the youngest listeners.

Hello, Baby Beluga *Informational picture book; Bedtime story; Early reader*

By Darrin P. Lunde. Illustrated by Patricia Wynne. Charlesbridge, 2011. Ages 2–5.

Subjects: White whale, Arctic mammals, Baby animals

Baby beluga introduces itself through its answers to questions from the young reader. This is the third in a series by a pair of American Museum of Natural History employees introducing uncommon animals to preschoolers. The increased public attention to Arctic animals makes this one particularly timely. The simple format addresses exactly the kind of thing youngsters want to know: What's your name? What do you look like? Where do you live? How do you sound? What do you eat? There is nothing fearful here; even the polar bear predator is safely at a distance. Wynne's softly rounded creatures have cheerful, smiling faces. Her watercolors are simple, but accurate, showing the whales, often in groups and surrounded by floating ice in the blue Arctic waters. This useful bedtime story for the young naturalist ends, fittingly, with a "Good night." *Hello, Mama Wallaroo* (2013) is annotated later in this chapter. *Hello, Bumblebee Bat* (annotated in chapter 11) and *Meet the Meerkat* were published by Charlesbridge in 2007.

Owlet's First Flight   *Picture book; Bedtime story*

By Mitra Modarressi. Illustrated by Mitra Modarressi. G. P. Putnam's Sons, 2012. Ages 2–5.
Subjects: Stories in rhyme, Owls, Flight, Fear of the dark

Fearful at first of setting out on his own, Little Owl braves a first nighttime flight. The scary shadows on the ground turn out to be tree branches; the popping noise just acorns falling. And there are other animals abroad at night, too. Readers will enjoy finding the squirrels, asleep in their nest, the kitten in the barn window, and the raccoons helping themselves to the corn from the basket they tipped over. At dawn, owlet returns to his heart-shaped hole in the tree, ready to go to sleep with his mother and siblings. Expressive owl faces translate animal emotions into human ones. The gentle rhyming

Toddler Activities

- Put mud in an aluminum pan or dishpan and let the child make handprints or, better, footprints. After they dry, compare them to animal tracks.
- Be a bird: fly (with scarves or arms for wings), eat with a beak (two fingers), make a nest.
- Trace the child's shadow with chalk on the sidewalk. Is it different in the morning and at night?
- Make a guessing game with a basket of natural materials and ask your blindfolded child to guess what you are holding by the smell.
- Walk like specific animals. (After a day at the zoo this can be a grand guessing game, too.)
- Make rock towers and art images with natural materials. Leaves put on paper covered with thick wet poster or finger paint will dry and stick.
- Walk in the rain and jump in puddles.
- Smell the flowers.
- **Go outside!**

text and muted watercolor illustrations add to the quiet feel of this sweet bedtime story which may reflect, and calm, some children's fears.

Little Owl's Night

Picture book; Bedtime story

By Divya Srinivasan. Illustrated by Divya Srinivasan. Viking Children's Books, 2011. Ages 2–5.

Subjects: Owls, Night, Forests and forestry, Forest animals

Here's an inverted bedtime story celebrating nocturnal animals and the beauties of the night. During Little Owl's wonderful night in the forest he watches night animals, including Hedgehog and Skunk; visits his friend Raccoon and the sleeping bear; hears Frog and Cricket; and listens to his mother describe dawn as he falls asleep. The writer-illustrator populates her shiny black pages with stylized animals with recognizable features and large eyes. Little Owl doesn't only enjoy seeing his friends. He admires the fog, the silver dust falling from moth wings, and the moon. Stars twinkle in the skies. Mama reminds him that the night has special plants, too. When dawn comes, "Moonflowers close and morning glories open." The endpapers reveal that even more goes on at night. The lyrical text of this gentle and appealing nighttime treat merits repeated readings.

Polar Bear Morning

Picture book

By Lauren Thompson. Illustrated by Stephen Savage. Scholastic Press, 2013. Ages 2–5.

Subjects: Polar bear, Bears, Friendship

Exploring his Arctic environment, a polar bear cub meets another cub covered with snow, a playmate for a joyful morning. "Snow, sea, and ice, and wide, blue sky" is the world Savage recreates in this appealing companion to the pair's *Polar Bear Night,* annotated next. Where the first was an award-winning celebration of home, this title celebrates friendship. And they both celebrate the bears' far-north surroundings. Here, the text and block print illustrations show the cubs meeting seagulls, seals, walruses, and whales. A background of sky and water in varying shades of blues and pinks suggests the vastness of the landscape. The bears tumble, roll, race, and leap. Their enthusiasm is catching. Like its predecessor, this is a perfect read-aloud, a grand example of youngsters' enjoyment of the natural world.

Polar Bear Night
Board book

By Lauren Thompson. Illustrated by Stephen Savage. Scholastic Press, 2004, 2013. Ages 0–3.
Subjects: Polar bears, Night

A polar bear cub wakes and goes exploring in the Arctic night. She sees sleeping walrus, seals, and whales; watches falling stars and northern lights; and then returns home to her sleeping mother. Throughout her trip, the moon follows. This comforting adventure for toddlers has been republished in a board book edition with padded covers for the very youngest readers and chewers. The story is the same, minus an opening showing cub and mom that sets the stage. One thing that distinguished this title was the range of colors— mostly, but not completely, variations on blue. This is also true in the board book, though some of the colors have changed slightly and the effect is less muted and hushed on the glossy paper. Still, it's an effective translation.

Baby Bear Sees Blue
Picture book; Bedtime story

By Ashley Wolff. Illustrated by Ashley Wolff. Beach Lane Books, 2012. Ages 2–5.
Subjects: Colors, Nature, Bears

Curious Baby Bear asks about the colors in his world all day long. Mama patiently answers each question, identifying yellow sunlight, green oak leaves, blue jays, brown trout, red strawberries, orange butterfly, stormy gray sky, and, finally, a rainbow. Other senses come into play, too. Baby Bear hears the thunder, smells the strawberries, and feels the splash of a fish. Watercolored block prints give these talking animals expressive faces, but they are portrayed in their natural world. Readers will enjoy finding other animals hiding in the pictures: a grey mouse appears in several, and there are several insects, a crayfish, a squirrel, a frog, and more. For very young lookers and listeners this gentle story will encourage conversations about colors as well as about the natural world. An effective read-aloud, this also works as a bedtime story, ending with Baby Bear's closed eyes, which "see nothing / but deep, soft black."

SPECIFIC ANIMALS

The Bear in the Book

Picture book; Bedtime story

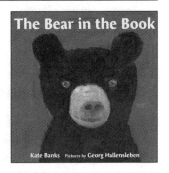

By Kate Banks. Illustrated by Georg Hallensleben. Farrar, Straus, Giroux, 2012. Ages 1–4.

Subjects: Reading, Bears, Hibernation

A small boy falls asleep listening to a bedtime story about a bear hibernating. This perfect picture book is a celebration of bedtime storytime. The listener is very young, maybe two or three. He names animals in the pictures and experiences the book-ness of the book, its sharp corners and pages that turn. He gets distracted, gets a drink, and pays attention again. The art is completely childlike, but the movement in these illustrations keeps you turning the pages. Along with the boy's story, there's the story of the bear, shown in a number of postures on the end pages. The bear goes to sleep for the winter; snow falls outside its den and animals cavort; children play on the ice and look out the window of a warm house into a snowy world. When spring comes, the bear wakes but the boy goes to sleep. Irresistible.

Old Bear

Picture book

By Kevin Henkes. Illustrated by Kevin Henkes. Greenwillow Books, 2008. Ages 2–6.

Subjects: Bears, Dreams, Seasons, Hibernation

Old Bear falls asleep for the winter and dreams of being a cub through four distinct seasons, waking up when it is spring again. The front dust cover of this beautifully made book shows a not-too-old bear walking on brown grass through falling red leaves; on the back, he travels through spring flowers. Fall and spring endpapers reinforce the message that this is a book about the passage of time. Henkes's familiar watercolors have heavy black outlines that make it easy for young children to see the images—and what splendid images they are! As Old Bear dreams through the winter, he enjoys the particular pleasures of each season, imagining himself young. Spring brings flowers "big as trees." In summer "it rained blueberries." Fall has its own vivid colors, and in winter "the sky was blazing with stars." And, when spring comes, it isn't a dream at all. Wonder-full.

Birds

Picture book

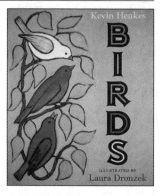

By Kevin Henkes. Illustrated by Laura Dronzek.
   Greenwillow Books, 2009. Ages 2–6.
Subject: Birds

A very young narrator listens to and watches birds through her window, noticing first that they differ in color, shape, and size. She thinks about a time when a group of birds instantly vanished. She imagines, she wonders, and she can pretend to be a bird, too. From the heard song at the beginning to the shared song at the end, Henkes's simple text moves through the stages of a young child's understanding. Simply portrayed, with heavy black outlines around each shape, Dronzek's brightly colored paintings nevertheless show recognizable birds. On rereading, the child will delight in joining the shouted "surprise" as a flock of blackbirds flies from a tree. While there is fanciful speculation from the observer, revealed as a girl only at the end, the text and illustrations are grounded in the facts of bird behavior.

Hello, Mama Wallaroo   *Informational picture book; Early reader*

By Darrin P. Lunde. Illustrated by Patricia Wynne. Charlesbridge, 2013.
   Ages 2–5.
Subject: Common wallaroo, Kangaroos, Australia

In the pattern of *Hello Baby Beluga* (2011), annotated earlier, Lunde and Wynne introduce another lesser known mother and child to preschoolers.

A kangaroo-like animal only three feet high, the mama wallaroo lives in Australia on rocky hillsides, hops away from dingoes, keeps her baby in her front pocket, and sleeps in the daytime. The simple text follows a predictable format: a question for the animal and a first person answer. "Mama Wallaroo, what do you eat?" "I graze on grass all day." Opposite the question-and-answer page is an ink-and-watercolor illustration showing the animal in action, in its appropriate environment. The text is large and readable and the illustrations clear and simple. It all looks inviting for the curious early reader as well.

Busy Gorillas   *Board book*

By John Schindel. Illustrated by Andy Rouse. Tricycle Press, 2010. Ages 0–3.
Subject: Gorilla behavior

Even very young babies respond to pictures of faces, and they can just as well belong to animals. This gorilla book is part of a charming series that began with *Busy Penguins* and *Busy Monkeys* published by Tricycle Press in 2002. In this one, each page shows a gorilla in action. The captions are only two words, and they rhyme: "Gorilla yawning, Gorilla gnawing," "Gorilla shoving, Gorilla loving." The verbs are unusual and interesting. Toddlers can imitate the actions. Sometimes the typography echoes the action, too. The photographs, taken by a British wildlife photographer, show gorillas up close. Often, we see just the faces, but the backgrounds suggest an appropriate habitat. Some backgrounds are blurred, suggesting motion. The small size is appropriate for small hands, and the series offers a natural way to help even the youngest humans make a connection to the animal world.

Fabulous Fishes   *Informational picture book; Board book (2012)*

By Susan Stockdale. Illustrated by Susan Stockdale. Peachtree, 2008.
   Ages 2–6.
Subject: Fish

"Fish that swim in numbers / fish that swim alone / no matter what they look like, they call the water home." Rhyming couplets and bright paintings introduce a wide variety of colorful fish. Page by page, different species appear in their usual environment, with a comment about behaviors or appearance. The pacing of these images supports the beginning reader. Their shapes have sharp edges and clear patterns for the younger viewer. The last spread includes a diver with mask and snorkel. In the back matter, in the order of presentation, thumbnail illustrations accompany the English name of each fish, and a bit more information. Except for the discus, all are saltwater fish, but most might well be seen in an aquarium. This ideal accompaniment to a field trip is also a grand read-aloud and early introduction to marine life at any time. A satisfying board book version was published in 2012.

Bring on the Birds   *Informational picture book; Board book (2013)*

By Susan Stockdale. Illustrated by Susan Stockdale. Peachtree, 2011.
    Ages 2–7.
Subject: Birds

The author of *Fabulous Fishes* uses the same approach to introduce the wide world of birds to the very youngest readers and listeners. Rhyming couplets and clear, identifiable illustrations remind readers that birds vary in many ways, but all have feathers and all hatched from eggs. The author-illustrator has chosen a splendid variety of real birds (named and briefly described in the back matter). Her rhymes work and the rhythm is infectious. "Swooping birds, / whooping birds, / birds with puffy chests." These lines open the narrative, each line illustrated with a framed image. Later, there are some full-bleed double-page spreads. The format provides predictability, the language is interesting, and the illustrations are excellent, often adding a bit of the bird's natural habitat. These bright, clear paintings will make readers and listeners want to see the real thing. A board book version, published in 2013, preserves the rhymes but speeds up the pacing.

I'm a Pill Bug

Informational picture book

By Yukihisa Tokuda. Illustrated by Kiyoshi
    Takahashi. Kane/Miller Book Publishers,
    2006. Ages 2–5.
Subject: Wood lice (Crustaceans)

"By the way, you don't think we're insects, do you?" A pill bug introduces itself to very young naturalists, describing where it lives, what it eats, how it reproduces and grows, and how it hibernates in winter. Illustrated with simple, flat shapes, this Japanese import provides the necessary facts in sentences addressed to the reader and simple enough to be understood by a toddler. The illustrations show the actual size of this curious nocturnal scavenger several times, once in a small child's hand, and the text gives instructions for keeping one for observation, temporarily. Roly-poly is another common name for this creature, found throughout the country and fascinating to small children, perhaps because of its habit of rolling up into an armored ball when threatened. This is a charming introduction to an unsung part of the natural world.

THE NATURAL WORLD IN GENERAL

Underground
Picture book

By Denise Fleming. Illustrated by Denise Fleming. Beach Lane Books, 2012. Ages 2–5.
Subjects: Stories in rhyme, Burrowing animals

"Low down. / Way down. / Under ground." Animals scamper to and fro and plants grow where a small boy plants a cherry tree. Fleming's colored paper-pulp stencil illustrations show a cross-section view of a boy planting a tree, admiring the creatures he sees in his garden world, and finally departing with the picked carrots while life goes on busily underground. The rhyming text is simple, and the creatures in the double-page illustrations are identifiable. A key, with just a bit of description of each of twenty-one creatures shown, is in the back. The end paper image reveals a monkey wrench in the soil, a clue to look for other buried treasures. With its simple rhyming text and somewhat complicated pictures, this works best as a lap read-aloud.

I Spy with My Little Eye   *Picture book*

By Edward Gibbs. Illustrated by Edward Gibbs. Templar, 2011. Ages 2–5.
Subjects: Animals—color, Animals

A guessing game introduces very young readers to iconic animals, including a whale, polar bear, elephant, lion, orangutan, fox, and frog. Sturdy pages, an inviting riddle, and a die-cut hole allow children to guess which animal will appear on the next page. An eye, a circle of color, and hint of the animal's surroundings appear on the page with the riddle along with the color name and one fact. "I spy with my little eye . . . something that is orange. I swing from tree to tree with my long arms." Simple but effective, this brings children into the game right up to the last page. Gibbs's digitally produced illustrations include large swaths of color and curly lines for the animals' fur. He has followed this successful title with two more: *I Spy Under the Sea* (Templar, 2012) and *I Spy on the Farm* (Templar, 2013).

Snow Rabbit, Spring Rabbit: A Book of Changing Seasons
Picture book; Board book (2013)

By Il Sung Na. Illustrated by Il Sung Na. Alfred A. Knopf, 2011. Ages 2–7.
Subjects: Rabbits, Winter, Animals

A rabbit observes all the preparations animals make for winter, and all the ways they spend this difficult season. Geese fly away, bears sleep in their dens, turtles swim to warmer waters, sheep enjoy their furry coats, squirrels gather acorns while deer forage further, crocodiles settle into the mud, and mice scurry about. Relatively sophisticated illustrations accompany the spare text of this story of changing seasons. Simplified animals and stylized snowflakes are more suggestive than realistic. Readers will want to look for the rabbit, watching and sometimes imitating on every page. Finally, it's spring. His brown coat turns to white and he turns to wink at the reader. The board book version works just as well as the original hardback and makes this even more accessible to toddlers.

Wait! Wait!

Picture book

By Hatsue Nakawaki. Illustrated by Komako Sakai. Enchanted Lion, 2013.
   Ages 1–5.
Subjects: Animals, Parent and child, Sense of wonder

Appealing illustrations and just a few, repeated words capture a toddler's sense of wonder at the natural world. This small child might be a boy or a girl; the experience is universal. Exploring the out-of-doors, she discovers first a butterfly, then a lizard, then pigeons, then cats. Though the animals escape her efforts to catch them, her father catches her up, puts her on his shoulders, and takes her off on an adventure, too. The body language in these illustrations is amazingly expressive. This child is all curiosity and yearning. The artist deftly indicates the animals' movements with simple oil-pencil lines: the butterfly flies up, the lizard skedaddles into the rocks, the birds flutter away, and the cats disappear off the page in mid leap. Perfectly sized for lap reading and irresistible.

Good Night, World

Picture book; Bedtime story

By Willa Perlman. Illustrated by Carolyn
   Fisher. Beach Lane Books, 2011. Ages 2–5.
Subject: Stories in rhyme

In this imagined journey, a bird flies around the world and a child says goodnight "to every living thing" and much of the inanimate natural world as well before curling up in bed to sleep. Beginning with stars and planets; passing

through deserts, mountains, and oceans; saying goodnight to rain forests and animals far away, the bird comes closer and closer to home, to the child's own street and house, yard animals and, finally, home. "Good night, sister, brother, friends. / Close your eyes as daytime ends." The rhyming couplets are set on slightly abstract images, a variety of patterns, textures, and surprising colors. Some images are childish scrawls, others sophisticated collage. There's much to look at and think about in these surreal illustrations before the listener nods off to sleep.

First the Egg

Picture book; Early reader

By Laura Vaccaro Seeger. Illustrated by Laura Vaccaro Seeger. Roaring
Brook Press, 2007. Ages 0–7.

Subject: Developmental biology

First things are revealed on page turns to be what follows, from egg to
chicken and back to chicken to egg. Seeger is a master of die-cuts, holes in
the page that reveal something unexpected when the page is turned. Not
only is this an enjoyable puzzle, it's an encouragement to read in a logical
order, teaching the very young child what to do with a book. The story is a
series of first-then events: egg to chicken, tadpole to frog, seed to flower, and
caterpillar to butterfly followed with word to story and paint to picture.
Each first has three stages; for example, the seed sprouts before it becomes
the flower. The final painting includes all the elements. Award-winning both
for its illustrations and for its encouraging-early-readers text, this has broad
appeal.

Stripes of All Types

Informational picture books

By Susan Stockdale. Illustrated by Susan
Stockdale. Peachtree, 2013. Ages 2–6.

Subjects: Animals—color, Camouflage (Biology), Stripes

This celebration of color and pattern introduces nineteen striped animals from around

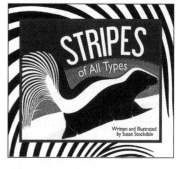

the world with a grand guessing game. The skunk on the front cover and
the zebra on the back may be familiar, but inside, readers will find bongos,
tree snails, tapirs, bitterns, and other unfamiliar creatures. Stockdale's bold
graphics emphasize their patterns but suggest their usual surroundings as
well. Bees crawl on a spiny cactus; a snake slides through weeds; kittens curl
in children's arms. The rhyme and rhythm of her simple text is easy to read
aloud. It doesn't include the animal's name but uses active verbs suggesting
the animal's behavior or movement. A tiger sprawls; a badger prowls. In the
back matter, short paragraphs give each animal's proper name, where it can
be found, and how its stripes support its life. A final identification puzzle
reinforces appreciation for patterns in the natural world.

What Will Hatch?   *Informational picture book*

By Jennifer Ward. Illustrated by Susie Ghahremani. Walker Books for
    Young Readers, 2013. Ages 2–5.
Subject: Eggs—incubation

For the youngest listeners, an interactive question-and-answer format introduces a variety of animals that start their lives in eggs. The title question
appears on a spread with a die-cut egg-shaped hole on the right-hand side.
Turn the page for the answer and the hole becomes some other element on
the left. The rhyming text includes at least one other fact about each egg's
appearance and the animal it will become. The animals introduced—sea
turtle, penguin, tadpole, crocodile, robin, caterpillar, platypus—have been
illustrated in stylized scenes and muted colors. Shown in their natural habitats, they are only slightly anthropomorphized by their smiles. The back
matter tells more about these oviparous creatures as well as the goldfinch on
the cover and explains chicken egg development. This quiet story is a pleasing introduction to an important event in the natural world.

Summer Days and Nights   *Picture book; Bedtime story*

By Wong Herbert Yee. Illustrated by Wong Herbert Yee. Henry Holt & Co.,
    2012. Ages 2–6.
Subjects: Stories in rhyme, Summer, Day, Night

Third in a series of child-sized books about seasons, this one presents sum-
mertime through the eyes of a small Asian girl. While the cat naps in the
morning light, she rises to explore her world. Butterfly net in hand, she
tiptoes through a daisy-covered meadow. She observes a bumblebee and,
later, black ants in a line. Some summer fun is provided by parents: a lem-
onade break, fun in a wading pool, a picnic in the park. Night comes, with
"winking, blinking fireflies," a mouse, and an owl, glimpsed on an evening
walk in the moonlight before bedtime dreams. More pictures than words,
this quiet celebration of the season and small wonders of natural world is a
worthy companion to *Who Likes Rain* (Henry Holt & Co., 2007) and *Tracks
in the Snow* (Henry Holt & Co., 2003). The soothing, rhyming words make it
a good bedtime read.

A beach walk with grandpa

Chapter 16

Books for Adults

SHARING BOOKS ABOUT THE NATURAL WORLD WITH CHILDREN CAN CER-tainly help kids connect with nature and reawaken your own interest and wonder. But in the end there's no substitute for looking and going outside. My husband and I are fortunate to live in an area where nature is close at hand. We can watch birds feed their babies from our feeders, we can swim or kayak in the creek that runs past our backyard. We can walk or bike a short distance to a wooded park near our home, and the Chesapeake Bay is close enough for us to stroll along the shoreline. The area is quiet enough that spring peepers and late-summer crickets are easily audible at night.

Not only in our present home, but wherever we've lived, throughout my adult life, as parent, teacher, librarian, and grandmother, I have been sharing nature with young people just as my parents and teachers shared it with me. I have accompanied children on walks through woods and in and along streams, picked berries for jam and weeds for winter arrangements from abandoned areas, and watched for falling stars. I've camped overnight with students on the banks of the Potomac River and in friendly farmers' fields. With school groups and family both, I've shared the wonder of the annual horseshoe crab spawning show under the full moon on Delaware Bay beaches, and we've made regular family trips to Cape May, New Jersey, to see the hawks and many other birds flying south in the fall. I have a treasure chest of memorable moments from many years and places. You can have such treasures, too.

Start in your own backyard and neighborhood. There's plenty to do and see. Several of the books annotated in this chapter have suggestions for simple activities (and some that might take more preparation). The U.S. Fish and Wildlife Service website (www.fws.gov/letsgooutside) and those of the National Wildlife Federation (www.nwf.org/Be-Out-There.aspx) and the Children and Nature Network (www.childrenandnature.org/naturestory) are only a fragment of the wealth of suggestions available on the Internet.

You and the children you know may want to participate in citizen science projects, reporting things you've observed to organizations that collect such information, usually through the Internet. Citizen science is thought by some to have begun formally with the Christmas Bird Count in 1900, though others date the use of crowd-sourced data to a U.S. Navy officer who collected wind, weather, and current data in the mid-nineteenth century or to similar activities even farther back in the past.[1] Whenever it began, the participation of ordinary citizens in collecting scientific data has had a long history. At the end of the twentieth century and into the twenty-first, my students and I participated some of in Journey North's studies of wildlife migrations and seasonal changes (www.learner.org/jnorth). You don't need to be a classroom teacher to do that. Plenty of material on its website will interest individual families as well.

For four days every February, people around the world participate in the Great Backyard Bird Count, submitting their sightings from that short period. Anyone, from beginners to experts, is welcome to participate—for as little as fifteen minutes on one day, or as long as you like. The sixteenth annual count, in 2013, was led by the Cornell Lab of Ornithology and National Audubon Society, with Canadian partner Bird Studies Canada and sponsorship from Wild Birds Unlimited. This count has been going on since 1999, and its data are publicly available (www.birdsource.org/gbbc). Our family also enjoys Project Feeder Watch, a winter bird-watching activity also sponsored by the Cornell Lab (www.birds.cornell.edu/pfw). *Citizen Science Guide for Families* (Landgraf, 2013) annotated below, has lots of suggestions for getting involved with wildlife-watching and environmental stewardship around the country.

With a balance of hands-on experience and shared reading, we can enhance and pass on our own appreciation of the natural world. What could be more important? In the words of Mary Oliver:

> Teach the children. We don't matter so much, but the children do. Show them daisies and the pale hepatica. Teach them the taste of sassafras and wintergreen. . . . Give them peppermint to put in their pockets as they go to school. Give them the fields and the woods and the possibility of the world salvaged from the lords of profit. Stand them in the stream, head them upstream, rejoice as they learn to love this green space they live in, its sticks and leaves and then the silent, beautiful blossoms.
>
> Attention is the beginning of devotion.[2]

ACTIVITIES

Go Outside! Over 130 Activities for Outdoor Adventures
Nonfiction

By Nancy Blakey. Illustrated with
 photographs by Dane Dean Doering.
 Tricycle Press, 2002. Adults.
Subjects: Outdoor education, Outdoor
 recreation, Amusements

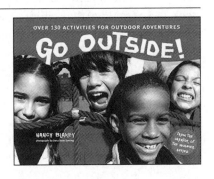

Over 130 outdoor activities, crafts, and games are presented here with clear recipe-style instructions and plentiful pictures of young people enjoying themselves. Organized seasonally, this has a grand range of projects from Flower Power Paper to Icicle Ice Cream. Some, like lap games and three-legged races, are games for groups; others, like fish prints or making dyes from natural materials, are projects for individuals. Some are tried-and-true outdoor skills, like telling time by using your hand against the horizon, cooking a biscuit on a stick, and finding edible weeds. There are suggestions for feeding the birds and for playing in a pool or in the snow. Some can be done in the backyard; others will take you further afield. Though no longer in print, Blakey's book is available at many libraries, and copies are still for sale on the Web.

Run Wild! Outdoor Games and Adventures

Nonfiction

By Fiona Danks and Jo Schofield. Illustrated with photographs by Jo Schofield and Fiona Danks. Frances Lincoln, 2011. Adults.
Subjects: Outdoor recreation for children, Outdoor games, Family recreation

Suggestions and instructions abound for all kinds of outdoor activities with children from preschool through high school. This British import describes parties, games, storytelling, theatre, treasure trails, hunting and tracking, and outdoor action of all kinds, both real and imagined. Photographs show children making pictures with river stones, running through the woods, dressing up with costumes made of natural materials, and playing games of all sorts. This is particularly useful for the clear instructions, though some games will be unfamiliar to American readers. Although stressing things children can do outside rather than the natural experiences themselves, this book is a reminder that children who are comfortable beyond the walls of their homes are more likely to enjoy the world outdoors. The introductory description of four- and five-year-olds on an outdoor walk in the rain chanting, "We're all going on a puddle hunt," is grand.

Celebrate Nature! Activities for Every Season
Nonfiction

By Angela Schmidt Fishbaugh. Redleaf Press, 2011. Adults.
Subjects: Science—study and teaching, Early childhood education—activity programs, Nature study, Teaching—aids and devices

Organized by seasons, this collection of simple nature study themes suggests connected activi-

ties for both indoor and outdoor use. Designed for educators of children aged three to eight, this offers plenty of ideas that would be helpful for parents, caregivers, and, especially, members of cooperative playgroups. Each section includes seven themes for coordinated studies such as leaves and squirrels in the fall, tracks and hibernators in the winter, stones and dandelions in the spring, grass and ants in the summer. Within each theme are suggestions for exploring outside, involving families, and integrated classroom activities, science and math, block building, art, language arts, and dramatic play. There are solid reading suggestions, mostly older titles appropriate for reading aloud. Each theme includes ideas for role play outside, a way to connect children even more closely to what they are seeing and hearing. Even browsing this collection should spark some ideas of your own.

Citizen Science Guide for Families: Taking Part in Real Science

Nonfiction

By Greg Landgraf. Huron Street Press, 2013.
   Adults.
Subjects: Research—United States—citizen participation, Science—general, Science—study and teaching

Count urban birds, record the dates the ice breaks and buds burst, join a group to watch squirrels or listen to frog calls or tag monarch butterflies. Record how many stars you can see in the constellation Orion or Leo. Landgraf has compiled an extensive listing of places where individuals, families, and groups can get involved in real scientific observation and data collection. After a brief introduction to the idea of citizen science, he organizes his programs by what they observe—birds, amphibians and reptiles, insects, plants—and where they work—beaches, wetlands, and all over. Some are specific to a particular part of the country; others are worldwide. In some cases, it is individuals and families who collect the data; in others, it is trained groups. Each has a website for further information, and each chapter includes some suggested reading. This is a gold mine of ideas for family activities.

I Love Dirt! 52 Activities to Help You and   *Nonfiction*
Your Kids Discover the Wonders of Nature

By Jennifer Ward. Illustrated by Susie Ghahremani. Trumpeter, 2008.
   Adults.
Subjects: Outdoor recreation for children, Children and the environment,
   Nature study, Activity programs

A collection of simple activities for young people and their adult caretakers designed to heighten appreciation for the natural world. The activities are open-ended, organized by season, and possible in many different settings. Besides intriguing things to do (most requiring no equipment at all) there are also "Help Me Understand" boxes adding information for the adult to share and answering possible children's questions. Each section concludes with a goal the activity encourages: stimulating curiosity, creative play, observational skills, problem solving, and so forth. Some ideas are obvious: watching ants and birds, for example. Others are more subtle: looking for your own shadow by the full moon or experimenting with dropping things to learn more about gravity. This title has been followed by two more: *Let's Go Outside* (Roost, 2009) for children eight to twelve years old, and, for city children, *It's a Jungle Out There* (Roost, 2011). Each one can stimulate hours of exploration.

FOOD FOR THOUGHT

The Sense of Wonder   *Nonfiction*

By Rachel Carson. Illustrated by Charles Pratt. Harper & Row, 1965.
   Adults.
Subject: Nature study

One of two published editions of Carson's *Women's Home Companion* essay, "Help Your Child to Wonder" with photographs, this one shows children in the natural world. This seminal essay on introducing children to the natural world describes Carson's own experiences with her nephew, Roger, at her summer place on the Maine coast. She describes walking with him in the woods, a nighttime beach visit during a storm, and the pleasures of a rainy day. Black-and-white and color photographs, mostly by Pratt, illustrate that world perfectly. Many show Pratt's own son; others are close-ups of beach and forest wonders. White-on-blue sun prints of leaves serve as the endpapers. Old as this edition is, it is still commonly available in public libraries though it is no longer in print.

The Sense of Wonder

Nonfiction

By Rachel Carson. Illustrated by Nick Kelsh. HarperCollins Publishers, 1998. Adults.

Subject: Nature study

A newer edition of Carson's influential essay, this takes advantage of more modern production possibilities and the talents of a renowned photographer. In planning an expansion of this essay, Carson told a friend "We plan for it to be rather lavishly illustrated with the most beautiful photographs we can find, some color and some black and white." This edition, with Kelsh's nature photographs on thick creamy paper and its thoughtful design, is likely how she envisioned her book, even though it doesn't expand on the text. From double-page color spreads to small sepia-toned images, these are breathtaking pictures of Carson's beloved Maine world. This edition is still in print.

Last Child in the Woods: Saving Our Children from Nature-Deficit Disorder
Nonfiction

By Richard Louv. Algonquin Books of Chapel Hill, 2005. Adults.

Subjects: Nature—psychological aspects, Children and the environment

An eloquent exposition of the modern-day distancing of children from the natural world and the physical and emotional benefits of connection. Louv coined the phrase *nature-deficit disorder*, hypothesizing that children's disconnection leads to all kinds of health and behavior problems. He builds on the work of others in this area: Wilson's biophilia, Gardner's naturalist intelligence, and Sobel's writings about ecophobia. He uses examples from all over the country to demonstrate ways we are currently disconnected and ways that we might reconnect in spite of societal and legal barriers, parent fears, and the attractions of the Internet and video games. He writes convincingly and with passion, using empirical examples, not research. This makes the book far more interesting to read, but research will be necessary, too. A 2008 edition (not seen) has been updated and expanded.

A Natural Sense of Wonder: Connecting Kids with Nature through the Seasons
Nonfiction

By Rick Van Noy. University of Georgia Press, 2008. Adults.

Subjects: Children and the environment, Philosophy of nature, Environmental psychology, Environmental education—study and teaching (Elementary)

A series of gracefully written essays about hikes, canoe trips, fishing, skiing, brook walking, and backyard explorations the author and his wife shared with their two young children in their efforts to give them some of the natural world experience they had in their childhoods. From their home in a small town in western Virginia, they explore locally and further afield throughout the year. Van Noy includes the failures as well as the successes—like the too-challenging camping trip—and he makes clear that it requires considerable effort on the part of parents to make time for this as well as the screens that are part of modern children's lives. Interspersed with the material about his family's activities are some thought-provoking quotations from Rachel Carson's unpublished notes for a longer version of the "sense of wonder" essay and other writers on connecting children with nature.

NOTES

1. Retro Science, Part 1, August 23, 2012, http://blogs.scientificamerican.com/guest-blog/2012/08/23/retro-science-part-1.

2. Mary Oliver, *Blue Iris: Poems and Essays* (Boston: Beacon Press, 2004), 55–56.

Subject Index

Author and Title Index